T0352362

THE PARATROOPER GENERALS

MATTHEW RIDGWAY, MAXWELL TAYLOR, AND THE AMERICAN AIRBORNE FROM D-DAY THROUGH NORMANDY

MITCHELL YOCKELSON

STACKPOLE
BOOKS

Guilford, Connecticut

Published by Stackpole Books
An imprint of The Rowman & Littlefield Publishing Group, Inc.
4501 Forbes Blvd., Ste. 200
Lanham, MD 20706
www.rowman.com

Distributed by NATIONAL BOOK NETWORK

Maps by Caroline Stover

British Library Cataloguing in Publication Information available

Library of Congress Cataloging-in-Publication Data

Names: Yockelson, Mitchell A., 1962– author.
Title: The Paratrooper Generals : Matthew Ridgway, Maxwell Taylor, and the American Airborne from D-Day through Normandy / Mitchell Yockelson.
Description: Guilford, Connecticut : Stackpole Books, [2020] | Includes bibliographical references and index. | Summary: "Jumping into Normandy during the early hours of D-Day, Matthew Ridgway and Maxwell Taylor fought on the ground for six weeks of combat that cost the airborne divisions more than 40 percent casualties. This is the first book to explore in depth the significant role these two division commanders played on D-Day."— Provided by publisher.
Identifiers: LCCN 2019048503 (print) | LCCN 2019048504 (ebook) | ISBN 9780811738552 (cloth) | ISBN 9780811768511 (epub)
Subjects: LCSH: Ridgway, Matthew B. (Matthew Bunker), 1895–1993—Military leadership. | Taylor, Maxwell D. (Maxwell Davenport), 1901–1987—Military leadership. | United States. Army—Airborne Troops—History. | United States. Army. Airborne Division, 82nd. | United States. Army. Airborne Division, 101st. | World War, 1939–1945—Campaigns—France—Normandy. | United States. Army—Biography. | Generals—United States—Biography.
Classification: LCC D769.345 .Y63 2020 (print) | LCC D769.345 (ebook) | DDC 940.54/21421092273—dc23
LC record available at https://lccn.loc.gov/2019048503
LC ebook record available at https://lccn.loc.gov/2019048504

Contents

Maps

Acknowledgments

Researching and writing *The Paratrooper Generals* involved the input of many people, and without them, this book would have never been completed. It started with my agent, E. J. McCarthy, who helped craft the idea for the book and put me in contact with Dave Reisch at Stackpole. It has been a pleasure working with Dave and his assistant, Stephanie Otto, as well as Rowman & Littlefield production editor Patricia Stevenson and copyeditor David Lampo.

I relied on a number of experts: Joe Balkoski, Mark Bando, Adam Berry, Tania M. Chacho, Roger Cirillo, Patrick Elie, Daniel Haulman, Kevin Hymel, David Keynon, Bob Leicht, Tom McCardle, Barney McCoy, Guillaume Marie, Marty Morgan, Tim Mulligan, and Steve Ossad, all of whom offered words of wisdom, read drafts of specific chapters, or provided invaluable comments.

Gina McNeely came to the rescue by finding photographs for the book, and Caroline Stover did a stellar job in creating the maps. Martha Baker carefully reviewed every word and offered solid wisdom that enhanced the writing. Her editorial advice is second to none.

At the National Archives, librarian Jeff Hartley responded to my numerous interlibrary loan requests for books and articles. Tim Nenninger weighed in with his military records' expertise when I needed it, Nick Natanson responded promptly to my frequent queries about photographs, and Rick Peuser was there as a good friend offering encouragement. I am grateful for the help and friendship of Tim Rives at the Eisenhower Library and Chis Belena at the FDR Library, who helped me with researching Wright Bryan. At the National Personnel Records Center, Theresa Fitzgerald came through with answers to my questions concerning service records.

I am very appreciative of Jim Gavin's daughters (Barbara, Chloe, and Caroline), who patiently answered questions I posed about their father. Similarly, I am grateful to Maxwell Taylor's son, John M. Taylor, and his granddaughter, Kathy Shaibani, for their insight into General Taylor's character. And thank you to Karen Costantini, John Cornish, Keely Jurgovan, Jen Rawley, Steve Pedone, David and Deanna Sullivan, and Mary Lane Sullivan for sharing personal accounts that relate to the airbornes' actions in Normandy.

I am also thankful for the help I received from staff members at the 82nd Airborne Division Memorial Museum at Fort Bragg, the Air Mobility Command Museum, Atlanta History Center, Don F. Pratt Museum, George C. Marshall Foundation Library, Nebraska Historical Museum, Ohio University Special Collections, Reuters, University of Texas–El Paso Special Collections, Upottery Air Field Heritage Trust, US Army History and Education Center, and the Utah Beach Landing Museum.

Individuals who provided much-needed research assistance include Ed Bradley, Doug Hartman, Sarah Minney, Kirk Mitchell, and Darby K. Ward.

Throughout the entire process of writing *The Paratrooper Generals*, I was so lucky to have the patience, support, love, and many other wonderful attributes of my mom, my wife Lynn, my daughter Lily, and Rosie. Despite all of the help and advice I received, I am solely to blame for any errors in this book.

Preface

They couldn't do it. Not Matthew Ridgway, not Maxwell Taylor.

They could not follow the path of other commanding generals who stayed out of harm's way, sent orders to the front lines from the rear, and polished their brass buttons with their khaki cuffs. They could not sit in the relative safety of their Jeeps, behind the lines. Not in Normandy.

Not in the most important campaign of World War II.

Instead, they chose to stand shoulder to shoulder with their troops: Ridgway with the 82nd Airborne Division, the "All-Americans"; Taylor with the 101st Airborne Division, the "Screaming Eagles."

Before daybreak on June 6, 1944, both major generals accepted the great risk of capture or death to drop alongside thirteen thousand other paratroopers into occupied Normandy. That day (and for the next six weeks), Ridgway and Taylor led their men—alongside their men—during fierce combat among the hedgerows, across canals, and through villages and city streets, eradicating German troops from Normandy.

And when situations dictated that these generals could not fight side by side with their men, Ridgway and Taylor remained in constant contact, never far from the front.

The Paratrooper Generals: Matthew Ridgway, Maxwell Taylor, and the American Airborne from D-Day through Normandy explores in depth the creation of the American Army airborne that led to the formation of the 82nd and 101st and the significant roles that these two division commanders played on D-Day as they demonstrated extraordinary courage and leadership throughout the most important campaign of World War II.

As West Point cadets, Ridgway and Taylor had learned that good army leaders should not only take a personal interest in the troops serving under them but also lead by example. Both generals followed these maxims to perfection, and no two commanders were more adored by their men.

During the months leading up to D-Day, Ridgway and Taylor were caught in an internal struggle with Supreme Headquarters Allied Expeditionary Force (SHAEF) commander General Dwight D. "Ike" Eisenhower and his immediate subordinates over the use of airborne troops for the initial attack. Their main sparring partner was Air Marshal Trafford Leigh-Mallory. The British air commander did not support troops landing by parachute before the Army's main thrust on the landing beaches.

Leigh-Mallory, convinced that such an operation would be a total failure, foresaw exorbitant casualties. He suggested leaving the airborne divisions behind during the initial attack and then bringing them in after the beaches were secure. This compromise was consonant with the original plan, which was handed to Eisenhower when he was appointed SHAEF commander.

That plan for the Allied liberation of Europe, known as Operation Overlord, was designed by a combined team of American and British officers. To them, the airborne landings were a mere afterthought to the infantry beach assault, with only a handful of British and some American parachutists considered as support to the amphibious landing forces.

As Eisenhower familiarized himself with the early Overlord plan, he was at least willing to listen to a larger airborne component of Neptune (the cross-channel phase of the Normandy attack). Ridgway and Taylor refused to stand down. They argued hard in meeting after meeting to convince the strategists that without a sizable airborne invasion in order to secure Utah Beach before the landings, the entire operation could fall apart on the first day.

Ridgway and Taylor—friendly but not friends—formed a strong alliance. They pushed back against detractors who lectured that an airborne drop in Normandy would cause more than 70 percent casualties (perhaps higher), and they won the argument. Their thinking benefited from the support of Chief of Staff George C. Marshall and First Army's General Omar Bradley. Bradley's support took the form of a threat to call off the Utah Beach assault unless his infantry divisions had full support from the 82nd and 101st divisions.

During the closing hours of June 5, 1944, Ridgway, Taylor, and thirteen thousand paratroopers aboard 820 Douglas C-47 transport airplanes—the workhorse of the Army Air Forces—took off from airfields throughout southern England. C-47s, flying in V formations of nine planes each, reached Normandy's Cotentin Peninsula ninety minutes later.

There, they encountered intense flak from German antiaircraft guns. As the planes approached the landing zones, the signal lights above the doorways flashed green. Jumpmasters ordered the soldiers to stand up, hook up, and jump out. Jumpmasters dropped first, followed by the paratrooper sticks—typically seventeen or eighteen men. Flying at a low altitude to avoid the enemy's radar, they exited the planes in many instances at only four hundred feet above ground that was to have been marked by pathfinder lights and navigational aids.

The airborne troops were part of US VII Corps, commanded by General J. Lawton Collins. Their mission, code named Boston (82nd Division) and Albany (101st Division), was to capture Cherbourg, the coastal city in Normandy that would serve as the Allied supply port once the infantry and support units had come ashore later on June 6. Paratroopers were also responsible for blocking approaches into the vicinity of the amphibious landings at Utah Beach, led by US 4th Division, as well as capturing causeway exits off the beach and establishing crossings over the Douve River to assist the US V Corps in conjoining the two American beachheads on Omaha and Utah.

A smaller contingent of British paratroopers (6th Airborne Division) was also incorporated into Neptune; it jumped around the same time as the American airborne divisions. Its mission was to protect the left flank of Sword Beach by seizing key points (bridges and terrain) in an area about five miles wide and seven miles deep between the Orne and Dives rivers.

As important as these objectives seemed in planning for Overlord, all eyes were riveted on the 82nd and 101st divisions that day. Ridgway's and Taylor's missions proved difficult and costly. Only part of the story is what occurred when just over thirteen thousand American paratroopers hit the ground, beaches, swamps, hedgerows, and trees.

German resistance was immediate, depending on where the paratroopers landed. Initial casualties were high, and the deaths included a significant loss of commanding officers. More than a few airborne soldiers were immediately taken prisoner by the Germans, and their accounts of capture and (in many cases) escape with help from French civilians add drama to the story.

Shortly after they landed, the paratroopers were met by gliders with reinforcements, antitank equipment, Jeeps, and artillery. The gliders had an even more difficult time landing at the designated zones—they were like clay pigeons to the German gunners. The flimsy planes that escaped antiaircraft fire still had to contend with obstacles such as poles and flooded marshland.

The story continued to unfold when the elements from their division, which had been scattered far and wide, eventually linked up to fight as regular infantry, carrying M-1 Garands and Thompson machine guns (tommy guns). Fighting at battalion level (roughly 37 officers and 669 men), they eventually accomplished every objective assigned over a relatively short period of just over a month and a half.

Ridgway and Taylor expected their men to be in action for no more than three days. They were supposed to be shock troops, stabilizing the areas behind Utah Beach to allow the amphibious forces to break free and then leaving. But they stayed in Normandy for several weeks and encountered daily combat.

By mid-July, the 82nd and 101st divisions had been relieved, so they returned to England. Statistics sum up a portion of their story: of the more than thirteen thousand paratroopers who had dropped a month before on D-Day, more than two thousand were killed and more than four thousand wounded during the entire Normandy campaign. About 60 percent of the divisional supplies and equipment delivered by the gliders was destroyed when the planes crashed or ended up in enemy hands.

The vast majority of Taylor's men had not previously seen action; the same could be said for some of Ridgway's troops. When they were withdrawn from the lines in July, however, they were battle-hardened veterans in two of the best divisions in the US Army.

Prologue: June 6, 1944

On Tuesday, June 6, 1944, at nearly three in the morning, Chicago native Lieutenant John E. Peters landed *Snooty*, his Douglas C-47 Skytrain, on the massive 5,800-foot runway at Greenham Common airfield in southern England.

A few hours earlier, around 10 p.m., Peters had taken off from there with a stick (A Air Corps designation for a group of paratroopers) of eighteen heavily armed paratroopers from 3rd Battalion, 502nd Parachute Infantry Regiment, 101st Airborne Division.[1]

After a one-day delay due to poor weather, Peters flew the soldiers across the English Channel and over the designated drop zone, from which they jumped into Normandy, which had been held by Germans for three years.

Returning to England after the drop, Peters carried two passengers besides his crew. The first was a "moody and glum" paratrooper, who had lined up with the last half-dozen soldiers to leave the plane. When his turn came, he had fallen, crashing into the rear door with such force that he was thrown into the back of the cabin. The men behind had shoved him aside to continue jumping.

Wright Bryan, the other passenger, was a war correspondent with the *Atlanta Journal-Constitution* and an NBC Radio stringer (freelance journalist). Later that morning, the charismatic, 6'5" Southern gentleman, who counted *Gone with the Wind* author Margaret Mitchell as one of his friends, would make history broadcasting the first eyewitness account of the Allied liberation of Fortress Europe. SHAEF knew that all eyes were on the paratroopers, so the veteran journalist, who had been in Europe for two years covering the war, was invited by NBC London manager Stan Richardson to report what he saw with his own eyes.[1]

For the past two days, Bryan had been living with pilots and crews of the 89th Troop Carrier Squadron, 53rd Troop Carrier Wing, commanded by Major Clement G. Richardson of Salinas, California.

Richardson's "combat crews had been fully briefed as to their initial mission, the course they would fly, all procedures they would follow." Bryan and the combat crews lived behind barbed wire surrounding their quarters, protected by guards to keep them from any contact with outsiders.[2]

After Peters returned to Greenham Common and brought *Snooty* to a stop, Bryan climbed out and headed into the control room, where he listened to C-47 crew interrogations. Then he went to the mess and ate beef stew and donuts, chased with a cup of coffee. From there, with journalist Demaree Bess from the *Saturday Evening Post*, Bryan was taken to a waiting Jeep and driven to London, fifty-five miles away. The chauffeur's erratic driving scared Bryan more than the flight to Normandy. Several times, he thought they were headed into a ditch or the Thames River.

Entering London just before daybreak, Bryan felt his fear surge when he saw "what seemed to be a paratrooper and his limp chute" dangling from an overhead trolley wire. He wondered whether the Germans had counterattacked and shot down a C-47. Bryan had his driver stop the Jeep. He shined a spotlight on the lifeless figure, but it turned out to be a cardboard dummy "advertising some show or carnival."

Bryan was dropped off at the Ministry of Information (MOI) office, located in Senate House of the University of London in Bloomsbury, "where the nerve center of handling war news had been established." The site contained a large newsroom for reporters, studios for broadcasting, and a War Room draped in maps that only the 533 accredited SHAEF journalists could enter.

A few people, most of them sound asleep in chairs, were there when Bryan arrived. The quiet didn't last. At 9:32 in London, or 3:32 Eastern War Time, Colonel Ernest Dupuy, a SHAEF press aide, read General Dwight D. Eisenhower's official communique announcing D-Day: "Under the command of General Eisenhower, Allied naval forces, supported by strong air forces, began landing Allied armies this morning on the northern coast of France."[3]

The announcement brought a hoard of press to the MOI newsroom accompanied by high-ranking army and naval officers to answer their questions. Bryan banged out his radio script on a typewriter in another room—ten pages, double spaced.

At 4:15 Eastern Time, he went on the air for just more than fourteen minutes, standing in front of the microphone, one hand cupping his left ear and the other holding his script. Barely pausing, Bryan's rich Southern drawl captivated listeners with prose worthy of William Faulkner: "The first spearhead of Allied forces for the liberation of Europe landed by parachute in northern France," he began. "In the first hour of D-Day by British Double Summer time, or a little more than an hour before D-Day began by Greenwich Mean Time, I rode . . . with the first group of planes to take our fighting men into Europe. . . . I watched from the rear door of our plane, named *Snooty*, as seventeen American paratroopers led by a lst. colonel jumped with their arms, ammunition and equipment into German-occupied France."

Before taking off for Fortress Europe, "long columns of airborne troops trudging slowly under their full loads of battle equipment from the bivouac area where they had been camped awaiting this day" moved toward the planes that would carry them into battle.

General Dwight D. Eisenhower, SHAEF commander, carrying the burden of the success of Overlord (code name for the invasion of Europe), "visited with the paratroopers during the afternoon, quietly passing among the men, and chatting with them, asking their names, their homes and their jobs. Outside the door of each C-47, the soldiers assembled and checked their equipment, while ground crews and combat crews gave the plane a final tuning up."

The paratroopers adjusted their packs, put on their Mae Wests (B-4 life jackets nicknamed for the Hollywood starlet inflated with compressed air, giving them an impressive torso profile) and chutes, and climbed into the planes. Each man was so heavily loaded that he had to be pushed from behind and pulled from above to mount the steps into the plane.

Bryan boarded last and spoke with some of the men, scribbling down their comments with pencil on sheets of paper or in his small pocket diary. Private Robert G. Hillman of Manchester, Connecticut, sitting farthest forward on the port side, proudly told the war correspondent, "I know my chute's o.k. because my mother checked it. She works in the Pioneer Parachute Company in our town and her job is giving the final once-over to all the chutes they manufacture." Before joining the Army, the blonde, blue-eyed paratrooper had also worked for a time at Pioneer.

As Peters readied for take-off, twenty-nine-year-old battalion commander Lieutenant Colonel Robert G. Cole from San Antonio, Texas, the senior officer aboard and future Medal of Honor recipient, moved quickly up and down the passenger compartment, asking each man whether he needed anything. As the men settled into their bucket seats, Colonel Cole said, "The doc is going to give you some pills to guard against airsickness. Make yourselves as comfortable as you can. Better try to sleep a little." Bryan noted that "quiet settled in the plane. These men had done their talking. Now they were grim and silent."

On the flight deck of *Snooty*, Peters and copilot Lieutenant B. E. Maxwell of Clave, Michigan, "muttered soft curses as their motors were slow to start after long pauses on the taxi strip. But when the engines did turn over, they droned steadily and powerfully. Almost before we knew it," Bryan projected, "we were trundling along past the operations buildings and control tower where the ground personnel of the base were standing. Some made the V-sign. Some waved." Lieutenant General Lewis M. Brereton, 9th Air Force commander, moved up and down the line of planes, giving the thumbs-up sign to his crews.

Then *Snooty*, marked like other C-47s with alternate white and black invasion stripes (to prevent friendly fire), rolled down the runway. As *Snooty* picked up speed, Bryan stood between the pilot and copilot and watched the formation lights of the ships ahead of them "slowly almost imperceptibly climbing, then gradually swinging into wide circles."

"This thing is really loaded down," Bryan heard Peters comment out loud, referring to the fact that each fully equipped paratrooper weighed about 150 pounds, and nestled underneath the plane were bundles containing radios, engineer equipment, heavy weapons and ammunition, and rations and medical supplies loaded onto racks.

When the plane became airborne, Bryan "could almost feel the sturdy transport strengthening its muscles shouldering its burden—then feet by feet, almost inch by inch rising above the fields and trees of southern England." Bryan had by then folded his lanky 6'5" frame into the navigating dome's forward roof of the fuselage, often referred to as a dome glass blister or an astral globe.

Snooty fell into a squadron formation of three Vs of three ships each in the first section, joined by Vs of three ships each in the second section, which led. The preceding squadron was already circling the airfield and rapidly gaining altitude.

Other squadrons followed. Bryan described the scene to the radio audience: "All about us and below us was such a glimmering fabric of lights as I had not seen in the eight months I had been in blacked-out England."

Snooty circled the field four times, "its runways and perimeter outlined in sparkling white lights. Through the sky the red and green formation lights of the planes strung out almost to the limit of vision, looking for all the world like holiday decorations stretching down the length of any American Main Street."

As the long procession straightened out on its preestablished course toward the shore of the English Channel, signal lights blinked in code, and navigators checked their speed and direction with the pilots, who were beginning the constant plotting of their position.

As *Snooty* flew toward the coast, "the bulky transport silhouetted against the sky as they greatly undulated in the prep wash of their companions."

"Right on course, and we're one minute early," navigator Robert E. Taylor of Altoona, Pennsylvania, reported to Peters.

At that moment, Bryan left the navigating dome "from which I had been watching the formations about me—too fascinated to feel the weight of the flak suit which I wore, like all crew members, or the steel helmet" tightly gripping his head.

Bryan walked down the long passenger cabin to see how the paratroopers were faring. More than half had taken their colonel's advice and were dozing, their heads back against the wall and their feet stretched in front. Others were sitting silently, except for two or three who whispered among themselves.

Bryan had perspired in the crew's cabin up front, but back where the colonel sat, by the open rear door, with wind whipping in, he was glad he'd worn heavy clothing.

More signal lights blinked as the plane pressed across the English Channel. "The sea was calm," Bryan described, "its steely grayness blending in the half-light with the dingier gray of the horizon, but soon the moon brightened the water and made the ripples below us twinkle."

The fuselage of a plane flew beside *Snooty* "outlined against the water," but its wings, obscured from Bryan's vision, "looked but for the high tail fin, like a giant whale, rising and falling in the easy swells."

Halfway across the channel, the planes, one by one, switched off most of their formation lights. Bryan could see a few ships in the channel below but could not be certain whether they were part of the armada carrying allied soldiers to the beaches for the attacks that would quickly follow the first landings of airborne troops.

Peters again muttered out loud, "Where is all this fighter protection we were going to have?" True, they had not seen a plane outside their own formations, but, Bryan thought to himself, "The fighters must have done their work well for there was no sign of enemy aircraft either."

"Tiny, tell the colonel it's thirty minutes till jump time," Peters yelled out, and Bryan watched as "the fat, husky crew chief, Staff Sergeant Richard A. Eberly of Indianapolis," the son of an Air Corps major, "shouldered his way back to give word to Colonel Cole." Before he knew it, Bryan turned his "eyes from the occasional lights and flares which glowed on the Channel Islands." As he looked straight ahead, he caught his first glimpse of the east coast of France. "I had never visited the continent of Europe in peacetime," he stated, "and I was waiting for invasion day to visit it in wartime. The pilot and copilot too were seeing this coast for the first time. None of us spoke, but each looked at the other."

Because of perfect navigation, they could now see the beach ahead, "precisely at the point we had studied it on the maps, an aerial photograph, and on carefully modeled relief maps."

Approaching the Normandy coastline, *Snooty* sailed straight into a thick fog bank. For the next two or three minutes, Peters flew blind, relying on his instruments to keep the plane on course. Emerging from the darkness, Peters was guided by a bright moon the rest of the way.

By now, he had reduced altitude so the plane was so low (about seven hundred feet) that, it seemed to Bryan, the ground was almost close enough for the men to jump without parachutes: "The small fields looked peaceful within their orderly hedge rows. It almost seemed you could see the furrows."

Snooty met with "only smattering small arms fire from the fields, which were dark and quiet as we entered enemy territory."

Now the paratroopers were on their feet, each adjusting his pack and snapping his ripcord over the static line cable running along the center of the cabin's ceiling. That way, each chute would open automatically as the paratrooper jumped through the door. Bryan stood by the rear door. Over the roaring engines, he could hear Colonel Cole ask his men, "Are you all set?" Heads nodded.

Another paratrooper hooked Cole onto the static cable, and he moved next to Bryan. Suddenly, Peters flipped the jump switch light to green.

The men began jumping quickly. In a matter of minutes, the empty plane flew back over the water, setting a course for home, while "a few tracer bullets curved up to the side of us and behind us." Because Bryan wanted to know how long it would take the eighteen men to jump, he tried to count—one hundred one, one hundred two, one hundred three— to estimate seconds. "Before I had counted to ten seconds—it may have been eleven or twelve, but no more—our passengers left us," Bryan said.

That is, all but one of them—the one who had fallen. He was miserable, thinking his comrades might call him yellow, but the plane's crew assured him that the other men would think no such thing.

As soon as Bryan had watched the jumps from the rear door, "tiny streams of tracer bullets were curving upward from the ground," but none hit *Snooty*. Perfect navigation had obscured the plane from known German batteries.

Snooty flew over France for only eleven minutes. With the C-47 lightened by unloaded men and cargo, it streaked for home. Behind the plane, Bryan "could still see the tracers and an occasional flare, below a few more ships: we couldn't tell what they were."

Flying back over the channel to Greenham Common, Bryan took his seat in the navigator's dome. He caught a glimpse of vessels below, ships probably loaded with troops storming the beaches. On *Snooty*'s starboard, a "continuous parade of C-47s" headed in the opposite direction.[4]

The battle of Europe was well under way.

1

General Lee's Airborne

Brigadier General Billy Mitchell was often found at General John J. ("Black Jack") Pershing's headquarters. Ever since Black Jack had put Mitchell in charge of the air service during World War I, Mitchell stopped by unannounced every week, sometimes more than once. He mostly ranted to the American Expeditionary Forces (AEF) commander about the value of air power. The flamboyant, cocky, and outspoken aviator continued this habit until the Army had suffered enough of his outlandish comments and booted him in 1925.

Mitchell came by one afternoon in mid-October 1918 when Pershing was in a particularly foul mood. After three weeks of continuous combat, his doughboys were struggling at Meuse-Argonne. Messages from the front told Pershing that their attacks had gained little ground. Casualties mounted. The other Allied commanders wanted Pershing's head, and he felt close to a nervous breakdown.

Mitchell boasted that he could break the stalemate and asked Pershing to hear him out. Black Jack nodded yes and listened:

"We should arm the men with a great number of machine guns and train them to go over the front in our large airplanes, which would carry ten or fifteen of these soldiers. We could equip each man with a parachute, so that when we desired to make a rear attack on the enemy, we could carry these men over the lines and drop them off in parachutes behind the German position."[1]

Pershing's reaction is unknown. Even had he approved, however, Mitchell couldn't have executed his scheme for at least several months: no parachutes were stored in the AEF stockpile, nor were there enough bombardment planes. Three weeks after Mitchell pitched his plan, Pershing's doughboys broke through enemy defenses, driving the Germans back into Germany and ending the war.[2]

One hundred and thirty-four years before Mitchell proposed the idea of airborne warfare, Benjamin Franklin—politician, inventor, scientist, and all-around renaissance man—advocated airborne warfare after witnessing the ascension of France's first hot-air balloon. Why not launch "five thousand balloons capable of raising two men each?" he suggested to his friend, Dutch plant physiologist Jan Ingenhouz, in 1784, so that "ten thousand men descending from the clouds might not in many places do an infinite deal of mischief before a force could be brought together to repel them?"[3] Franklin's idea, like Mitchell's, went nowhere, and parachutes continued to be used strictly for recreation.

Who precisely invented the parachute, which led to thirteen thousand American paratroopers dropping into Normandy, is debatable—although the credit should most likely go to the ancient Chinese: legend has it that four thousand years ago, Emperor Shun escaped his father's attempt to burn him by jumping off a roof using two cone-shaped bamboo hats to cushion the fall.

Vertical envelopment is far better associated with Europeans. In the fifteenth century, Leonardo da Vinci invented a parachute design. As Franklin witnessed firsthand four hundred years later, the French turned jumping from balloons into a spectator sport. In 1785, noted French hot-air balloon adventurer Jean-Pierre Blanchard threw a parachute-equipped dog over the side of his balloon. The dog landed safely and took off running with the parachute still attached.[4]

Around 1907, American Charles Broadwick devised his own method of parachuting. He jumped from underneath the balloon, using a parachute folded into a pack, strapped to his back and opened by a static line attached to the balloon. Not only was Broadwick a daredevil, performing for large crowds at fairs, but, like the parachutists who came before him, he was also a pioneer.

Finally, in 1929, the US Army briefly tested what Franklin and Mitchell had envisioned: exploiting parachutes for military operations. At Brooks Field in San Antonio, Texas, three soldiers wearing goggles and parachute backpacks climbed onto the top of four de Havillands (two-pilot biplanes) and, when ordered, jumped from the wings.

Between the biplanes, Claire Lee Chennault (the future commander of the Flying Tigers but then a training instructor at Brooks) flew a Ford trimotor transport carrying machine guns, ammunition, water, and food, which were dropped where the paratroopers intended to land. The landings didn't go entirely as planned, however.

Soldiers drifted over power lines or landed in mesquite trees; yet in short order the soldiers had reassembled at the designated landing zone and had the machine guns operational. None of this, however, impressed the Army's chief of staff, General Charles P. Summerall. On hand to watch the event, he was heard murmuring, "Some more of this damned aviation nonsense."[5]

Under his watch and the inaction of two chiefs of staff who followed, the War Department mostly chose to just watch as the French, Germans, Italians, and Soviets gave substantial attention to parachuting—that is, until General George C. Marshall was appointed to the coveted post in 1939.[6]

A brilliant, forward-looking thinker, Marshall was fifty-nine when he took charge of the Army (coincidentally, the same day Adolf Hitler invaded Poland). Much like his mentor John J. Pershing, whom President Theodore Roosevelt had catapulted from captain to brigadier general over 835 senior officers, Marshall became brigadier general, the Army's highest-ranking officer, under the command of Teddy Roosevelt's distant cousin, President Franklin D. Roosevelt, who chose Marshall over twenty more senior generals.

Born in 1880, George Catlett Marshall Jr. was raised forty-six miles southeast of Pittsburgh in Uniontown, Pennsylvania. His father, who partly owned several coke ovens and coal fields, came from a long lineage of Virginians, including the first chief justice, John Marshall.[7]

Marshall was closer to his mother, Laura, than to his father. She was the opposite of her husband, who had a quick temper. "She was both gentle and firm," Marshall remembered, "very understanding, and had a keen, but quiet sense of humor."[8] Each Christmas, she placed a special gift for Marshall under the Christmas tree, and every year on his New Year's Eve birthday, a week later, he could count on $10 from his mother.

Marshall was a mediocre student. He loved history, especially stories about Benjamin Franklin and Robert E. Lee, while finding math, grammar, and spelling tough going.[9] Approaching graduation from public school, Marshall weighed his options. College and military service topped the list; attending West Point seemed a good idea.

Before applying to take the competitive exam, he had to secure a political recommendation. Uniontown, a largely conservative part of Pennsylvania set in Fayette County, had sent a Republican senator and congressman to Washington. Marshall's father, an outspoken Democrat, told George Jr. not to even bother applying.

So George Jr. attended Virginia Military Institute (VMI) in Lexington, where his older brother had gone, and where, many years before, Thomas J. ("Stonewall") Jackson, a boyhood hero of Marshall's, had taught. Just steps from the school's gate, General Robert E. Lee, another of his heroes, lay enshrined in the Washington and Lee University chapel.

Entering VMI in September 1897, Marshall turned heads as "a lean and gawky cadet, sensitive and shy, a Pennsylvania Yankee in a Southern school." In the classroom, he floundered, but on the parade ground, he shined and was made first captain his last year. In Lexington, Marshall met Lily Coles. They married in 1901, right after his graduation.[10]

Marshall launched his long public career a year later as a second lieutenant in the infantry. He seesawed between assignments in the Philippines and garrison duty in the United States. Between overseas posts, he enrolled in Fort Leavenworth's officer-training school, the path to advancement in the Army.

To get through the rigorous two-year program, Marshall had to break his poor study habits, and, in his second year, he was ranked number one in his class. Afterward, Leavenworth hired him as an instructor.

When the United States entered World War I, Marshall became a G-3, or operations officer, with 1st Division and designed the AEF's first major battle, a limited but stunning victory at Cantigny, France, in May 1918. General Pershing noticed and transferred him to American First Army. There, Marshall was architect of the war's last two operations: St. Mihiel and Meuse-Argonne. Not only a superb staff officer, Marshall was also noted for his loyalty and outspoken candor.

One such example of Marshall's frankness occurred when he confronted Pershing in 1918, something few officers dared to do. During an inspection of 1st Division, Black Jack publicly complained that the unit was poorly trained; Pershing blamed its commanding general. Marshall stepped forward, placed his hand on Pershing's arm to prevent him from leaving, and corrected his boss: AEF headquarters was the problem, he declared, not the division.

Startled by the audacity of the young officer and eager to escape, Pershing promised to look into the matter. "There was no need to look into it," Marshall bluntly retorted. "It's a fact." Pershing calmly replied that Marshall needed to appreciate the troubles his GHQ faced. Marshall, now growing angrier, fired back: "We have them [problems] every day and many a day and we have to solve every one of them by night."

Marshall expected a reprimand for his outburst. Instead, Pershing respected his openness and, from then on, took Marshall under his wing. After the war, Black Jack assigned him as his aide-de-camp.

Twenty years later, his star on the rise, Marshall continued to speak bluntly with his superiors. Summoned to the White House by FDR in April 1939, Marshall presented himself to the president, who said, "General Marshall, I have it in mind to choose you as the next chief of staff of the United States Army. What do you think of that?"

"Nothing, Mr. President," Marshall replied, "except to remind you that I have the habit of saying exactly what I think. And that, as you know," he added, "can often be unpleasing. Is that all right?"

Marshall remembered that Roosevelt flashed his famous grin and said, "Yes." Marshall, not happy with the minimal response, replied, "Mr. President, you said yes pleasantly. But I have to remind you again that it may be unpleasant." The president continued to grin. "I know," he said. But he did not add "George."[11]

When Marshall became chief of staff in September 1939, he piled his desk with attaché intelligence reports describing foreign armies' use of parachutes: the Russians drew the most attention. They had dropped more than five thousand paratroopers during 1936 maneuvers at Kiev; three months after Hitler's invasion of Poland, the Russians went to war with Finland and were the first belligerent to exploit airborne troops in combat.

The Russians were proudly ahead of everyone else in developing airborne troops, even inviting foreign military attaches to witness their maneuvers.[12]

Unlike his predecessors, Marshall paid attention to these events. He directed the chief of infantry, Major General George A. Lynch, to study the possibility of "organizing, training and conducting an air infantry." Lynch knew this directive meant "Right away!"[13]

He replied in five days and told Marshall about four scenarios in which troops could be transported by air: depositing small combat groups for special missions like blowing up enemy factories and munitions, delivering small raiding parties for reconnaissance, dropping combat groups to hold key objectives, and working side by side with mechanized forces.

Marshall sent Lynch's recommendations to Air Corps commander Major General Henry "Hap" Arnold, who had become an early aviation pioneer after Wilbur and Orville Wright taught him to fly in 1911. But Arnold had other priorities. He asked his Air Corps Board and Plans Division to weigh in.

Seven months passed before Lynch heard back. Even then, the response was lukewarm. Simply put, the board decided, the Air Corps' meager resources were already stretched thin, and the Corps did not have enough air transport planes in its fleet. Marshall shelved the plan to use an air infantry—for now.

In a strange way, it was Adolf Hitler who lit a fire under the War Department to jumpstart its parachute program. He launched two successful airborne operations in Denmark and Norway in April 1940 and two others, in Holland and Belgium, the following month.

Suddenly, Arnold offered Marshall a few transport planes, and Marshall then told Lynch to make air infantry a top priority. One of Lynch's most experienced officers on the Infantry Board, forty-three-year-old Major William C. Lee, took charge of the task.

Later called the "Father of Airborne," Bill Lee not only took this new instrument of war forward but also refined it. Described by one historian as "homely and lanky," Lee attended North Carolina State College, about thirty miles from his hometown of Dunn, where he'd joined the school's Reserve Officers' Training Corps (ROTC). Second Lieutenant Lee graduated in 1917, and the Army assigned him to 3rd Division as a platoon and company commander during World War I.

After the war, Lee stayed in the Army as an armored-warfare specialist. Twice in the early 1930s, he went to Europe as an observer and peeked at Germany's airborne-training program. This alone made him the most qualified officer to launch a similar project in the United States. In July 1940, Lee created a Parachute Test Platoon at Fort Benning. Forty-eight men, all volunteers, were divided into four squads that underwent a rigorous six weeks of three-mile runs, calisthenics, tumbling, and hand-to-hand combat.

They also had classroom instruction. Lieutenant William P. Yarborough, one of the squad leaders, recalled sitting in Fort Benning's main theater with a half-dozen other parachute battalion recruits. When the lights dimmed, they stopped talking and stared straight ahead. On the screen, a German newsreel, obtained through American intelligence, titled *Deutsche Wochenschau,* with Wagner's music in the background, showed "in some detail" the Third Reich training paratroopers.

The opening scenes filled the screen "with undulating parachute canopies," Yarborough remembered, "drifting slowly like swarms of poisonous jellyfish across the field of vision." No dialogue—only a "sound track that vibrated and thundered with Wagner's music as the *fallschirmjaeger* came to earth, slipped free from their parachute harnesses and assembled quickly into fighting formations."

Yarborough and the others watched the film over and over. By the fourth time, they knew "every detail—the boots, the helmet straps and the aerial delivery packages."[14]

During the last phase of training, soldiers spent more than forty hours learning to pack their own chutes and, over the course of instruction, jumped four times off a 250-foot tower. A fifth and final jump involved the entire platoon dropping from three aircraft. Once they reached the drop zone (DZ), the paratroopers seized "enemy" positions, using weapons, ammunition, and equipment dropped in separate parachute bundles.

On a warm day in August 1940, practically the entire War Department, including Marshall and Secretary of War Henry L. Stimson, flew from Washington to witness the event. Of course, Major Lee was also there.

The jump was nearly perfect. Other than a couple of paratroopers drifting off course, the majority landed precisely in the DZ and quickly assembled their weapons to attack the objective with vigor.

Marshall was so impressed that he declared the battalion be activated as a permanent tactical army unit the very same day. Before the end of September 1940, the training unit was designated the 501st Parachute Infantry Battalion. The wheels were set in motion for the eventual formation of two airborne divisions, one of which Lee commanded; General Matthew Ridgway, a Marshall protégé, commanded the other. Major Albert Wedemyer, in the War Plans Division and the architect of the so-called "Victory Plan" (a blueprint for how the Army would mobilize and fight should it become a belligerent in World War II) calculated a powerful army to include seven airborne divisions.[15]

While the United States made great progress with air infantry even though it was not yet at war, the Germans regressed: On May 20, 1941, Hitler directed fifteen thousand paratroopers with glider support to assault the Greek island of Crete. This time, the results proved disastrous. Hundreds of transport planes and many paratroopers were shot out of the sky. Fifteen hundred German soldiers who landed were killed by waiting British Commonwealth and Greek troops and armed civilians. Another fifteen hundred Germans were reported missing, but the British and Greek forces also suffered substantial losses. Of the thirty-two thousand British Commonwealth troops and the ten thousand to fifteen thousand Greek troops, the British lost 1,742 killed and roughly the same number wounded, as well as 11,800 captured. Almost the entire Greek force was either killed or captured. After eight days of intense fighting, the Germans took the island, but from then on, Hitler forbade further large-scale airborne operations, but Allied leaders vowed to learn from Crete. For the Americans, Chief of Staff Marshall in particular, it was a true wake-up call. It wasn't until after the war that the full extent of German losses and Hitler's reluctance to employ further large-scale airborne operations became known. Crete had represented the first time that a full division of paratroopers and glider units had been deployed in a single, concentrated operation. It remained the largest airborne operation until Normandy.[16]

2

Matthew Bunker Ridgway

Future 82nd Division commander Matthew Ridgway belonged on the battlefield and led his men from the front in Normandy. He belonged in the midst of his troops, sharing their hardships, discomforts, and dangers.

James Gavin, who served under Ridgway during World War II, said this about him: "A great combat commander. Lots of courage. He was right up front every minute. Hard as flint and full of intensity; so much so I thought the man's going to have a heart attack before it's over."

But Gavin also worried about his commander: "Sometimes it seems as though it was a personal thing. Ridgway versus the Wehrmacht. He'd stand in the middle of the road and urinate. 'I'd say, Matt, get the hell out of there. You'll get shot.' No! He was defiant. Even with his penis he was defiant."[1]

When another officer questioned why Ridgway put himself in harm's way, Ridgway replied that it "won't hurt troop morale to see a dead general from time to time."[2]

Ridgway inherited his devotion to soldiering from his father, Thomas. The 1883 West Point graduate retired as a colonel after thirty-six years in the coast artillery. On March 3, 1895, during the first of Thomas Ridgway's two assignments at Fort Monroe, Virginia, his son, Matthew Bunker, was born.

Typical of military families, the Ridgways traveled the country from one army post to another. Garrisons out West, where Thomas Ridgway commanded artillery batteries, were often the most primitive: they had changed little since they were constructed soon after the Civil War.

Ridgway's parents made an otherwise dreary existence comfortable for him and his younger sister, Ruth.

Their mother Julia, a concert pianist and art collector from Long Island, filled each of their temporary quarters with music and shelves full of books, while their father displayed love, respect, and kindness to his wife and children.

They lived for four years at Fort Snelling, Minnesota. The quarters assigned to the Ridgways had been vacant (except for rodents) for more than a decade.

Winters there were especially harsh, little helped by having only one room heated by a fireplace. Each evening, the family congregated around Julia, seated at her piano. The quartet sang loudly, their voices rising, according to Ridgway, "above the shriek of the whistling wind that blew the snow in drifts against the doorway."

In these remote parts of the United States, Ridgway learned to hunt and fish (his lifelong passions) from his father, from whom Ridgway also learned "to love the open country in all its myriad forms." Matthew Ridgway learned from his family's peripatetic life that no matter where he was—mountains, plains, prairies, or seashore—he could "make myself at home."[3]

In 1900, the United States became involved in the Boxer Rebellion in China. Thomas Ridgway left his family behind to go there with an artillery regiment. Returning after a year, he filled his son's head with rousing stories of American cannon fire smashing down the walls of Tientsin in northern China.

As an army brat, Ridgway changed schools often. He started grammar school in St. Paul, Minnesota, and finished in North Carolina. He did the same thing with high school, starting in Virginia when his father went back to Fort Monroe and then graduating in Boston, where Thomas Ridgway led a coast artillery unit.

Matthew Ridgway easily adapted to the Army life he was born into. Waking up to reveille and falling asleep to "Taps" seemed as natural to him as the sun's rising and setting each day. Yet he displayed only a minimal interest in joining the military, and his father never pushed him in that direction. Thomas Ridgway believed "that a boy was an individual, a new being on earth, with his own traits of character and personality, and he should be allowed to choose his life work without interference."[4]

Ridgway, like most children, longed to please his father. For that reason, and despite his own slight ambition to become a soldier, he applied for appointment to the United States Military Academy in 1912. It remained to be seen whether he could pass the demanding entrance exams, since constantly changing schools had left alarmingly wide gaps in his education.

He was especially delinquent in math, but Thomas Ridgway, an artilleryman, knew this subject well and patiently tutored his boy in the evenings. Young Matt still floundered, however, and remained "exceptionally ill informed" in algebra and geometry. His parents then turned to Swavely's, a preparatory school in Washington, where other academy aspirants studied.

The extra help did little good. Ridgway entered the academy around Christmas 1911, took his exams in May, and "to my bitter disappointment," he recalled, "I failed in Geometry."

Back to Swavely's he went. For the next year, Ridgway studied hard. "Night and day, Saturdays, Sundays and holidays included, I pored over my math books until I felt that Euclid himself would have been hard put to find a proposition that would stump me."

His studying finally paid off: he earned a presidential appointment. He averaged 96 in geometry and algebra, a high enough score to best thirteen other candidates. Walking on to the West Point Plain for the first time on June 14, 1913, Ridgway looked like a model plebe, as first-year cadets were called.

A biographer described Ridgway's hazel eyes as "piercing, deep, and wide-set," which accented a "sharply chiseled and well-proportioned cheekbones and chin, a thin Roman nose and remarkably unblemished, swarthy skin."

Standing 5'10" and weighing 175 pounds, Ridgway effected near-perfect posture. His athletic physique and huge, powerful hands made him a natural at horseback riding, running, swimming, and playing handball and tennis.[5]

Besides his handsome physique, Ridgway's presence radiated toward everyone who encountered him. "He'd come into a room and you immediately felt it," said a close associate. "He couldn't have gotten lost in a crowd if he tried."[6]

To the grinning first classmen, his dashing good looks and rugged appearance meant nothing. They could hardly wait to introduce Ridgway and the other plebes to "Beast Barracks." No sooner had he laid down his bags than he was plunged into "six weeks of rigorous mental, physical and spiritual testing."

Ridgway never forgot that "there is many a night when a man, sore and bruised both physically and emotionally, doubts the wisdom of ever having entered West Point at all." He certainly did. Each night while lying in bed during this anxious period, when a plebe's character is put to test, Ridgway reminded himself, "Your father endured this thing and thousands of other men went through it without breaking down. And if they did it, you can."[7]

Once the hazing ritual ended, Ridgway tried to make the most of his plebe year. He competed for varsity football but showed little aptitude on the gridiron, so he was cut from the team.

While horseback riding, Ridgway was thrown twice into a wooden box painted to resemble a stone fence; during his second fall, while the instructor loudly pointed out his clumsiness, Ridgway suffered an obvious injury to his lower spine, although he walked away as if unharmed. Fearful of being dismissed from West Point, Ridgway kept quiet about the excruciating distress that made walking and sitting uncomfortable.

Eventually, the agony dissipated but never completely disappeared, plaguing Ridgway for the remainder of his life. Once, while bending over a billiard table to make a shot, he felt the pain return with such force that he was brought to his knees.

Another time, when he was on a training mission before the Normandy invasion, Ridgway hopped over a low fence and, as he landed, slipped on the icy ground, which shot a tremor of pain from his head to his toe.[8]

Ridgway continued to thirst for reading at West Point, where he devoted his free time to military biographies and memorizing Rudyard Kipling's poems. Thus, Ridgway behaved in exemplary fashion for most of his four years at the academy.[9]

His only disciplinary infraction occurred during the latter half of his first year: the commandant of cadets caught him inflicting a relatively mild form of Beast Barracks on a plebe. Ridgway was sentenced to a month of walking the grounds during leisure hour and a slew of demerits.

During his last year at the academy, 1918, Ridgway was voted cadet adjutant and managed the football team. Because the United States had just entered the war and needed officers, West Point graduated Ridgway's class of 139 cadets six weeks early.

He ranked somewhere around the top of the middle third of his class. His rank, considered only "fairly good," prevented him from receiving first choice of service. Ridgway wanted the artillery, as his father had selected, but by the time his name was called for assignment, that branch was filled. He settled for infantry. Reflecting on that moment, Ridgway allowed that he had no regrets, not even for a moment, that he "ended up with the riflemen."

Right after graduation, Ridgway married Julia Caroline Blunt in the West Point chapel. Oddly, in his memoir, *Soldier*, published thirty-nine years later, Ridgway never mentions Julia by name, nor their two daughters, Constance and Shirley. The Ridgways divorced in 1930. Five days later, he married again, this time in New York City to Margaret (Peggy) Howard Wilson Dabney, the widow of a West Point classmate, Henry H. Dabney.[10]

Ridgway vaguely cites this second marriage, which lasted sixteen years, in *Soldier*. Without mentioning Peggy by name, Ridgway wrote, "My earlier marriage could no longer survive the long years of separation. The only answer lay in divorce." He married a third and final time in 1947, to divorcée Mary Princess "Penny" Anthony Long.

They had one son, Matty. He and his mother take up much space in the memoir. Ridgway seemed to try to keep his first two marriages hidden, but what makes Ridgway's stance peculiar is that in speeches and memoir, he often touted his strong moral and religious upbringing, which included a boyhood of regularly attending church on Sundays services.[11]

In 1918, the Army allowed Ridgway a two-week leave before reporting to the 3rd Infantry on the Mexican border. Ridgway had hoped the regiment would fight on Europe's Western Front battlefields, but the

Army kept the unit three thousand miles from the muddy trenches of France to protect Eagle Pass, Texas, from bandits.

Thanks to a belligerent noncommissioned officer, Ridgway's first few weeks with the 3rd were tense. The sergeant, who had been in the regiment far longer than Ridgway, had little respect for his green commander. Whenever Ridgway gave him an order, the NCO "would drag his feet" and "offer a half-dozen plausible reasons why it couldn't be carried out."

Although he hesitated to take action at first, Ridgway figured, "If I were ever going to be a leader of troops I had to begin now," and he busted the unruly sergeant. From then on, Ridgway commanded his company without contradiction.[12]

Ridgway never did get to France in World War I. The Army pulled him out of Texas to report to West Point as an instructor. Crushed, he bemoaned in his memoir, "The last great war the world would ever see was drawing to an end and there would never be another." Naively, he thought at the time, "Once the Hun was beaten, the world would live in peace throughout my lifetime."[13]

At the academy, Ridgway hoped he'd be assigned to teach English or law, or maybe Spanish—all subjects in which he had succeeded fairly well as a cadet. The chair of the Department of Modern Languages, one Colonel Wilcox, thought differently.

Wilcox informed Ridgway that he would teach French. Wilcox had shoved Spanish aside because French was the preferred language for future officers who might go to war. Ridgway politely told Wilcox that, one, he hadn't spoken French since his first year as a cadet and, two, he "hadn't been particularly good in it then." Those reasons didn't matter to Wilcox, who told him, "Your classes start tomorrow."

For three weeks, Ridgway stayed up late practicing French grammar. During the day, he bluffed his way through classrooms full of "bright youngsters who from the start had known more about the language then their instructor." The following year, he was allowed to teach Spanish since the war had ended and French no longer seemed a priority. Ridgway stayed at West Point another five years as a tactical instructor, then as director of athletics.

West Point superintendent General Douglas MacArthur took a liking to Ridgway and called him "one of the finest officers I have ever known." The two men didn't cross paths again until decades later during the Korean War, when Ridgway first served under MacArthur as Eighth Army commander and then replaced him as head of United Nations' forces in 1951.[14]

From West Point, the Army transferred Ridgway to Fort Benning to take the company officers' course, from which he graduated second in the class of 1924–1925. His next assignment had far greater significance, as it placed him back with the infantry.

At this time, tensions were running high in north China, where bandit commanders had violated the 1901 Protocol forbidding Chinese forces to enter a several-square-mile area surrounding Tientsin, where Ridgway's father had briefly served during the Boxer Rebellion.

The 15th US Infantry, under command of then-Lieutenant Colonel George C. Marshall, was on duty in the city with a British unit trying to enforce the protocol and to protect Westerners and their property.

Ridgway served as one of Marshall's regimental company commanders. Extending their friendship, Marshall became more than just a mentor to Ridgway: Marshall had "a profound effect" on Ridgway's career. The 15th had suffered from poor morale, a lack of training, and a high rate of venereal disease. Marshall trusted Ridgway to help turn the regiment around. Ridgway did just that in short order: the 15th became a well-disciplined outfit thanks to Ridgway's ability to communicate with the men.

For the next couple of years, until 1928, Ridgway moved back and forth between China and the United States for more regimental command. Then Major General Frank McCoy asked Ridgway to join him on an American mission to war-torn Nicaragua to oversee free elections.

The relationship defined Ridgway: observing McCoy's honesty, integrity, and assurance taught Ridgway to be not only a soldier but also a diplomat.

While in Nicaragua, Ridgway fulfilled his appetite for hunting. The country's lakes were teeming with crocodiles, which Ridgway jumped at the chance to hunt. He sneaked up on the "wary creatures," crawling on his belly through the shallow, slimy, coffee-colored water.

Taking careful aim, he fired between the crocs' eyes. This aim was "a fine test of marksmanship," he later bragged, "for it was all offhand shooting at unknown ranges, at a very small target."[15]

Ridgway was next assigned to the Philippines in 1932 to serve as technical advisor on military matters to the governor general, Theodore Roosevelt Jr. The "warm friendship" they established grew: twelve years later, Ridgway jumped into Normandy and Roosevelt came ashore at Utah Beach.

In 1935, Ridgway was enrolled in Fort Leavenworth's Command and General Staff College in the same class as Maxwell Taylor. They had first met fifteen years before when Ridgway was Taylor's language instructor at West Point.

Also at Leavenworth were Mark Clark, future commander of Fifth Army, and Walter Bedell Smith, Eisenhower's chief of staff for much of World War II. By the mid-1930s, Taylor and Ridgway had developed a close, professional relationship and from then on crossed paths frequently. In a sense, the slightly older Ridgway looked after Taylor. Together, they took the first steps to destroy Hitler's Fortress Europe.

As the 1930s drew to a close, Ridgway attended the Army's prestigious War College, a necessary step for promotion to a higher command. After a brief posting at the Presidio in San Francisco, where he organized a large field exercise, Chief of Staff Marshall brought Ridgway with him on a diplomatic mission to Brazil in spring 1939. The following year Marshall sent Ridgway to Washington to be on the War Plans Division staff in Washington.

Along with fourteen other officers, Ridgway drew up plans in the event of war with either Germany or Japan. "It was an exhilarating experience," he later wrote in his memoir, "to shift armies about, even if they were only on paper."[16]

Not much later, he actually commanded one of these armies in combat.

3

Maxwell Davenport Taylor

If not for his grandfather, it's unlikely that Maxwell D. Taylor would have heroically jumped into Normandy with the 101st Airborne on D-Day.

As a boy, Taylor spent every summer vacation with his maternal grandparents, Milton and Maryellen Davenport. The school year couldn't go by fast enough for young Taylor, for when it finally ended, he could head to his grandparents' Missouri farm near Keytesville in north-central Missouri on the Lewis and Clark Trail.

Taylor adored his grandfather (he was the "greatest man in the world," Taylor once wrote) and was profoundly influenced by him. Davenport had lost an arm in a sawmill accident, not during the Civil War, as one might have guessed. He had proudly served in the Confederate Army under generals Sterling Price (also born in Keytesville) and Joe Shelby, seeing action in Arkansas and Missouri. He started in the cavalry and reached the rank of sergeant; then his horse died, so he switched to the infantry.[1]

Each evening, after long hours working together in the field, Taylor sat beside his grandfather, listening to records on the RCA Victor phonograph and to his war stories. The tales gripped the boy, although they were not fanciful—the old veteran refused to glorify the rebellion. On the contrary, he preferred telling his grandson "how shared hardships and dangers bind men together in the camaraderie of arms."[2] Taylor never forgot how those precious moments with his grandfather steered him toward a military career.

Taylor's parents, John Earle Maxwell and Pearle Davenport, lived in the small town of Keytesville when their only child Max was born on August 26, 1901. Soon after, the Taylors moved to Joplin, then Kansas

City, which became their permanent residence. John Maxwell scratched out a living as a "young country lawyer" even though he had never attended law school. Working for other attorneys meant he earned little money—certainly not enough to buy a house for the family. Throughout his childhood, Taylor lived in a series of small but comfortable houses. He described his family later as "poor-middle class."[3]

John Taylor was a mild-mannered fellow who enjoyed a cigar now and then. Pearle Taylor, by contrast, was "strict and humorless" and doted on her son to the point of possessiveness. The Taylors attended the Disciples of Christ church every Sunday.[4]

At Northeast High School in Kansas City, Taylor proved to be a stellar student. He had an extraordinary aptitude for foreign languages, breezing through classes in Greek and Spanish. Taylor also wanted to learn German, but his mother insisted he take Latin because she thought it was the foundation of the classical education that her generation had received. Not until preparing to face the German Army in World War II did Taylor finally study German.[5]

Taylor was a confident debater: During one particular oration, he spoke about Robert E. Lee's personal integrity and devotion to duty. Lee's greatness as a general was not measured by ultimate success, Taylor believed, but "by the love and devotion given him by his whole army."[6]

In 1917, the United States entered World War I. At age sixteen that year, Taylor had enough credits to graduate early from high school. His father hoped Max would follow him into the legal field, but his grandfather's influence pulled him strongly toward the military. Taylor was more excited by witnessing other young men marching off to war, as his grandfather Milton had done five decades before, than he was by practicing law. His aim was to attend West Point.[7]

Before applying to the military academy, Taylor had to improve his skills in mathematics and science. In high school, he had taken only a few classes in these disciplines. His parents enrolled him in a junior college, Kansas City Polytechnic Institute, where a Professor Lusby enthusiastically taught mathematics. Lusby "would look at a solved equation on the board and crow to his students: 'Now stand back, isn't that beautiful?'" Taylor embraced Lusby's inspiration that math "can indeed be beautiful."[8]

Taylor secured the recommendation of a Missouri congressman to attend either the naval academy or West Point. The entrance exams at both service academies were virtually the same—with one exception: the naval academy required a more extensive understanding of geography, which Taylor lacked. Fortunately, however, he passed the West Point test, and in late October 1918, his father carefully mapped out an itinerary that would haul him up the Hudson River in plenty of time to begin classes. This trip east would be his first time out of Missouri (heretofore, he had ventured only across the Kansas River a few times to visit relatives in Kansas City, Kansas).

Leaving Kansas City's Union rail station, Taylor traveled in a Pullman to New York City, spent one night at the Astor Hotel, and then took a ferry to Weehawken, New Jersey, the next day. That evening, he boarded the *West Shore*, back then the only direct route to the military academy other than river boats. "There were a few other young men on the train," Taylor wrote, imagining his fellow travelers as his future classmates. They "looked just about as uncertain of what they were going to do as I felt."[9]

Taylor arrived at West Point in time to watch a graduation of cadets, who left early after two and a half years so they could fight in France. His class of just more than one hundred cadets was also slated to leave early for the same reason, but World War I ended quicker than anyone thought it would, whereupon the academy reverted to its four-year program.[10]

The first couple of weeks wrecked Taylor's nerves. Before arriving at West Point, he had never met anyone who had attended the academy and could give him some pointers. The next best thing was a handful of books he'd read, which provided a vague idea of how to prepare for plebe year. One of them warned that it would be "something other than mother welcoming home the prodigal son," likely a veiled reference to dreaded Beast Barracks.

Although Taylor endured harassment "morning and night" on the drill field and in the barracks, he came through the ritual unscathed. Beast Barracks, at least for him, proved far less grueling than what his West Point history books had predicted.

It was the same with the academy's notoriously stiff academic program. Professor Lusby had prepared Taylor well for the engineering-based curriculum, which included a heavy load of math. Taylor blew through homework and spent his spare time reading in the small but well-stocked cadet library. [11]

The first year went by quickly with only one minor irritation—the plebes' temporary uniform. Since the academy first opened in 1802, cadets had dressed in gray jackets and pants. Taylor wanted to uphold this tradition, but because of the war, the plebes were clad like General John J. Pershing's "doughboys" on the Western Front for the first few weeks in session. The men wore drab olive blouses and trousers, topped with large campaign hats wrapped in a two-inchwide orange band. The class, forever known as "the Oriole Class," "stood out like barber poles," Taylor recalled years later. After an armistice ended the Great War, the class changed to the gray uniform.

Beginning with Taylor's second year, Douglas MacArthur took over as academy superintendent. The larger-than-life, highly decorated war hero instituted diverse reforms, such as promoting athletics, increasing the number of required classes in the social sciences, and allowing cadets to smoke in their rooms.

Outside his office, MacArthur could be aloof, rarely interacting with the cadets. Taylor recalled him as "a very glamorous figure, a handsome officer of good build and with an impeccable uniform"; when Taylor and the other cadets saluted him with "great decorum," MacArthur returned the salute "with equal decorum, but never spoke to us."[12]

Standing six feet tall and weighing around 155 pounds, Taylor played on intramural sports teams. Tennis appealed to him more; he progressed to become captain of the academy squad. The highlight of Taylor's time at West Point by far, however, was meeting Lydia Happer of Washington, DC. During the fall of his second year, she came up with a group of other young women to attend one of the academy's weekly hops, where Taylor saw her as she entered the hall. After swapping his dance card with another cadet, he pursued her vigorously, and she returned the interest in kind.[13]

Records show that Taylor had very few infractions or demerits throughout his four years at West Point. Two particular incidents, however, bear noting. One time, he received a demerit for "allowing disorder and boisterous conduct in the mess hall" after he had been required to keep good order, while another time an upperclassman saw him make "an improper expression at 8 a.m."[14]

Taylor's most egregious violation, at least according to Major Simon Bolivar Buckner Jr., occurred in his last year during graduation week. Buckner later became a three-star general and was killed at Okinawa, but at the time, he commanded the cadets. Lydia Happer had witnessed the commissioning ceremony, and Buckner learned that the soon-to-be lieutenant and Lydia were seen "showing affection" in public.[15]

Ordered to cadet headquarters, Taylor answered to Buckner's charge of *"flagrante delicto."* Then Buckner asked him whether, based on the circumstances, he should be allowed to graduate. Without batting an eye, Taylor responded, "I hope so."[16]

On June 13, 1922, after two days of uncertainty, Buckner dropped the charges. Taylor graduated number four in a class of 102. MacArthur handed him his diploma and, for the first time, addressed the fresh lieutenant by name: "Congratulations, Mr. Taylor." Taylor's high class ranking earned him the right to choose his branch of service; he selected the engineers for two reasons: first, Robert E. Lee had been an engineer, and second—and more obvious—he would be sent to Engineer School at Camp Humphreys, Virginia, located just outside Washington, where Lydia lived.[17]

Fifty years later, Taylor summed up his West Point experience: "I still dream about being a cadet. The experience is like being dropped on your head when you're a baby. You never quite recover from it in certain ways."[18]

The newly minted lieutenant set foot into a service branch that initially proved more discouraging than promising. Like the uniform he'd briefly worn at West Point, the postwar uniform was "drab and un-exhilarating." The Army overflowed with temporary officers who'd stayed and become regulars after the fighting stopped, so advancement for new officers in the Army was rare and slow in coming: Taylor did not become a captain for thirteen years.[19] He admitted years later that he contemplated leaving the military, but the hard times of the Depression meant that resigning his commission would have been foolhardy.

In 1925, Lydia Happer and Max Taylor married and later raised two sons. Lydia Taylor never complained about being an Army wife, her husband told an interviewer, adding that she "fitted in well. People liked her. We were just a congenial Army family in a congenial environment."[20] Had she been unhappy with their military life, Taylor said, he would have reconsidered staying in.

Despite the lack of promotions, the Army offered Taylor ample opportunity to build his résumé. Besides attending the Engineer School in Virginia, he also went to the Artillery School in Oklahoma and the General Staff School at Leavenworth, Kansas. Between these assignments, Taylor returned to West Point for five years to teach French and Spanish.

In October 1935, right after school in Leavenworth, Taylor went to Yokohama, Japan, to learn Japanese; his wife and sons accompanied him. They lived in a Western-style house with Japanese servants who spoke no English. His classes, held at the American embassy, consisted of two years of formal tutoring, followed by a six-month assignment with a Japanese regiment.

The Japanese fascinated Taylor. He immersed himself in the language every day for a year and a half. Not surprising given his gift for foreign dialects, he excelled to the point that he could carry on a conversation, read the newspaper, and "understand the radio pretty well, provided it did not deal with some esoteric subject." The Army allowed Taylor to leave his studies early to join the Imperial Guards Artillery Regiment in Tokyo as an observer.[21]

Before reporting for duty, Taylor had to speak formally in Japanese before several senior officers at the regimental mess, and he began by expressing his deep honor for being attached to such an esteemed unit. Taylor noted later that he had memorized his talk "so thoroughly in advance" that for years afterward he could it recite it verbatim.[22]

For a long time, Taylor accompanied the Japanese regiment on field exercises, evaluating it at the same time the soldiers were sizing up their foreign guest. The assignment came to an abrupt halt in July 1937, however, when Japanese forces invaded north China. Taylor was sent to Peking to assist the military attaché there, Colonel Joseph Stillwell.

Better known by the nickname "Vinegar Joe" for his harsh treatment of subordinates, Stillwell took Taylor along, traveling by automobile, crowded troop trains, and (not infrequently) foot, throughout north China to watch the Japanese troops on campaign. Taylor never fought the Japanese in World War II, but Stillwell commanded the China/Burma/ India theater. Taylor's experience there proved invaluable, and Stillwell rated him as "one of the finest officers I have ever known."[23]

At the end of that year, Taylor returned to Tokyo for two years and then to the United States in time to enter the War College. There, he first encountered General George C. Marshall, who gave one of the welcoming addresses to the new class.

What Marshall said that day was not memorable, but to Taylor, Marshall's delivery captivated his audience. No one "could ever imagine questioning the accuracy of his facts or challenging the soundness of his conclusions on any subject he undertook to discuss," Taylor recalled.[24]

The Army pulled Taylor out of the War College in spring 1940 just before graduation to send him to Central and South America with a group of Army and Navy officers. They were tasked with determining the "military needs of hemispheric defense" against a probable Nazi threat.

Six months had gone by since Adolf Hitler had invaded Poland to start World War II, and the Germans wanted neutral Latin America to side with them. Leading the project was Taylor's former Leavenworth classmate, Lieutenant Colonel Matthew B. Ridgway, who arranged for most of the Spanish-speaking countries they visited to receive military aid and funds from the United States.[25]

In Taylor's last post before the war, he reported directly to Marshall as his military secretariat. Primarily, Taylor shuttled messages between the chief of staff and the White House. One day, in Marshall's office, Taylor met Dwight D. Eisenhower for the first time. Eisenhower, recently called back from Fort Sam Houston, Texas, had just made brigadier general and been appointed to head the War Plans Division. Taylor took him to see President Franklin Roosevelt.

Whether Eisenhower formed an opinion of Taylor then is unknown, but a few years later, Eisenhower knew Taylor well enough to tap him as division commander.[26]

Taylor's beloved grandfather would have been proud.

4

War

On Sunday afternoon, December 7, 1941, Max and Lydia Taylor were cleaning closets upstairs in their northwest Washington, DC, row house. Downstairs in the living room, their two boys listened to the Redskins versus Eagles football game on radio station WOL. Part-way through the first quarter, a bulletin interrupted the broadcast. Jack, the older son, repeated the announcement, yelling upstairs to his folks, "The Japanese are attacking Pearl Harbor!"[1]

Taylor ran downstairs to try to call General George Marshall's office. No luck. All circuits were busy. No matter—Marshall wasn't in his office. He was across the Potomac River, riding his horse at Fort Myer.[2]

Taylor hopped into the family Chevy and sped down Military Road. Washington's streets had little traffic that Sunday afternoon, so he quickly reached his office. The Munitions Building on Constitution Avenue was hunched among other run-down structures that had been hurriedly constructed during World War I and now served as headquarters for the Navy and War departments.[3]

Major William Sexton, Marshall's assistant secretary, had been on duty all night. Sexton greeted Taylor with an update on the attack. When Marshall showed up, he went right to work.[4]

Taylor spent the rest of the day sorting through the communiqués pouring in on the wire with the latest information. At eight o'clock that night, Taylor delivered a summary report to the White House from Marshall to President Roosevelt's military aide, General Edwin Martin "Pa" Watson. Taylor drove home, changed from civilian clothes into his Army uniform, and returned to the Munitions Building. He stayed there for the next several days.[5]

Colonel Matt Ridgway learned about the Pearl Harbor attack around the same time as Taylor. Ridgway had just entered the familiar grounds of Fort Benning, Georgia, where he was about to start the Infantry School's refresher course. Ridgway, unaware of the news unfolding in Hawaii, couldn't have been more delighted to be far from Washington, DC.

His job had become tediously routine: Every day, Ridgway sat behind the same desk to carry out the same duties. His chores, which started at 6:00 a.m., involved reviewing overnight reports on the fighting in Europe. By eight, he'd complete a summary for Marshall, Secretary of War Henry L. Stimson, and President Franklin Roosevelt. For the remainder of the day, Ridgway recalled in his memoir, "I would go ahead with my regular duties until ten or eleven o'clock at night, a routine that left me a little hollow-eyed."[6]

More than twenty years had passed since his post as a company commander on the Mexican border, his first assignment after West Point. Ridgway, longing for another field command, was not shy about asking Marshall for help. The chief of staff promised him a regiment more than once, but first, Marshall would add, a position had to open.

Ridgway persisted. Every day, he hounded Marshall's staff secretary, Walter Bedell Smith, with the same question: "Any word for me?" Each time, the answer remained the same. Finally, Smith had had enough. He shot back at Ridgway's demand: "Yes, this morning, General Marshall said, and I quote, 'Tell Ridgway I'm tired of seeing him hanging around out there every time my door opens. When I have something for him, I'll send for him.'" Ridgway backed off.

At the end of November 1941, Chief of Infantry Major General George A. Lynch offered Ridgway command of a Philippine regiment. Ridgway didn't inquire further about the assignment. He figured it had to be with one of the new Scout units forming to bolster the Philippines' meager defenses.

Ridgway turned Lynch down. Leading a bunch of raw recruits with questionable ability sounded unappealing. Reflecting on the decision two years later, Ridgway sighed with relief, for accepting the command probably would have resulted in his being captured or killed at either Bataan or Corregidor.

Ridgway remained chained to his desk until the Infantry School's refresher course was scheduled, and Marshall granted him a week's leave to attend. Not only would this offer a respite from his monotonous (yet grueling) schedule, but the class could also provide Ridgway a leg up when competing for eventual command assignments.

Ridgway arrived in Georgia around midday on December 7. Cooling his heels until lunch, Ridgway caught the approach of another officer, a sullen expression on his face. Something was wrong.

Ridgway learned that the situation at Pearl Harbor was bad, but just how bad nobody knew for sure. Rumors spread like jam among the clatter of flatware hitting plates in the Benning Mess Hall: waves of Japanese planes were striking the naval fleet lying exposed in water, once blue but now oily. The reality turned out to be far worse than the rumors.

Before Ridgway settled into his quarters, a phone call from Washington ordered him back to the White House immediately. The next morning, December 8, he was once again at his desk, shuffling papers. Later that day across town on Capitol Hill, President Roosevelt addressed Congress to ask for that body to declare war on Japan. Both the House and the Senate unanimously approved.

Three days later, on December 11, Nazi Germany declared war on the United States.

Marshall had at his disposal a meager army, just a tad more than 1,500,000 troops led by around 120,000 officers. The War Department moved swiftly to mobilize three or four divisions per month. Most, such as the 82nd "All-American" Division, had originally been formed at the outbreak of World War I but had lain dormant since the armistice. They were composed of drafted troops, who their commander boasted were the "best men from every state in the Union." In 1918, the division had included Medal of Honor recipient, Alvin York, within its ranks.[7]

Marshall picked forty-eight-year-old Omar Bradley as the 82nd's new commander. At that time, Bradley presided over both the Infantry School and the post at Fort Benning. Bradley had met Marshall about fifteen years earlier as a student in the 1925–1927 Company Commanders' Course at Benning. In Marshall's efficiency report, the general had rated Bradley upon graduation a "superior officer."

"Quiet, unassuming, capable, sound, common sense," Marshall wrote glowingly about the up-and-coming officer. "Absolute dependability. Give him a job and forget about it. Recommended command: regiment in peace, division in war."[8]

Bradley had grown up in humble, Midwest surroundings. Both of his parents were raised in Randolph County, Missouri, in the north-central part of the state. Bradley's father John farmed a bit, but mostly he taught school (he was self-educated).

Between the two occupations, he made little money, so the family struggled. John married one of his students, sixteen-year-old Bessie Hubbard, who gave birth to Omar exactly nine months after their wedding. Bradley's parents named him after a local newspaper editor whom his father had befriended.[9]

In 1907, when Bradley turned fourteen, his father died, leaving his family destitute. Like many soldiers who'd grown up impoverished, Bradley could attend college only by securing a slot in one of the two service academies. Through an appointment from a local Democratic congressman, Bradley went to West Point. He graduated in 1915, along with Dwight Eisenhower and fifty-seven other future generals. They composed what one historian called the "Class the Stars Fell On."[10]

Like Eisenhower and Ridgway, Bradley had served during World War I but never overseas. His career trajectory followed a similar path as others who were guided by George C. Marshall. The chief of staff promoted Bradley to general and placed him in charge of Benning before appointing him 82nd Division commander.[11]

Bradley needed an assistant division commander (ADC). Marshall wanted Ridgway, and in mid-January, Ridgway eagerly accepted the job. Now "Brigadier General Matthew Ridgway," his dream of returning as a field commander had come true. Doing well under Bradley's guidance boosted the chance that one day he might be assigned his own division.

Two hours after meeting with Marshall, Ridgway cleared his desk and marched out of the Munitions Building for the last time. He then rushed across the Memorial Bridge to Fort Humphreys, where he had once been assigned to the Engineer School. Army Ground Forces (AGF) had its headquarters there with the mission of overseeing the organization of Army divisions.

Ridgway's final instructions informed him that the 82nd would assemble at Camp Claiborne on the Red River in central Louisiana. Since he would pass Fort Benning on the way to Claiborne, Ridgway followed the suggestion of the AGF staff to take the week-long refresher course that he had dropped out of on December 7.

Bradley had remained at Benning, so Ridgway's stop-over would be an opportunity for the two soldiers to meet, which made sense to Ridgway. He headed south after a quick stop home to say good-bye to his wife Peggy.[12]

Major Max Taylor's career ambitions differed little from Ridgway's, but he vocalized them far less. He, too, desired to be far from the dingy Munitions Building, out of Washington and leading a combat unit as his grandfather had some seventy-five years before. Taylor thought his break had come around the same time Ridgway left for Louisiana.

Major General Joseph Stillwell, with whom Taylor had served briefly in China, was visiting the War Department. During lunch, Stillwell proposed that Taylor join the staff of his new command, what would ultimately become the China/Burma/India theater.

By the time they left the restaurant in southeast Washington, Taylor thought he had locked up a staff assignment halfway around the world. But a few weeks later, when Stillwell's list of staff officers reached Marshall for approval, Taylor's name did not appear. As it later turned out, Marshall had other plans for Taylor.

Down in Camp Claiborne, Ridgway's tenure as ADC ended abruptly—for good reason. When he had first arrived in Louisiana, Ridgway smartly took responsibility for training the draftees who filled the rosters of the 82nd's three regiments, while Bradley dealt with more time-consuming administrative matters.

Ridgway's dedication and hard work paid off. The AGF moved Bradley to command another remnant from World War I, the 28th National Guard Division, which was showing little promise. After just ninety days, Ridgway assumed leadership of the entire division.[13]

Ridgway's devotion to the Army and his growth as an officer had paid off. Lieutenant Melvin Zais, an 101st Airborne division battalion commander for a brief period, was immediately taken with Ridgway and thought he fit the mold of a model commander:

General Ridgway, from the moment I first set eyes on him, had extraordinary daring, magnetism, and strength of character, and looked like my idea of a leader and an officer. When he walked into the Officers' mess you could feel his presence. He had this look of eagles in his eyes. There was a certain vibrancy that exuded from him. He was broad chested and square shouldered. He walked with a bounce and had a wonderful jaw and aquiline nose. He just looked like a fantastic officer. He spoke in lofty terms and said the right things. He was physically fit. He exercised and had a demeanor and a bearing that was very inspiring.[14]

Now, as commander of the 82nd, Ridgway had the approval to select his own officers: for chief of staff, he added Max Taylor's name on a list sent to Marshall. Ridgway had remembered Taylor from Leavenworth and was impressed by his mission to Latin America.

Marshall wasted little time in selecting Taylor out of the half-dozen other candidates. As Taylor set out for Louisiana, he had no idea—nor did Ridgway, for that matter—that in a matter of months, the 82nd would soon be converted into the US Army's first airborne division.[15]

The Birth of American Airborne Divisions

On a hot, sultry, summer day in 1942, newly minted colonel Maxwell Taylor entered Camp Claiborne, Louisiana, to join Matthew Ridgway's 82nd Division.

Although they were well acquainted, Taylor had not served under Ridgway until then, and the experience taught him much about troop leadership. Taylor later described Ridgway as "very impressive, very intense. He was highly ambitious, determined to be a great general, go all the way to the top."

As divisional chief of staff, Taylor was to handle administrative matters, but Ridgway urgently needed him to help prepare the men for combat. So Taylor immediately spent more time outside than behind a desk. Ridgway oversaw the troops' training. Seven days a week, the troops "worked in the field from morning till night," their uniforms soaked from perspiration brought on by "sizzling Louisiana temperatures."

Sometimes Taylor accompanied Ridgway during inspections.[1] They'd review one company and then jog elsewhere in the camp to observe another group of men. Taylor, who carried no fat on his 175-pound frame, could barely keep pace with his boss. After one of these visits, a junior officer exclaimed, "My God! I saw the chief of staff *chasing* the Old Man around the camp."[2]

Ridgway "drove his men hard," but he also treated them respectfully—a trademark of his command style. "He'd offer constructive criticism," one of his officers remembered, "but would always end up with some sort of compliment. He never talked down to us, but spoke as though we were on his level." Ridgway would emphasize to his officers that they needed to coax soldiers to "exceed their best efforts through the desire to do better than before, not through fear." However, there was to be "unfailing compliance with orders."[3]

Toward the end of July, General Lesley McNair, Army Ground Forces commander in Washington, surprised Ridgway with news that his 82nd would transform from a typical infantry division to a motorized division and move to Camp Atterbury, Indiana, for more training. Motorized infantry divisions ride in trucks alongside armored forces. Ridgway took the change in stride. It made no difference to him whether the 82nd was composed of "foot-slogging infantry" or "troops that rode to battle on wheels."[4]

Hundreds of trucks and vehicles appeared at Claiborne to move Ridgway's men, but before a single bag was packed and the equipment sheds emptied, Major General Floyd Parks arrived unexpectedly to speak with Ridgway. Parks and Ridgway had known each other early in their careers; now Ridgway served as a major general under McNair. Parks entered Ridgway's office, closed the door, and, according to Ridgway, "looked about him cautiously, and then in a voice that was almost a whisper asked his old friend, 'How would you like to command an airborne division?'"[5]

Ridgway, probably dumbfounded, told Parks that he "didn't know what an airborne division was." Parks replied, "Don't worry. Nobody else knows much about it either." Parks claimed that all the brass back in Washington understood about "airborne" was that the Germans had deployed paratroopers and glider men with some success until the disaster at Crete.

Parks's dismissive comment was not entirely correct. Thanks to Bill Lee, the anointed Father of the Airborne, the paratrooper program had blossomed since Chief of Staff Marshall had given a thumbs-up after witnessing the successful parachute jump exhibition in August 1940. Under Lee's leadership, four paratrooper battalions had been created in a little more than a year.

One of Lee's staff officers witnessed how his boss almost single-handedly grew the airborne. The officer called Lee a "smart, patient, tolerant, considerate, intelligent and kind man." The officer added that, although Lee allowed his staff to be creative and try just about anything, "he applied a governing hand—and good common sense."[6]

Despite Lee's brilliant work, the fledgling airborne program experienced significant growing pains. There was a limited stockpile of rifles, pistols, machine guns, mortars, helmets, and communication equipment from which to draw. Acquiring parachutes (the Air Force's responsibility) became a greater headache. Not only were thousands needed to accommodate Fort Benning's volunteer trainees, who needed two parachutes (main and reserve chutes), but just as many were also required for the regiments now under Lee's command.

The Air Force adopted the T-5 parachute, which has a twenty-eight-foot canopy with the same number of panels and an open apex that allowed air to escape and that reduced oscillation. Parachutist Leslie Irvin, a former film industry stunt man, developed the T-5. His Irving Parachute Company in Buffalo, New York, couldn't meet the heavy demand as stipulated in its War Department contract, however, so the Air Force called on the Switlik Parachute Company out of New Jersey to assist in production.

Started by Polish immigrant Stanley Switlik in 1920, the company first manufactured canvas and leather goods, including collapsible hampers, golf bags, coal bags, and pork roll casings. Fourteen years later, George Palmer Putnam, Amelia Earhart's husband, collaborated with Switlik on a joint venture to train airmen in parachuting and, from there, started making parachutes. By 1942, Irvin and Switlik were producing twenty thousand parachutes per month.[7]

The British airborne program started in June 1942, around the same time that the American program began. To observe how the Brits maintained their program, Lee, who had been promoted to brigadier general on April 19, 1942, traveled to England to meet his counterpart, Lieutenant General Sir Frederick Browning.

Not only did Lee and Browning visit British units, but they also saw Polish, Free French, Norwegian, Belgian, and Dutch airborne outfits that were training in the United Kingdom. Lee and Browning shared ideas and mutual admiration that, as one historian noted, "laid the foundation of the close co-operation and affection" between American and British paratroopers.[8]

Browning was raised in a distinguished, middle-class family. He attended Sandhurst, a secondary school, in 1914, and then he accepted a commission with the Grenadier Guards. In that organization, Browning was first called "Boy." Browning's family had called him "Tommy" when he was a boy, and he'd bestowed that name on his constant companion as a child, a toy pet monkey, but "Boy" lasted the rest of his life.[9] Major Brian Urquhart, who served under Browning for three years, suggested that "Boy" resulted from Browning's never quite growing up, as well as from his "dashing appearance, his perfectly harmless vanity, his enthusiasm. And hyperactivity."[10]

Never a healthy child, Browning's sickliness followed him into the Army. During World War I, he was too ill to fight at the Somme in 1916. He did see heavy combat at Passchendaele in 1917, however, as well as action near Amiens during the German 1918 spring offensives.

In October 1941, during World War II, Boy was promoted to major general and appointed commander of the Parachute Troops and Airborne Troops. Browning became the face of the British airborne divisions for creating the maroon beret his men wore draped to the right and for designing a distinctive uniform made of barathea, a fine, woven cloth, with a false, Uhlan-style front, reminiscent of Polish cavalry uniforms, which incorporated a zipper.

After Lee had returned home, Field Marshal General Sir John Dill, vice chief of the Imperial General Staff, visited Washington as head of Joint Staff Mission. He suggested that Browning come to the United States to meet the American paratroopers. Browning arrived on July 20, 1942, and was welcomed warmly by Lee and his staff. He spent most of the time with Lee, touring fields in Texas and Florida, but he also found a moment to meet with George C. Marshall, who impressed him a great deal. By and large, Browning liked what he saw, particularly the abundance of support equipment.

Browning's visit was marred, however, by what his biographer, Richard Meade, described as his "seemingly condescending manner, which ruffled American feathers and was recalled in all of their dealings with him over the coming years."[11] Meade suggests Browning never intended to offend his American hosts: "But it was his manner to adopt a certain professional coldness when in uniform and express his opinions with considerable force, traits which were often mistaken for arrogance by those who had not had the opportunity to know him better." Browning later admitted that his opinions may have been misunderstood and that perhaps "Americans did not like being lectured by people whose experience was not significantly greater than their own."

In Browning's report, submitted after returning to England, he agreed that the limited experience of the British gave them no right to tell the Americans how to do things, but the Brits could advise the Yanks how *not* to do things. Browning concluded, "I personally would have no qualms, from what I have seen of the [US] Army, about the amount of co-operation which can be expected as long as we know their outlook and meet them more than half-way, which is not always easy for an Englishman."[12]

Because the decision to form an airborne division had been crafted in complete secrecy, Browning likely had had no idea regarding the plan when he visited the United States.

On advice from Lee, Leslie McNair had selected the 82nd "to be the guinea pig division."[13] Clay Blair, one of Ridgway's biographers, cites several reasons: "It was a problem-free division nearing the end of its training cycle; Ridgway was intelligent, dynamic and flexible; and the division was conveniently situated near the Paratrooper School at Fort Benning."[14]

Even though Ridgway later remarked that "my knowledge of airborne operations at that moment was exactly nil," he was flattered that his 82nd had been selected, so he quickly warmed to the idea of being an airborne division commander. With division artillery commander Brigadier General Joe Swing, he made an excuse to "slip off down to Benning."

In Columbus, Georgia, Ridgway met with General Bud Miley, who had organized and led the 501st Parachute Infantry Battalion. Miley gave Ridgway and Swing a crash course in parachuting. Ridgway reportedly had told him, "If anybody in my division was going to jump, I wanted to be the first to do it."

The jump was far from pleasant for Ridgway: he hit the ground with a "tumbling, bruising roll." Next, it was on to Wright Field in Dayton, Ohio, to fly in a glider. That experience also caused Ridgway a great injury. As the glider attempted to land, the wheels failed to drop, so the pilot yelled for Ridgway to jump. As they approached the runway going thirty miles an hour, Ridgway "made the damnedest two-point landing you ever saw," ripping all the skin off his left ankle and the right cheek of his behind.[15] He returned to his division, now training at Fort Bragg, North Carolina, bruised and sore.

During the first week of March 1943, General Marshall called Ridgway to Washington. There, the chief of staff informed him that he had planned a quick trip to Africa and wanted Ridgway and two or three of his staff to come along so they could start the preliminary plans for an airborne drop into Sicily.

They flew overseas by way of the South Atlantic route, which took them from Florida, over Puerto Rico, and onto South America. Over the three-day flight, the longest stretch was over water, Brazil to the Ascension Island, in the middle of the South Atlantic, one thousand miles from the west coast of Africa. This leg of the flight scared Ridgway so much that he recited an "old, simple prayer of the Breton fisherman": "Oh Lord, be good to me, for Thy sea is so wide, and my ship is so small."[16]

Reaching Africa, Ridgway saw for the first time "the loneliest and most ominous of all landscapes, a battlefield." He visited with General George S. Patton, who was in command of II Corps, and General Omar Bradley, who was on hand as Patton's understudy since he would take over the corps after Patton's promotion to Seventh Army command took effect.

For an entire week, Ridgway observed fighting on the Tunisian front. Not much "hard fighting," as he put it, but plenty of patrols by 1st and 9th Infantry divisions in which he took part. Ridgway saw German soldiers for the first time when a Messerschmidt strafed his convoy.

More important, on the trip he met British general Harold R. L. G. Alexander, who now commanded 18th Army Group, who would take charge of all ground forces at Sicily. Ridgway and Alexander briefly discussed the airborne plan, and Ridgway was not at all happy with what he learned. The 82nd would play a minimal role after the British 1st Airborne had jumped. But the plans for now were preliminary, and there would be plenty of chances for Ridgway to argue for a bigger piece of the operation after he returned to Fort Bragg on March 24.[17]

It was there that he received orders to split his division in two. Another airborne division, the 101st, would be formed with Bill Lee as its commander. Lee came up to Bragg from Benning to discuss how to separate the 82nd. He was even more banged up than Ridgway after breaking his back in a parachute jump. Lee spent a few weeks in the hospital and had to wear a cast—from his chin to his waist—for months. The two maimed soldiers quickly decided to divide the 82nd equally.[18]

On August 15, 1942, the 82nd had been scheduled for a full-dress review. Ridgway took advantage of the occasion to announce the split to his men. He stood on a raised platform, and, like Shakespeare's Henry V before the Battle of Agincourt, Ridgway delivered a rousing speech, his voice booming over a public address system. He regaled the men with how important and unique their mission had become:

> *This I do know, and you know it, too, that never in the history of our Army will one unit go into battle with so many eyes upon it as we will. New weapons, new organization, new technique, new tactics in the hands of the first American airborne division ever tested will turn the spotlight on us, and we can be sure that our enemies will watch us even more intently than do our comrades.*[19]

Many of the new tactics Ridgway crowed about had been developed by a young upstart officer named James Gavin (a protégé of Bill Lee's), who, his biographers rightfully acknowledge, deserves a place on the same stage as his mentor for defining the airborne concept and fighting "fiercely for its acceptance."[20]

6

"Become a Paratrooper!"

Not long after Pearl Harbor was attacked, Father Francis L. Sampson exchanged his black cassock and white, starched clerical collar for a chaplain's green uniform. He said goodbye to his bishop of the Roman Catholic Diocese of Des Moines and reported for duty as a first lieutenant in the 90th Infantry Division.

In August 1942, after completing thirteen weeks of basic training, Frank Sampson attended Chaplain School on Harvard University's campus to learn military law, map reading, defense against gas warfare, discipline, close-order drill, and grave registering.[1] One day, Sampson and the other chaplains were asked whether they wanted to volunteer as paratroopers. "Like a zealous young business man starting out in a strange town," Sampson remembered that he swiftly responded, "Yes!" "I was ready to join anything out of the sheer sense of civic duty," he wrote in his memoir.[2]

He immediately regretted his snap decision. He had not realized that all paratroopers—even their chaplains—jumped from airplanes into battle. He also found out that training for airborne divisions would be far more strenuous than he'd imagined.

"Had I known this beforehand, and particularly had I known the tortures of mind and body prepared at Fort Benning for those who sought the coveted parachute wings," Sampson would later say, "I am positive that I should have turned a deaf ear to the plea for Airborne chaplains."

Pride wouldn't allow him to back out. Besides, airborne divisions were "elite troops of the Army." He thought, "I'll enjoy the prestige and glamour that goes with belonging to such an outfit."[3] Sampson would soon not only join the select group of paratroopers but also become part of the elite

101st Airborne Division and take part in one of the war's most dangerous missions.

Sampson was born in 1912 in Cherokee, Iowa. For much of his childhood, Sampson moved often with his family. Sampson's father was a "hotel man": he bought a hotel every year and a half and renovated it. After turning a profit, he moved on to the next hotel with his family in tow. Frank Sampson attended eight different grammar schools and five different high schools. He attended Notre Dame University and, afterward, St. Paul Seminary. Ordained on June 1, 1941, he served as a parish priest and taught high school until the surprise Japanese attack on Pearl Harbor six months later changed his career. Sampson didn't wait to be drafted into the Army; he voluntarily joined up.

Thanks to its aggressive campaign, the Army lured him and thousands of other soldiers to volunteer as paratroopers. Some were drawn by recruitment flyers strategically placed throughout Army posts; others might have joined after reading *Life* magazine's eight-page article "U.S. Army Parachutist." The May 12, 1941, cover story, packed with photos, hyped that "day after day, at peril of their lives," brave men jumped from 750 feet into the "dusty Georgia air above Camp Benning."[4]

Four months later, Hollywood did its part and rushed out an epic film, *Parachute Battalion*. Only seventy-five minutes long, the documentary-style film starred Robert Preston, Buddy Ebsen, and Edmond O'Brien as three strangers who meet on a train headed to Fort Benning for paratroopers' school. To add a bit of realism to its story, RKO Productions sent a camera crew to Benning, where Colonel Bill Lee doubled for Robert Preston in some scenes.[5]

Outside the Cincinnati, Ohio, post office, Robert L. Williams gazed at a poster beckoning him to "Become a Paratrooper: Jump into the Fight." The colorful illustration by Harry Steele Savage showed a tough-looking soldier dominating the foreground with a Thompson machine gun; behind him, a half-dozen paratroopers floated from the sky. This image was all it took for Williams to join the 506th Parachute Infantry.

Wanting to became a paratrooper, willing to fight and to accept the hazardous risks of jumping from a plane, was one thing. Meeting the Army's strict physical standards was another.

Paratroopers had to be active, alert, and flexible; they had to possess firm muscles and sound limbs. They needed to be capable of developing into an aggressive, individual fighter with great endurance. They could not be younger than twenty or older than thirty. Weight was capped at 185 pounds, and eyesight had to be at least 20/40 in each eye. Systolic blood pressure could not exceed 140. Failure to meet any of these criteria meant instant disqualification.[6]

Sampson reported to paratrooper school in late 1942. Like others before and after him, he would have entered through a gate embossed at the top with the words "Through these portals pass the toughest paratroopers in the world." On Lieutenant Sampson's first day, the smiling school adjutant told him rather flippantly, "You know, the previous two chaplains were hospitalized! One broke his leg and the other suffered a back injury!" Sampson said nothing, but he later described his face as turning both "comic and tragic." After laughing, the adjutant added, "but three or four chaplains came through with hardly a scratch!"[7]

Officers were housed in wooden barracks huts, while enlisted men slept in tents. Officers and enlisted men also did not train together, although everyone went through the same grueling process. Training was divided into four stages: A, B, C, and D. Sergeants led stage A, a rare opportunity for them to oversee higher-ranking officers attending the school. Sampson learned of one lieutenant colonel who refused to obey a training sergeant; as punishment, the colonel had to apologize publicly before the Army kicked him out of school.

Instructors dressed identically: jump boots, trousers, and white T-shirts that "showed their bulging muscles and slim waists to good advantage"—so remembered Private Spencer F. Wurst.[8] Private Bob Bearden marveled at how the tough sergeants partied all night at drinking holes in Columbus, Georgia, or nearby Phenix, Alabama, yet still rose early to lead recruits on a five-mile run, "barking commands all the way."[9]

Each day started with reveille at 5:00 a.m. Sixty minutes later, forty-five-man platoons engaged in intense, three-hour-long calisthenics. As many as two-thirds of the recruits would pass out from the heat or physical exhaustion. NCOs punished them by shouting, "Gimme 25!" (meaning twenty-five push-ups).

Lieutenant Sampson admitted that he was among those who "did rather badly with calisthenics." He "could never seem to get the hang of climbing the rope." He got very accustomed to doing fifty push-ups. The only thing that prevented Sampson from washing out was that he never dropped from a run. By the end of his first week, he noted that the once-crowded barracks where he had been quartered with seventy-seven other officers "had slipped to a comfortable thirty-eight."[10]

During stage A, men also learned how to leave from a plane door in order to be in the correct position when their parachutes opened. This exit involved climbing a set of steps leading six feet from the ground into an open door nearest to the cockpit. Once inside the plane, they turned around to exit from the rear door while counting: "One thousand, two thousand, three thousand . . ." They repeated the exercise over and over, first slowly, and then increasing the pace while two or three instructors corrected and harassed them.

Soaked with sweat after four hours of training, the men hustled back to the barracks to shower. In their coveralls. That way they washed their bodies and clothes at the same time since the coveralls had to be clean the next morning. They spent the remainder of the day at Lawson Field in hangars, learning to pack their parachutes on long, narrow tables. Afternoons, they repeated the schedule, adding judo, multiple attempts at the obstacle course, and another long, hot run.

Up to this point, most of the parachutes used in training were made of silk that had been imported from Japan, and some were manufactured with cotton. But once the United States entered the war and no longer traded with Japan, the Dupont Company helped develop a nylon parachute. Dupont teamed with the Pioneer Parachute Company (the same company in Connecticut where paratrooper Robert Hillman had worked before the war and that still employed his mother) and a silkmaker, the Cheney Brothers Company, to create a durable parachute.[11]

Stage B focused on landing correctly. Class was held in a wide shed with a fifteen-foot platform at one end. The students stood on the platform and put on their harnesses, which the instructors attached to an apparatus with roller wheels and a quick-release mechanism. This contraption was attached to an I-beam mounted on an angle running about fifteen feet above the ground. As the soldiers jumped from the platform, forward momentum simulated the speed of actually jumping from a high altitude.

"Land on the balls of both feet!" the instructors bellowed. "Tumble forward to either the right or left." Corporal Wurst remarked that it was difficult during practice to land properly without wearing combat gear but added that landing was "impossible when loaded down with equipment."[12] Next, they jumped from a ten-foot tower and then from forty feet. Punishment for not jumping correctly was harsh criticism— and fifteen to twenty push-ups.

During stage C, the men jumped from two types of 250-foot towers: controlled and free. The towers were the idea of Colonel Bill Lee, now leading Airborne Command. Lee had seen a similar contraption at the 1939 World's Fair in New York before which people lined up to be hoisted to the top of the tower by cable and then dropped by parachute. A year later, Lee took a paratrooper platoon to the Safe Parachute Company in Highstown, New Jersey, and trained on the towers. Convinced that they were essential for practicing jumps, Lee had the Army buy four of them, and they were reassembled at Fort Benning.[13]

The controlled tower had four cables that opened the canopies from the outer edge; on the free tower, students were hoisted to the top and released while the instructor shouted through the loudspeaker, "Don't stretch for the ground! Make a half-turn to the right!" The objective for jumping from both towers was to accustom the men to heights and to teach them how to place their bodies in the correct position when they hit the ground. Sampson, who failed to heed the advice, "landed like a sack of flour."[14]

At the end of stage C, men were placed in front of a wind machine so they could discover how to return to their feet while being dragged. Wurst had a tough time with this exercise. His small stature made it hard for him not to be blown around. After many attempts, he figured out how to stand up and collapse his chute, but not without incurring the wrath of his instructors, as well as "many scrapes, scratches and bruises from head to foot."[15]

Finally, stage D. This last phase of training made or broke a recruit. Beginning bright and early the first day, the men were assigned to a group that occupied one plane and jumped together. These groups were called "sticks." To get through this last stage and earn paratrooper wings, Wurst remembered, they had to "pack [their] parachutes and jump out of an airplane five days in a row." It sounds easy, but Wurst and most of the others in his stick who had never flown before were petrified.

Lieutenant Sampson was just as frightened. Even though "we would be experiencing the grand-daddy of all thrills," Sampson remembered, "we were 'sweating the jump out.'"

That first morning, hardly anyone touched his eggs at breakfast. The jumpmasters offered all kinds of instructions to ease their nervousness: "Don't get excited. Stay cool. Just remember what you have been taught."[16]

The men were loaded into trucks, taken to the Fort Benning runway, and boarded onto the planes. They took off. Sampson recalled spotting a Catholic chapel from the air, "and for a moment in spirit he knelt before the Blessed Sacrament." Once the planes reached the drop zones, jumpmasters barked: "Stand up, hook up, check your equipment, close up and stand at the door." Lastly, when the green signal light came on, their final command was "Let's go!"

Sampson's jumpmaster slapped his leg. Out he went. The same for Wurst and all the other recruits making their first jumps. Sampson floated down to the Georgia soil rapidly. He thought he felt something snap in his leg when he hit the ground. The chute dragged him for almost a hundred feet before he could disengage from the harness. Secretly, he was hoping he had broken his leg or damaged his knee—either would have given him a chance to "back out of this foolish business gracefully." No such luck. His leg felt fine when he stood up.[17]

Wurst landed more smoothly, although the shock jolted extreme pain through his joints and lower back. Agony aside, he jumped four other times that week as required during stage D in order to pass the course. [18]

After the fifth jump, the men were loaded into trucks and taken back to the packing shed, where a grinning school commandant waited. Certificates were handed out, and jump wings pinned on the left breast pockets. Lastly, the moment all the students waited for: the commandant issued each man a pair of jump boots manufactured especially for the Army by the Corcoran Shoe Company of Massachusetts.[19] To fully expose his new prize for everyone to see, Wurst tucked his trouser cuffs into the boot tops. He was now, he crowed, one of the "top dogs in the Army."[20]

When the ceremony ended, the men broke into song: "Glory, Glory, What a Helluva Way to Die," ending with a strong chorus of "They Poured Him from His Boots."[21]

7

James Gavin

Next to George C. Marshall and Bill Lee, no other US Army officer had as much passion for airborne warfare as James Maurice Gavin.

Although Matthew Ridgway and Maxwell Taylor were the division commanders during the Normandy campaign and became better known later in their careers, Gavin became an innovative and towering presence in the deployment of paratroopers and gliders during combat, as well as a competent general adored by his men.

Tall, slender (one of his nicknames was "Slim Jim"), handsome, and intelligent, Gavin's soft voice belied his robust personality. Kind and considerate, he never offered a negative comment. Gavin never even openly uttered foul language or told an off-color joke, an aide-de-camp remembered. Bill Lee marveled at "his keen and penetrating mind" that transformed him into a "dynamo of intelligent energy." Matthew Ridgway described Gavin as "one of the most brilliant thinkers the Army has produced."[1]

Gavin's career is even more remarkable considering his painful childhood, which could easily have stunted his intellectual growth. Gavin's biographers rightfully label his life a Horatio Alger, "rags to riches" story.[2]

Gavin's early years present a nearly blank canvas. Through bits and pieces gathered from his own painstaking research with help from the Pinkerton Detective Agency and the Catholic Church, Gavin learned that a twenty-three-year-old Irish immigrant named Kate Ryan gave birth to him on March 22, 1907, at Holy Hospital in Brooklyn, New York. His father remains a mystery.

Gavin often told people his parents died before he turned two because he was humiliated by having been an orphan.

Kate Ryan briefly cared for her son but then, probably destitute with no support from the boy's father, placed him in the Angel Guardian Branch of the Convent of Mercy in Brooklyn. Two years later, Martin and Mary Gavin from the small coal mining town of Mount Carmel, Pennsylvania, adopted him. They also adopted a girl around the same time, but even less is known about her other than that she died at an early age.

The Gavins were simple folks with modest means. First-generation Irish, Martin Gavin spoke with a bit of an accent. Like almost every male in Mount Carmel, he worked as a miner. His adopted son remembered him as a "kind, generous and gentle God-fearing man." Others in town who knew Martin Gavin painted him as weak—hardly a father figure.

As a mother, Mary Gavin proved far worse. She drank heavily and often beat her adopted son for any "not-too-minor misdemeanor." She didn't work outside the home beyond earning money by reading tarot cards and renting rooms to male boarders.

Mary had an unhappy, unfulfilled life, for which she punished her son. Gavin never forgot the hair brush with which she beat him. Not satisfied with the results, she persuaded one of her boarders to go to the harness shop at the mine and have a cat o' nine tails made. She applied the heavy leather strap frequently until Gavin figured out where she stored it. One night, while she slept, he stuffed the whip down an opening in the wall by the staircase. According to Gavin's memoir, his mother screamed and carried on when she couldn't find it for the next beating. He never revealed the hiding place.

Martin Gavin made no attempt to intervene when his wife raged, even though he, too, found home life miserable. Once, Gavin remembered, his father suggested that they leave, but Martin never followed through on the idea.

Throughout his life, Gavin understandably harbored deep-seated anger toward his adoptive parents. As an adult with a family of his own, he hardly ever talked about his childhood. His oldest daughter, Barbara, once asked why she had never met her grandparents. Gavin didn't respond and changed the subject. However, on the rare occasions he spoke about his childhood, Gavin's anger toward his adoptive mother came barreling out. When an interviewer asked about her, he replied acidly, "That slut." He had always thought she had sex with some of the male boarders.

When Gavin was ten, a man and an attractive, tall woman representing the Catholic Home Bureau appeared at the house to interview him in front of his parents.

At the end of the conversation, the bureau's representatives asked whether he'd like to go with the woman. Gavin hesitated, knowing his answer would anger his parents. Still, he said yes. The question was apparently rhetorical since she didn't take him with her, but the woman left an indelible mark on the young man. She didn't identify herself, but Gavin thought she might have been his biological mother, Kate Ryan.[3]

Many years later, he walked into the living room and saw his daughter Chloe sitting on an old Victorian couch. Her hair was tied into a bun, not hanging down as she normally wore it. Shaking, Gavin ran upstairs. Later, he claimed to have experienced a moment of déjà vu. Chloe looked exactly like the woman who had come to his Mount Carmel home many decades before. That moment convinced him that he had met his real mother at that interview.

As he grew older, conditions at home deteriorated. Gavin had to fend for himself when he was hungry. At lunchtime, he'd leave school to hike up to the coal mines to wait for the miners to ascend above ground to eat their noon meal. They generously shared their food with the poor boy.

Gavin loved school, especially history class. Reading about great military figures provided a momentary escape from his traumatic home life. The First Presbyterian Church of Mount Carmel kept an extensive library of "boys' books." Raised as a strict Roman Catholic, Gavin had to be convinced by a friend to enter the church for fear that "God would strike him dead."

On the eve of his seventeenth birthday, Gavin witnessed a fierce argument between his violent mother and passive father. He stayed sequestered in his bedroom. The fighting lasted until midnight, and at that moment, he decided it was time to break away from this wretched situation.

Armed with $2.75 earned from a paper route, plus more funds squirreled away in a bank account, Gavin sneaked out of the house at 1:30 a.m.

so he could catch a Pennsylvania Railroad train leaving thirty minutes later for New York. Several years passed before Gavin returned to Mount Carmel.

Arriving in New York around daylight on March 22, 1924, he immediately sent a telegram to his parents saying he was in good health so they wouldn't call the police. He then set out to find work. Gavin wandered around Manhattan, but employers found his lack of experience unemployable. Gavin never said where he slept or ate.

After a week of rejections, he stumbled upon an Army recruiting office in Battery Park. He told the sergeant on duty that he'd like to join up and confessed to being under age and an orphan who could not secure his adoptive parents' consent to enlist. The recruiting sergeant told him not to worry. He led the lad to a nearby building where other boys in a similar predicament waited. They were taken to a lawyer, who first asked the young men a slew of questions before having them sign papers declaring him their guardian.

Now a soldier, Gavin was sent to the Canal Zone in Panama for rudimentary training under a sergeant named McCarthy. The "hard as nails" sergeant took an instant liking to Gavin, and he became a father figure whom Gavin could trust and in whom he could confide.

Within a year, Gavin was promoted to corporal. Another sergeant also saw the young soldier's potential and put his name in to take the West Point entrance exam. The Army wanted to recognize talent from the enlisted ranks as a way to fast-track those men into officers.

Gavin had left home before completing high school, so he was petrified that he would flunk the exam. But, again, a mentor in the form of a lieutenant charged with administering the test helped Gavin prepare, and he passed.

During his four years at the academy, Gavin rested in the bottom two-thirds of his class. He graduated in 1929, 185th out of 299. He would have ranked lower but for stellar grades in history classes.

Gavin often referred to West Point as his "Spartan Mother." For Gavin, West Point was more than a stepping-stone to becoming an officer. The academy certainly helped propel his military career, but, even more so, it gave him the sense of belonging that had eluded him thus far in his life.[4]

At West Point, Gavin met his first wife, Irma "Peggy" Baulsir. With his Hollywood good looks and quiet demeanor, he had little trouble attracting the attention of the young women who showed up at the academy to attend dances, or "hops," held in the spring. Baulsir came to one of them before Gavin's senior year. The pretty Washington, DC, resident and the good-looking cadet were instantly drawn to each other. She visited a couple of times the following year, and they corresponded steadily. They married immediately after he graduated.

The Gavins raised a daughter, Barbara, but they were never a perfect fit. The marriage dissolved in 1946, and he carried on numerous affairs during and after the war, including with actress Marlene Dietrich and journalist Martha Gellhorn. During World War II, Gavin became fodder for gossip columnists, who widely reported on his amorous liaisons.[5]

In 1947, he married Jean Emert, although he continued to have extramarital affairs. He and Jean eventually had four children, and they remained together until his death in 1990.

Gavin's first post after graduation took him to Arizona along the Mexican border. Life there proved dreary, and there was little to do. Three years later, in 1932, Gavin jumped at the chance to attend the Infantry School at Fort Benning, Georgia. There, he learned the rudiments of becoming an effective officer under the guidance of General Joseph Stillwell, who had mentored many other young officers, like Maxwell Taylor. The veteran officer taught Gavin that "anything you ask the troops to do, you must do yourself."

After Benning, Gavin served at Fort Sill in the Philippines and Fort Ord; then the Army sent him back to West Point in 1940 as a tactics instructor. Gavin possessed a gift for teaching. With dramatic flair, the thirty-three-year-old captain enthralled future officers, and they packed his classrooms. Gavin believed in hands-on, active learning to captivate his students. He showed combat films and employed "props" in his lectures on the war in Europe, by then in its second year. To demonstrate how Hitler's forces were steamrolling through the European continent, for example, Gavin placed sand tables in front of the classroom to serve as mock battlefields.

During one memorable discussion, Gavin knocked the red arrows off the by-then-outdated war maps of Europe. They crash-landed on the classroom floor in front of his startled cadets. "They were too small," he warned them.[6]

Gavin prepared for classes by memorizing military attaché reports on the war, paying close attention to the German airborne assaults in Holland and Crete. He read and reread the documents the same way that, as a boy, he had studied his hero Thomas "Stonewall" Jackson in the 1862 Shenandoah Valley campaign. Gavin delighted in telling about the Confederate commander's skillful maneuvering that allowed him to evade capture by Union forces.[7]

The more Gavin read and then taught his cadets about the German airborne operation, the more he longed to become a paratrooper. In April 1941, he applied to attend parachute school at Fort Benning. Initially, West Point prevented him from going: he was much too valuable as an instructor.

It took a letter-writing campaign and several trips to see the chief of infantry staff in Washington before West Point relented. In August, Gavin graduated from airborne school. Earning his paratrooper's wings and a new pair of jump boots, however, was not enough, and he strived for more. He wanted to be both a leader and a teacher. The Army listened. Gavin, assigned as a 503rd Parachute Infantry Battalion company commander, proceeded to develop theories on tactics and airborne combat doctrine.[8]

Colonel Bill Lee noticed the rising star, helping to promote Gavin to major and then placing him on his staff as an operations and training officer. Serving with Lee provided Gavin with clout—a lot of it. Lee and his protégé brainstormed to develop the first airborne division. They also significantly aided in selecting Ridgway's 82nd for this unique designation.

In August 1942, after Gavin took a shortened version of the Command and Staff College course at Fort Leavenworth, Colonel Lee saw to it that he received command of the newly formed 505th Parachute Infantry Regiment with the rank of colonel. Lee's vote of confidence for his young protégé spoke volumes about Gavin's abilities.

Gavin's days were frequently interrupted by visits from dignitaries who wanted to witness in person the progress of the American Army's airborne program. General Boy Browning arrived first. Although initially charmed by the British paratrooper's kind remarks, Gavin came to loathe Browning for openly criticizing Matt Ridgway. Next, Secretary of War Henry Stimson stopped by, and after him, George C. Marshall and Winston Churchill showed up together.

The old adage, "a soldier's soldier," described Gavin perfectly. Rank made little difference to him. His loyalty to his men was showcased when someone in the Benning commandant's office complained about a paratrooper in the 505th who had ventured across the Chattahoochee River to Phenix City and was arrested for having sexual intercourse with a young woman on the courthouse lawn. Gavin's adjutant handled the problem until he was asked what the regimental commander planned to do about it. Gavin's response was to the point: "In view of the fact that that young man will be asked to give his life for his country in the next few months, I suggest we give him a medal." Gavin's adjutant heard nothing further.[9]

After taking command, Gavin placed his stamp on the regiment by repeating to his battalion and company commanders what General Stillwell once had told him: "In this outfit, an officer is the first man out of the airplane and the last man in the chow line."

Gavin also expected a lot from the enlisted men, as they were the backbone of the unit. How well the regiment performed in battle largely depended on its level of preparedness. Most of his men had just completed the four-week Paratrooper School, which must have seemed like summer camp compared to the brutal physical training Gavin put them through.[10] Regardless of how hard he pushed his men, however, Gavin was seen by the regiment as a fair and compassionate commander. An awe-struck paratrooper who saw Gavin walking ahead of him remarked to another soldier, "I'd follow that guy through hell."[11]

Sicily and Italy

A Dress Rehearsal for Normandy

In January 1943, President Franklin D. Roosevelt and Prime Minister Winston Churchill and their staffs met in the Casablanca suburb of Anfa to discuss the next phase of the war. Invading the island of Sicily, they decided, was the next major objective and would commence as soon as the African campaign concluded. Code named Operation Husky, the Sicily campaign had three main objectives: clear the lines of communication in the Mediterranean, divert German forces from the Russian front, and increase pressure on Italy.[1]

The amphibious landings on Sicily would be the first joint Allied airborne operation of the war. The British 1st Airborne Division was assigned to land near Syracuse in July to seize a key bridge and points south of the city, while elements of Ridgway's US 82nd were to land behind the US Army beachhead at Gela to block the advance of Axis forces. Ridgway's men were placed under the command of Lieutenant General George S. Patton.[2]

Husky would be the baptism of fire for the 82nd but not the first time a US Army airborne unit jumped into combat. On the night of November 7, 1942, during Operation Torch, thirty-seven C-47s carried the 509th Parachute Infantry Battalion (formerly designated as 2nd Battalion, 503rd Parachute Infantry Regiment), led by Lieutenant Colonel Edson D. Raff, 1,500 miles nonstop from England. Its mission was to seize two pro-Axis, French-controlled airfields, Tafaraoui and La Sénia, south of Oran, Algeria, hours before an Allied amphibious invasion began.

Poor weather, as well as navigational and communication issues, hampered the attack. Several C-47s were downed by enemy fighters, and some planes ran low on fuel and were forced to land in a dry salt lake to the west of the target. After Colonel Raff jumped from his plane, he landed on a large rock, breaking two ribs. He was also thirty-five miles from his destination. It took a full day for the scattered paratroopers to reach Tafaraoui; Raff arrived by Jeep. By then, both airfields were already in the hands of the seaborne troops. Casualties were few. Between Raff's paratroopers and the troop carrier crews, five were killed and fifteen wounded.[3]

At this point, Colonel James Gavin's 505th Regimental Combat Team (RCT) counted as a recent addition to the 82nd. Gavin's unit replaced the 326th Glider Regiment, which had transferred out of the division. Addition of this unit meant that the All-Americans had three of the Army's best officers: Gavin, Ridgway, and Taylor. One historian described them as "magnetic, handsome, dynamic, literate and ambitious."[4]

An 82nd signal officer by the name of Frank Willoughby "Bill" Moorman, a close associate of Ridgway's, sarcastically compared all three officers' unique personalities: "Ridgway would cut your throat and then burst into tears. Taylor would cut your throat and think nothing about it, and Gavin would cut your throat and then laugh."[5]

On March 24, 1943, General Ridgway returned to Fort Bragg after a whirlwind, week-long trip to North Africa to discuss the preliminary plans for Operation Husky. Once back, he had less than a month to prepare his division for Sicily and its first taste of combat. During this rushed time frame, he put his men through a series of exercises, including a mock glider assault, in front of Chief of Staff George C. Marshall, Air Force Chief General Hap Arnold, and two British dignitaries.

Marshall and Arnold were not pleased. They berated Ridgway, accusing him of softening realism by placing the gliders down on "nice, smooth runways" instead of "small fields, onto rough ground."

Ridgway shrugged off the criticism. He had only four Waco CG-4As and didn't want to risk damaging them. In his head, he thought, "If they'd just give us the gliders, and plenty of replacements for the ones we'd wreck, we'd use them realistically all right."[6]

More exercises filled the 82nd's last days before it headed to the Mediterranean. One involved dropping Colonel Gavin's entire 505th RCT[7] into mock-enemy territory, the first time a complete unit had jumped all at once. One hundred thirty C-47s successfully took Gavin's men over three drop zones near Camden, South Carolina. A tragedy marred the practice jump however: Both engines on a C-47 lost power due to mechanical failure. As the plane sputtered toward the ground, it ran into a mass of paratroopers heading in the same direction. Three men were chopped up in the propellers before the C-47 forced-landed in a field.[8]

Movement orders, which had arrived during the first week of April, told Ridgway that his division would depart Fort Bragg on the 20th and board trains to Camp Edwards, Massachusetts. Before leaving North Carolina, Ridgway instructed the men to disguise themselves: their parachute badges and other obvious signs that they were anything but a normal infantry outfit had to go. But the men refused to pull off their paratrooper boots—a dead giveaway as to the division's real identity.[9]

On April 29, Ridgway's paratroopers boarded three troopships for Casablanca, and they entered the Mediterranean on May 10. Maxwell Taylor had already flown to North Africa a few days before to pave the way for the division's arrival.

Preparing for Operation Husky, Ridgway's men trained in Morocco. They were, Gavin later wrote, subjected to a "fiery furnace, where the hot wind carried a fine dust that clogged the nostrils, burned the eyes and cut into the throat like an abrasive."[10]

Technical Sergeant Bing Wood was a C-47 aerial engineer with the 314th Troop Carrier Group, 52nd Troop Carrier Wing, the outfit designated to the paratroopers for Sicily. He remembered North Africa much the same way as Gavin: "Sand, flies, filth, a lack of water, bad food, terrific heat, cold, the sirocco wind, and boredom."[11]

Dismal conditions aside, General Ridgway put his men through rigorous physical conditioning, weapons firing, command tactics, bayonet exercises, and grenade practice. Small units were formed and sent out at night to drill in defensive tactics.

The 52nd Troop Carrier Wing had recently arrived from the United States, its pilots well-versed in daylight operations but not night flying.

Regular nighttime practice runs by the C-47s were conducted throughout much of June 1943, with mixed results. During one nighttime parachute jump, a couple of paratroopers dropped into a cluster of giant cactus trees, but a more serious incident involved a C-47 crew chief.

After the paratroopers jumped, one of the transport planes came back without its crew chief. The next day, a search team canvassed the desert in the drop zone area and found his body, without a parachute attached. It was concluded that one of the inexperienced paratroopers saw the crew chief standing by the door, hadn't noticed he wasn't hooked up to jump since he wasn't a paratrooper, and pulled him out the door upon exiting. From then on, crew chiefs were directed to stand by the bulkhead near the cockpit, and they were now equipped to wear backpack parachutes. [12]

Husky's airborne operational plan was not complicated. There would be two drops. First, Gavin's 505th would land behind the projected amphibious beaches at Gela to protect the city against counterattack. The next day, a battalion from the 504th RCT, led by Colonel Reuben Tucker, would reinforce Gavin's paratroopers along with artillery; meanwhile, the remainder of the 82nd, including Ridgway, would come ashore by landing craft.[13]

Back in North Carolina, Bill Lee's Screaming Eagle regiments remained in the background, training in anticipation of one day seeing combat. Why Bill Lee's paratroopers were passed over in favor of the 82nd to go into Sicily has never been explained. Lee never privately or publicly expressed anger over the decision, but he had to have been disappointed at the very least. The airborne community considered him its father, so allowing him and his regiment to test their skills in combat would have been appropriate. In fact, Lee never got the chance to jump into enemy territory.[14]

On the night of 1943, just before the C-47s carrying Gavin's 505th rolled down the runway in Tunisia, an airman from the weather station ran up to the door of the plane where the colonel was seated. The airman hollered to him, Gavin recalled: "Colonel Gavin, is Colonel Gavin here?"

"'Here I am,' I answered, and he yelled, 'I was told to tell you that the wind is going to be thirty-five miles an hour, west to east.' He added, 'They thought you'd want to know.'"

What could Gavin do about wind?

"We couldn't change plans now. Besides, there were many other hazards of greater danger in prospect than the thirty-five-mile-an-hour wind."[15]

Around 10 p.m. on July 9, 226 C-47s, each one carrying a stick of about sixteen paratroopers, flew toward Sicily. Pilots ran into trouble right away. Because of the high winds Gavin had been warned about, some of the pilots turned away from the formation to avoid midair collisions; others, the ones with too few hours of experience flying at night, became lost.

Practically all of the planes reached Sicily, but an estimated 80 percent of the sticks were dropped far from the landing zones. Some paratroopers ended up sixty-five miles from where they were supposed to be. Soldiers fought in small bands—never linking up with their units—until they reached the beachhead.

When the paratroopers entered Sicily, they found the Sicilian people unwelcoming. Simply asking the native people where to find food and water or asking for directions elicited no response. Many ran in the other direction from the soldiers.

Gavin learned that the Germans had stoked the flames of fear by indoctrinating the Sicilians into believing American paratroopers were criminals on probation and placed in parachute units as punishment. Be wary of them, the Germans had warned: paratroopers will "loot and rob," and, by all means, don't help them. To these frightened Italians, one paratrooper with a shaved head looked convincingly like a criminal.[16]

Taylor had stayed behind in Tunisia to oversee the launching of Colonel Tucker's 504th on the evening of the second day. Tucker's paratroopers, as it turned out, had a worse experience than Gavin's men. That night, one of the worst cases of friendly fire in military history exploded.

After Taylor saw the final C-47 take off, he went to bed. A few hours later, a staff member woke him with word that planes were returning badly damaged with wounded paratroopers on board.

Ridgway had done his best to warn Allied naval units to look out for C-47s bringing in reinforcements. Some of the units thought the planes were German, however, and shot them out of the sky. Twenty-three C-47s were downed. Fortunately, many of the paratroopers were able to parachute out safely, but the 504th still lost 229 men, including 81 killed. An investigation failed to determine exact fault for the friendly-fire fiasco; the Navy blamed poor navigation by inexperienced pilots who flew off-course.

Ridgway was beside himself with anger. "The responsibility for loss of life and material resulting from this operation is so divided," he wrote in his 1972 memoir. "So difficult to fix with impartial justice and so questionable of ultimate value to the service because of the acrimonious debates which would follow . . . that disciplinary action is of doubtful wisdom."[17]

Over the next few days, with the horror of the air drops behind it, Ridgway's 82nd now fought its way northward up Sicily's west coast. During one minor engagement, near Trapani, Taylor impressed Ridgway with his coolness under fire and his willingness to lead from the front and not the rear. That placement, after all, served as a trademark of both generals nine months later at Normandy. Ridgway recorded:

> I was up with the advance guard, expecting momentarily to get a salvo on the road, when I looked around to see General Maxwell Taylor, my assistant division commander, standing by my side, watching the shell bursts casually, with an artillery man's appraising eye. . . . It distressed me to see Max up there, for one shell could have gotten us both, leaving the division without a top command. So I told Max, by God, he was to get back until I sent for him. . . . I talked pretty strongly to Max, for I knew he had all the courage in the world . . . but someone had to stay back at CP and I knew it wasn't going to be me.[18]

Soon after, Taylor proved his bravery on a larger stage when General Eisenhower sent him on a secret mission to Rome. This daring escapade came about after the Allied invasion of Italy, a day after the Italians secretly agreed to lay down their arms and surrender. A plan to help safeguard the Italian royal family was put in place: the operation called Giant II dropped part of the 82nd near Rome just before the formal announcement of Italy's armistice with the Allies.

Eisenhower agreed as part of the armistice that the Allies would provide military support to Italy to defend Rome from German occupation. Giant II was, therefore, planned as the drop of one regiment from

Ridgway's division in the area to the northwest of Rome in order to help four Italian division seize the Italian capital.

As the time for the operation grew closer, however, the Allies began seriously to doubt the ability of the Italian forces to cooperate or to deliver. Ridgway and Taylor were among those who shouted the loudest since they had much to lose in terms of manpower should the operation fall apart.

Taylor, along with Air Force intelligence officer Colonel William T. Gardiner, was ordered on a reconnaissance mission to Rome to report on the operation's chances of success. Taylor's background in languages and his expertise in dealing with foreign armies made him a natural for the assignment. The pair left Palermo, Italy, at 2 a.m. on September 7, 1943, in a British PT boat. They had stripped their American uniforms of any sign of rank since they were going to pretend to be two enemy airmen pulled from the Mediterranean.

For much of the day, they negotiated with General Giacomo Carboni, commander of the Italian corps defending Rome. Carboni convinced the Americans that a landing by US airborne troops would only provoke the Germans into retaliating. Carboni added that he couldn't guarantee that the Italians would be able to cover the airfield to provide necessary logistical support to the paratroopers.

Taylor and Gardiner then insisted upon seeing the new Italian premier, Pietro Badoglio, who had replaced the ousted Fascist leader, Benito Mussolini, in July. Badoglio, clad in his pajamas, met with the Americans in the middle of the night. He confirmed what Carboni had already told them. Taylor rushed to file a report, transmitted by radio, urging Eisenhower to cancel Giant II. The following day, even as the transport aircraft carrying two battalions of the 504th RPT was being prepared for take-off, the operation was called off.[19]

Taylor would later stay in Italy as an Italian expert with the Allied Control Commission, organized to oversee the Badoglio government. The 82nd also stayed in Italy as ground reinforcement to General Mark Clark's Fifth Army operation at Salerno.[20]

On September 9, 1943, Clark launched Operation Avalanche. Four days later, his forces on the beachhead were pushed back by persistent

German counterattacks. Clark sent an urgent request to Ridgway, still in Sicily with the 82nd.

On September 13, 1943, Colonel Reuben Tucker, still shaken from the horrific incident in Sicily two months earlier, led his 504th combat team (minus the 3rd Battalion) on a parachute assault at Paestum, south of Salerno. Within an hour and a half of Clark's appeal, 1,300 paratroopers from the 505th, carried by eighty-five troop transports, jumped onto the beachhead the next day.

The paratroopers were rushed to the front line, where they engaged the enemy in the rocky hills and drove them back. On September 15, the 504th conducted an amphibious landing near Salerno. Throughout this period, Ridgway's men conducted operations around the Salerno and Naples area. The 82nd was the first unit to enter Naples, and it then advanced north to the Volturno River and cleared the area of the enemy.[21]

In December 1943, Ridgway moved his division (the 504th RCT remained behind) to Northern Ireland to begin preparations for Operation Overlord. During the D-Day planning, he could not ignore the lessons learned from Sicily. In case Ridgway forgot, however, he could always turn to Colonel Gavin for advice.

As Gavin would later write, "We learned what could be done by parachute troops and troop carrier pilots, but, more important, we learned what they could not do." Specifically, he cited that when on the ground, "airborne troops had more than held their own against infantry."

Looking ahead to Normandy, Gavin feared that "meeting German armor in good tank country could be disastrous." He also pointed out the obvious: "The airborne-troop carrier team had to be thoroughly trained and honed to a keen edge. Small mistakes could lead to disaster, with airborne troops badly scattered and heavy troop carrier losses."

Although the first major American airborne operation, Sicily and Salerno were relatively small battles compared to what the Overlord planners had in mind for Normandy, fewer than six months away.

9

Eisenhower

"This is the best officer in the Army."

So declared Chief of Staff Douglas MacArthur in 1934, speaking of his military aide, Major Dwight D. Eisenhower. MacArthur added, "When the next war comes, he should go right to the top."[1]

Such strong words from the vain and egotistical MacArthur surprised his readers, no doubt, given that MacArthur, soon to be commander of the Southwest Pacific Area Theater, rarely heaped praise on officers of his own rank, much less subordinates.

MacArthur saw in Eisenhower the same thing others in the Army recognized: he was efficient, loyal, congenial, and smart. Eisenhower knew how to take orders but never shrank from questioning a superior's decisions. Such attributes define a great soldier.

Nine years after MacArthur made his prediction, it became true as a result of the meeting of the Big Three. In 1943, President Franklin D. Roosevelt, Prime Minister Winston Churchill, and Marshal Joseph Stalin met in Tehran, Iran, from late November to early December. The chief topic of discussion revolved around creating a second front to alleviate military pressure on Russia. FDR and Stalin favored the cross-channel operation to liberate northwestern Europe, code named Overlord and previously discussed when Churchill and Roosevelt had met in August 1943.

Churchill had been reluctant to launch such a large-scale invasion across the English Channel, and he would not budge in Tehran. He stubbornly held out for alternative methods to choke Hitler's forces by way of the Mediterranean. When FDR and Stalin finally wore him down, the Allies set Operation Overlord for May 1, 1944.

Who would command the operation was their next decision.[2]

Overlord had to be led by an American because of "the very great preponderance of American troops that would be employed after the original landing." FDR had a long list of some four hundred officers to choose from. George C. Marshall certainly headed the pack, but the chief of staff was far too valuable in that post, so the president didn't want Marshall to leave Washington.

At a later conference in Cairo, Marshall urged FDR to select fifty-four-year-old Eisenhower to command Overlord.[3]

Eisenhower was thus appointed to "the most important field command of World War II." In January 1944, when they met in the White House, the president asked Eisenhower, "Do you like the title of supreme commander?" "I like the title very much, Mr. President," Eisenhower replied. "It has the ring of importance—something like 'Sultan.'"[4]

Eisenhower's response reflected his modest but self-assured personality—humble, friendly, and unassuming. His face seemed stamped with a permanent, wide grin, and he laughed effortlessly. However, he could just as easily lose his temper, and that's when his brightly smiling face turned beet red.

As commander of the Supreme Headquarters Allied Expeditionary Force (SHAEF), Ike captivated the public's imagination. His celebrity, already on the rise after successful campaigns in North Africa and the Mediterranean, now reached Hollywood-movie-star level. Eisenhower also looked the part. Just two inches under six feet, he had sparkling blue eyes, light brown hair, broad shoulders, and a muscular frame. "Handsome" was the only way to describe the army commander and future president of the United States.[5]

His mother, Ida Elizabeth (Stover) Eisenhower, gave birth to the third of her seven sons on October 14, 1890, in Dennison, Texas, and named him David Dwight, but she soon reversed his given names to avoid confusion with his father, David Jacob Eisenhower.

When Dwight turned two, his family moved to Abilene, Kansas, where the "Eisenhauers" (as the name was originally spelled) had settled a few decades earlier with a Mennonite colony. Long before that, Abilene had been a small Midwestern railroad town of four thousand on the northern end of the Chisholm Trail. Before Ike, Abilene's most celebrated son was "Wild Bill" Hickok.

David Eisenhower, his father, worked as a mechanic at a creamery on the outside of town. Ida raised the boys, each of whom was nicknamed "Ike," an abbreviation of their surname; later on, as young adults, Ike's six brothers relinquished that nickname, leaving it for Dwight alone.

All seven sons were competitive and athletic. Passionate about baseball and football, Ike played both sports in high school. Of all the Eisenhower boys, only he entered the military: the chance to play on a college team led to his decision to attend the US Military Academy in 1911. "One of my reasons for going to West Point," he explained in his memoir, "was the hope that I could continue an athletic career."

During plebe year, West Point's football coach thought Eisenhower too small and light for the varsity team. He eventually joined, however, playing in several games until a knee injury sent him to the sidelines. An average student, Eisenhower excelled in English—about the only class he did well in. As a cadet, he took up smoking (even though the Army forbade it) and became a decent poker player.

Eisenhower graduated from the academy in 1915, 61st out of 164, in the same class as Omar Bradley and James Van Fleet; fifty-seven other classmates later attained the rank of general.

While stationed at Fort Sam Houston in 1916, Ike met Marie Geneva "Mamie" Doud, the second of four daughters of a meat-packing executive. Dwight and Mamie married on July 1, 1916. Their long, loving marriage ended with his death in 1969. While overseas during the World War II, Eisenhower wrote his wife 319 times.

A year after marrying, they had a son, Doud Dwight, or "Icky," who died at age four from scarlet fever. In 1922, Mamie gave birth to a second son, John Sheldon Doud, who, like his father, attended West Point and then enjoyed a long career in the Army.

The United States entered World War I in April 1917, with General John J. Pershing forming the American Expeditionary Forces (AEF) to fight alongside the British and French. Ike wanted to be among Pershing's warriors, but the War Department sent him instead to Fort Oglethorpe, Georgia, and then on to Fort Leavenworth, Kansas, as a training officer.

In February 1918, Eisenhower took command of a tank battalion at Fort Meade, Maryland, slated for overseas duty, but the battalion went without him because after a month in Maryland, he was sent to Camp Colt in Gettysburg, Pennsylvania, to direct tank training. Instead of driving tanks across the shell-pocked no-man's land in Europe, Eisenhower taught others to steer the flimsy machines on a former Civil War battlefield in the United States.

Finally, in October 1918, orders arrived for Eisenhower to ship to France on November 18. Much to his dismay—although to the delight of the more than two million American soldiers in Europe—Eisenhower's chance to see combat died when the Germans and Allies signed an armistice on November 11. Eisenhower remarked to another officer, also slated for Europe, "I suppose we'll spend the rest of our lives explaining why we didn't get into this war."

In 1919, with his future unclear, Eisenhower volunteered for an Army convoy that spent the summer traveling across the United States along the Lincoln Highway (US Highway 30). Its objective was to study the time it took to move fourteen pieces of military equipment coast to coast. Throughout the two-month trip, "roads varied from average to non-existent," and the motor trucks frequently broke down. Ike never forgot the "difficult, fun and tiring" excursion. The 1919 expedition influenced his decision as president to secure funding to pave 41,000 miles of highways across America.[6]

Eisenhower did get to the Western Front, but not until five years after the armistice. General Pershing tapped him to write a battlefield guide for the American Battle Monuments Commission (ABMC), the newly formed government agency responsible for placing memorials and markers where US soldiers and marines fought and for maintaining eight veterans' cemeteries.

In 1926, with Mamie and John by his side, Eisenhower visited practically every piece of European ground where American doughboys had shed blood. He compiled his notes into the first edition of *American Armies and Battlefields in Europe*; he returned two years later to revise the guide.

In 1929, he worked for the assistant secretary of war, primarily writing reports, speeches, memos, and letters.[7] Most important, he also created the war plans for mobilizing American personnel and industry in the event of war. His plan would be implemented after the attack on Pearl Harbor more than a decade later.

By virtue of his job, Eisenhower also served at the pleasure of the chief of staff. This position resulted in one of the more embarrassing moments in Douglas MacArthur's stellar career and also stained President Herbert Hoover's administration. In the midst of the Depression, on a hot July day in 1932, the chief of staff ordered a garrison of cavalry (Major George S. Patton among them) at Fort Myer to assist Washington, DC, police in rounding up a group of hungry, unemployed World War I veterans squatting in tents and vacant buildings.

Some of the former doughboys had been in DC since May, trying to lobby Congress for early payment of their $1,000 war bonus. Tied to 1924 legislation, the funds would come from a bond not set to mature until 1945. Congress turned a blind eye to their pleas. So did Hoover, who referred to the so-called "Bonus Marchers" as "rabble-rousers" and "communists."

On July 28, MacArthur insisted upon leaving his office to stand in solidarity with the horse soldiers and cops as they swept homeless World War I heroes from Washington's streets. Eisenhower, no lackey for the strong-willed MacArthur, warned him to stay away. The junior officer predicted that the day would turn into a "riot rather than a big military movement"; Eisenhower warned further that it was "highly inappropriate for the Chief of Staff of the Army to be involved in anything like a local or street-corner embroilment."

MacArthur ignored him, exchanged his civilian clothes for a fresh uniform, and directed Eisenhower to do the same. An iconic photograph taken that day, shows MacArthur looking proud, a cigarette clenched between his lips. Major Eisenhower stands next to him—angry and embarrassed.[8]

Eisenhower was proved right: the forced removal turned violent. Veterans were tear-gassed and shoved across the Anacostia River to their tent city, known as a "Hooverville," and eventually into Maryland. Spectators threw bricks and rocks at attacking soldiers. When the unrest ended that night, MacArthur not only declared the operation a success but also defended his use of the army.

Although he never forgot MacArthur's ill treatment of the Bonus Marchers, Eisenhower became his aide in 1934. His tiny office, "no larger than a broom closet," stood adjacent to the general's colossal room in the War and State Building next to the White House. Within constant shouting distance of his boss, Eisenhower busied himself with helping MacArthur untangle the bureaucracy of budgets and staffing issues. From his first day, Eisenhower recognized the role of a chief of staff as more political than military.

Around then, Eisenhower's health turned ugly. "Lots of trouble with my insides lately," he recorded in his diary. "Have been bothered for 5-6 years with something that seems to border upon dysentery." His doctors blamed his misery on too many nerves but not enough exercise. For the next decade, he suffered from bouts of acute gastroenteritis, colitis, hemorrhoids, arthritis, and, worst of all, chronic back pain.[9]

In 1935, after extending his chief-of-staff tour for another year, MacArthur left Washington for the Philippines to serve as a military adviser. Eisenhower went with him and, with another staff officer, ran the day-to-day operations of preparing the Philippine Army and the island country for the next war. He often clashed with MacArthur over minor things, like the number of Filipino army units that should be allowed to parade through the streets of Manila as a morale booster, and over more serious issues, like funding. In early September 1939, Ike ended his seven-year working relationship with MacArthur.

By then a full colonel, Eisenhower returned to the United States to take field command at Fort Lewis, Washington, before moving on to Fort Sam Houston as 3rd Army chief of staff.

When World War II started in Europe, Eisenhower played a crucial role in preparing the Army should the United States join the fray. He participated in the 1941 Louisiana Maneuvers, a full-scale war-game exercise. His big break came when Chief of Staff George C. Marshall brought him back to Washington as deputy chief of the War Plans Division for the Pacific and Far East.

Like so many officers of his era, Eisenhower became one of Marshall's protégés. Eisenhower's more laid-back style fit with Marshall's "brusque" managerial style. Marshall quickly promoted him to major general and head of the War Department Operations Division. Eisenhower had naturally been concerned that not having seen combat in World War I would hinder his military career, but he need not have worried.

Marshall sent Eisenhower to London, where he led the newly formed European Theater of Operations. The ETO had been organized to ease the US Army toward an eventual invasion of the continent. Marshall favored a direct approach by concentrating American troops in England prior to a cross-channel invasion of France. Churchill still held on to his belief that wearing down the Germans in North Africa or the Mediterranean would prove to be a more logical strategy.

Marshall appointed Eisenhower as commander of Operation Torch, an Allied invasion of North Africa. The Eisenhower-led forces captured key North African ports but were defeated at Kasserine Pass in February 1943. In response, Eisenhower sacked an ineffective corps commander, strengthened his alliance with the British, and led the Allies to victory over the Axis forces at Tunisia.

Later in 1943, he retained command of operations in the Mediterranean, including the invasion of Sicily in July and the landings at Salerno in September. All the while, he was building relations with the British, especially with General Bernard Montgomery, who liked Eisenhower personally but distrusted his strategic judgment since he had not seen World War I combat (just as Eisenhower had feared). Montgomery would have no choice but to get over this ill-conceived opinion of Ike. Soon, "Monty" would be subordinate to "Ike" when the Brit became 12th Army commander for Overlord.[10]

That moment came on January 15, 1944. After a lengthy trip back to the United States, when he saw Mamie and his son John for the first time in almost two years, Eisenhower arrived in London by train after his plane had been diverted to Scotland because of fog. He jumped into his new duties as the head of the SHAEF at 20 Grosvenor Square. He dissected the existing Overlord plan that had been conceived the previous year by the British, and he selected his team of advisers to meet the unprecedented challenges associated with assembling the largest multinational force in history.[11]

10

Planning for Neptune

"Impractical."

So declared 21st Army Group Commander General Sir Bernard Law Montgomery after exhaustively reading General Frederick Morgan's Operation Overlord plan for the first time.

Who received Montgomery's icy dismissal of the magnum opus of the Chief of Staff Supreme Allied Commander (COSSAC)? None other than Prime Minister Winston Churchill.

Flying back to London from Italy on New Year's Eve 1943, Montgomery (only a few close associates dared call him "Monty" to his face), stopped off in Marrakech, where the prime minister had been recuperating from a bout of pneumonia. Montgomery handed Churchill his first written impression of Morgan's plan: "The initial landing is on too narrow a front," the army group commander wrote, "and is confined to too small an area. . . . This would lead to the most appalling confusion on the beaches."

Montgomery returned to London on January 2, 1944. Churchill stayed behind, where he cabled his chiefs of staff: "I was encouraged to hear General Montgomery's arguments that many landing points should be chosen instead of concentration as at present proposed through one narrow funnel."

That Montgomery had the prime minister's ear says more about Churchill's respect for his ability than about his personal feelings toward Montgomery. In actuality, the prime minister stood in a long line of people who privately disliked him.[1] One of Montgomery's biographers wrote that most of his contemporaries "either worshipped or despised him," adding that few regarded the fifty-seven-year-old 21st Army Group commander "dispassionately."

A bishop's son, Montgomery attended St. Paul's School in London, then Sandhurst, followed by an army commission. Like his father, he neither drank nor smoked and frowned on those habits when in the company of others who embraced them.[2]

Eisenhower and Montgomery first met in spring 1942 at a south England farmhouse. As they started to discuss the war in North Africa, Eisenhower instinctively lit up a cigarette, never considering that this action might offend his host. The smell of smoke agitated Montgomery. He abruptly stopped speaking. After a silence, Montgomery queried, "Who is smoking?" Ike confessed, "I am, sir." Montgomery admonished him for lighting up in his presence. Eisenhower, his face glowing "beet-red," tapped out the cigarette.[3]

Montgomery, although badly wounded in 1914 during the Great War, recovered in short order, and he ended the war as a battalion commander with the rank of lieutenant colonel. Despite that, he was relatively unknown at the outbreak of World War II; yet he commanded a division. He moved to direct anti-invasion preparations in southern England. Churchill, appreciating Montgomery's attention to detail, appointed him commander of the British Eighth Army in Egypt.

In the Middle East, Montgomery turned a downtrodden force into an effective combat unit, twice defeating the "Desert Fox," Field Marshal Erwin Rommel, once at Alam Halfa and then, more decisively, at El Alamein. While in the desert, Montgomery got his first look at Americans. He turned his nose up at this bunch of amateurs, and his opinion hardly wavered throughout the war.

Returning to London in early January 1944, Montgomery worked to further mark up and expand Morgan's Overlord plan. This process exhausted Montgomery and reminded him of the lengthy time it took to put Operation Husky together. "But this time it is very serious as if Overlord were to fail, or to be only a partial success," Montgomery recorded, "it would put the war back months and months."[4]

As Overlord's ground forces' commander, Montgomery primarily concerned himself with how to move his men off the beaches into the open Normandy countryside. Morgan had allocated only enough landing craft for three divisions on a thirty-mile front.

Code named Neptune, the amphibious phase of Overlord lumped together the navy, ground troops, and airborne. Montgomery convinced Eisenhower that he (Ike) needed to muscle more leverage with the Combined Chiefs of Staff; this body comprised American and British staff officers, who had authority to set major policy issues, subject to approval from Prime Minister Churchill and President Roosevelt. Montgomery's goal was to secure additional logistics for a powerful assault.

Thus, the invasion front broadened, the assault force grew, and three airborne divisions were included to secure the flank: the 6th British Airborne Division around Caen and the American 82nd and 101st to protect the newly added Utah beachhead to seal off the Cotentin Peninsula. Also known as the Cherbourg Peninsula, this stretch of land along the French coast extends in a northwest direction toward the English Channel.

Air Marshal Trafford Leigh-Mallory oversaw the airborne portion of Neptune. An Anglican priest's son, fifty-two-year-old Trafford Leigh-Mallory was "round-faced, with a neat toothbrush moustache," so described by a historian, who added that Leigh-Mallory had the "soulful eyes of a well-fed spaniel." He studied history and law at Magdalen College, Cambridge, and considered becoming a barrister. World War I shelved that career plan: he joined the infantry in 1914. Wounded at Second Ypres a year later, he recovered and received a promotion to first lieutenant. He transferred to the Royal Flying Corps and stayed with the air service for the remainder of his military career.

Early in the next world war, Leigh-Mallory commanded a fighter group during the Battle of Britain. He gained notice after introducing the unorthodox strategy of attacking the German Luftwaffe with "big wings"—that is, three to five squadrons—as they returned from raiding England, rather than shooting down enemy planes before they reached their targets.[5] Although his innovative tactics barely dented Hitler's air force, the War Office promoted Leigh-Mallory to head fighter command with the temporary rank of air marshal. This led to his appointment in August 1943 as air marshal and commander-in-chief of the Allied Expeditionary Air Forces.

Gavin, representing the 82nd, and Lee, the 101st, served on the committee. Lieutenant General Frederick "Boy" Browning spoke for the British. Lee confessed to Gavin that he felt nervous that his inexperienced troops wouldn't be able to handle the ground operation after landing.[6]

Leigh-Mallory convened the first few airborne meetings at Bentley Priory, a stately home spanning the eighteenth and nineteenth centuries in the London borough of Harrow. Gavin attended and came away concerned "that the employment of the airborne troops in the coming operation lacks vision and boldness." Major General William O. Butler, a senior US Air Corps officer assigned to Leigh-Mallory's staff, concurred with Gavin: "It is like having Michaelangelo paint a barn."

Leigh-Mallory made no decisions or commitments about how he would like to use the airborne, but he encouraged further discussion. After another meeting, Gavin grew concerned that the 82nd might not get into the fight, having been replaced by additional British airborne units thanks to Boy Browning's influence with Montgomery.[7]

Gavin had been long suspicious of Browning. When they first met in London in November 1943 to advise General Morgan on the American airborne participation, Browning made a crack about Ridgway not having parachuted when in Sicily. Major General Ray Barker, COSSAC's American deputy-chief of staff, told Gavin to watch out for Browning: he was "an empire builder."[8]

The airborne would fly from bases in southern England to the Cotentin Peninsula. Specifically, the American airborne was composed of more than thirteen thousand men from the 82nd and 101st divisions, including six paratrooper regiments, parachute field artillery, and engineers. Additionally, another four thousand men, consisting of glider infantry with supporting weapons and medical and signal units, would arrive in five hundred gliders later on D-Day and on D+1 to reinforce the paratroopers already on the ground. Small groups of airborne would join the 82nd and 101st on D+1 by landing craft.

VII Corps comprised Ridgway's and Taylor's airbornes and Raymond Barton's 4th Infantry Division, the amphibious force scheduled to come ashore a few hours after the paratroopers secured the exits and causeways leading from Utah Beach. VII Corps was led by General J. Lawton

Collins, fresh from commanding the 25th Division on Guadalcanal in the Pacific, where his men relieved the Marines and cleaned up that island. Collins, a forty-eight-year-old Louisianan, had been eager to leave the Pacific and command his own corps. He was a youngster compared to MacArthur's other divisional and corps leaders, and General Bradley, who had served with Collins on the West Point faculty, gladly accepted him for Overlord.[9]

British airborne units under Major General Richard N. Gale's 6th Airborne Division would land on the eastern end of the beachhead near Caen. Once on the ground, Gale's paratrooper and glider battalions would secure crossings over the Orne River and Caen Canal, knock out large German coastal guns that could wreak havoc on amphibious troops coming ashore at Gold, Juno, and Sword beaches, and block the movement of German reinforcements.

General Friedrich Dollmann's second-rate, poorly equipped German Seventh Army defended the Cotentin Peninsula with only two infantry divisions. Hitler and his commanders expected the Allied invasion force to come ashore at the Pas-de-Calais sector, so that's where he sent his best divisions.

One of Dollmann's divisions, the 709th, filled its ranks with Ostlegionen, captured Soviet soldiers from the East. Rather than rot away in a prison camp, the prisoners chose to fight with the Germans. Dollmann placed them along the beach's defenses. Another division, the 243rd Division, was located to the rear of the 709th, assigned to defend the western portion of the peninsula.

Beside dealing with Dollmann's men, the Allied invasion forces would have to contend with the so-called Atlantic Wall. First started by German occupation troops in spring 1942, the wall spanned from Spain to Norway. Field Marshall Erwin Rommel's name is synonymous with the Atlantic Wall because as chief of operations to Field Marshal Gerd von Runstedt, commander of German forces in the west, he took charge of the wall's construction in fall of 1943. A half-million men, some as young as fifteen, helped build it.

Although unfinished, by June 6, 1944, the series of defensive structures consisted of twelve thousand bunkers constructed from thirteen million tons of reinforced concrete and one million tons of steel. Hitler believed his Festung Europa impregnable. "No nation on earth can drive us out of this region against our will," he proclaimed.

The Allies proved him wrong on June 6.

One paratrooper remarked sarcastically, "Hitler made only one big mistake when he built Fortress Europe—he forgot to put a roof on it."[10]

Paratroopers and gliders landing behind the Atlantic Wall encountered hedgerows, another form of defensive structure, which the Germans used to their advantage. Since at least the days of William the Conqueror, who defeated the English at the Battle of Hastings in 1066, Normandy has been a dairy and farming region. To prevent cattle from roaming from one field to another, farmers constructed great hedges using piles of stones and brush incorporated into vines, topped by "ghostly-looking trees."

Some of the hedges or hedgerows that Captain Sam Gibbons of the 501st PIR encountered rose six to eight feet from the base and as wide as six feet. Instead of removing the hedgerows to make way for a road or highway, the Norman people historically had cut right through them.[11]

For the Allied soldiers fighting in so-called "hedgerow country," the obstacles were a blessing and a curse. In the dark, early morning hours of June 6, paratroopers used the hedgerows as protection while they fought to dislodge their chutes and establish their bearings. Yet, often on the other side of these peculiar barriers, "a single German soldier or an entire company of 150 men—or perhaps none at all" might be lurking, their weapons ready.[12]

Other obstacles designed to impede the paratroopers were long, wooden poles Rommel had planted as preventive measures against the expected airborne landings. Rommelspargel, or "Rommel's asparagus," measured six to twelve inches in diameter and eight to twelve feet in length stretching across miles of open fields. Rommel ordered the poles to be planted two feet deep, roughly thirty feet apart. Local peasants performed much of the labor to place the poles in the ground. Since there weren't any forests in the vicinity, the tree trunks (usually pine) had to be brought in from great distances away by horse and cart.

If that wasn't enough, the field marshal ordered mines secured to the tops of each pole and wires crisscrossed along the tops of clusters of poles.

That way, if paratroopers landed in bunches, the "spider's web" would blow them to pieces. For their own safety, the Germans marked the poles with little yellow flags with crossbones drawn on them.[13]

Two weeks after D-Day, a Reuters correspondent came across a French laborer who had been hired by the Germans, still digging holes and planting the poles. When asked what he was doing, the Frenchman explained that he had been told to plant the poles a couple of weeks before, but he got sick and was home in bed. Although he had heard some excitement, he didn't know the Allies had landed, and no one told him to stop digging.[14]

Flooded marshlands presented another daunting obstacle. The Douve River flows through the south Cotentin; its main tributary, the Merderet River, flows south and southeast before veering toward the sea. Neither of these rivers is very wide or has high banks, but each one floods where it flows through flat bottom lands and watery meadows. Flooding is controlled by a lock and dam at La Barquette, north of Carentan. At high tide, the low marshland lies below sea level but transforms into shallow lakes when the locks are open. Other areas of the Cotentin Peninsula formed low-lying meadows and were also easily flooded.

Movement around the Cotentin was largely over causeways first built during the eighteenth century in the time of Louis XIV, when large-scale drainage work was undertaken to clean up the swamps at the base of the peninsula. They were simple dirt roads, barely three meters wide, just enough room for a farmer's horse and carts to pass over to reach their grasslands in the marshes and fields in the coastal dunes, as well as for fisherman heading to sea. When in need of repair, sand and stone were used to fill in holes.

More than a century later, in the 1930s, the roads were paved with a layer of stone or sometimes bitumen for use by automobiles, but they were never widened. Because the causeways led from the beaches and were essential for the amphibious forces to access as they broke out into the open, securing the causeways was a key D-Day airborne objective.[14]

These impediments—the hedgerows, the poles, and the flooded areas—meant, essentially, that the airborne had to capture the La Barquette lock before the Germans controlled the water heights and trapped the amphibious troops on the beach.

The final Utah Beach operational plan turned into a bold attempt to use airborne units to overcome the difficult terrain behind the beachhead. This combat air drop would be the largest of the war so far: two airborne divisions delivered at night behind enemy lines with the aim of securing bridges and access points.[15]

Ultimately, Leigh-Mallory spoke up about the airborne. In a February 1944 meeting attended by Bradley and Montgomery, Leigh-Mallory insisted that they should "spike the airborne plan for Utah." Not only had the air commander soured on the course taken by the C-47s, "but he insisted that the risks of an air drop on Utah outweighed the advantages to be gained there."

Bradley had insisted all along that without airborne support before the amphibious landing, Utah Beach would have to be subtracted from the Overlord plan. "I'm sorry, General Bradley," Leigh-Mallory half-heartedly apologized, "but I cannot go along with you." Bradley responded, "Very well, sir," but "I am not going to land on that beach without making sure we've got the exits behind it."

Like a boxer ready to strike the next punch, Leigh-Mallory stared briefly across the table. Then he hit back with force: "Let me make it clear," he said, "that if you insist upon this airborne operation, you'll do it in spite of my opposition."

Satisfied, as though he'd landed the knockout blow, Leigh-Mallory, according to Bradley, "squared himself in his chair, turned to Montgomery, who so far had been uncharacteristically silent, and added: 'If General Bradley insists upon going ahead, he will have to accept full responsibility for the operation, for I don't believe it will work.'"

"That's agreeable to me," Bradley retorted. "I'm in the habit of accepting responsibility for my operations."

Montgomery interjected as though he were the peacemaker: "That's not at all necessary, gentlemen. I shall assume full responsibility for the operation."[16]

With that—and later with Eisenhower's approval—the airborne operation was a go.

11

The American Airborne in England

They started arriving in 1943.

The first echelon of the 101st Airborne docked at Liverpool on August 21. More Screaming Eagles came throughout the early fall, and the last of General Bill Lee's paratroopers set foot on English soil in late January 1944.[1]

Ridgway's 82nd came to England a month later in February 1944, after some of his paratroopers had been in Sicily and then Northern Ireland. C-47 and glider pilots and their crews from Troop Carrier Command had shown up in December 1943.

The US Army, especially its airborne, took over every square inch of the British Isles—or so it seemed to the British people. One historian cites the figure of 113,350 private properties requisitioned by the War Office for use by the Armed Forces, both Britain's and other nations'. "Great Britain became one big army camp," said one historian—especially among the American servicemen like the airborne. For them, "England was a home away from home."[2]

General Bill Lee was ordered to London in March 1943 as the American airborne representative during Overlord's early planning stages. Just before leaving, he was handed a packing list prepared by his staff with an eye toward the frigid temperatures in the War Office, like other poorly heated English buildings.

The offices were also cold and damp because windows that were damaged during the Battle of Britain in 1940, had yet to be repaired. Lee was instructed to bring a sweater, overshoes, and a raincoat, along with woolen, olive drab uniforms, socks, overcoat, underwear, and a muffler. His staff told him not to bother bringing his electric razor since it wouldn't operate on British circuitry. And should he want cigarettes, his staff said, he'd better bring his own since "British brands are inferior and costly."[3]

In February 1944, when C-47 radio operator Martin Wolfe arrived at Bottesford Airfield, six miles northwest of Grantham, rain fell most of the month. "British rain," as Wolfe described it: "cold, windswept, foggy, incessant." Trying to stay warm proved quite a chore for him and the others in his squadron. Their barracks were heated by potbellied iron stoves fueled by either coke or charcoal briquettes, "spheres of compressed coal dust," which were difficult to set afire, even with lighter fluid, paper, and matches.

Almost right away, Americans complained about the weather and the food. Wolfe also had a lot to say about food prepared by British cooks. Victuals were "not only strange," he remembered, but also "sloppily cooked and unappetizing-looking." Breakfast might be powdered eggs, fried Spam, brussels sprouts, and creamed chicken on toast—the English version of "SOS" (shit on a shingle). Tea was "strong enough to drink until you could float a spoon on it"—same with the coffee, Wolfe reported.

With all the sheep farms in England, mutton turned up for dinner frequently. By most accounts, the lamb tasted as bad as it smelled. On days when mutton was served in the mess hall, the Post Exchanges (PXs) emptied of cookies, potato chips, and candy. Resourceful soldiers took potatoes, bread, and marmalade from the kitchen to make their own dinners in their barracks.

Complaints about the food aside, American soldiers adored the British people and their beautiful countryside. Wolfe recognized "the rich green color in the checkerboard fields, the neat hedgerows and fences, the stone farmhouses with their thatched roofs, and the soft, undulating hills and valleys" from illustrations in a half-forgotten children's book. Another soldier remarked that "he felt he had passed out and awakened on a Hollywood movie set."[4]

Before stepping onto the British docks, American troops were expected to have read the War Department brochure, "Guide to Britain," passed out on the troopships. The guidebook offered GIs sensible advice on how not to offend their British hosts. These were basically the rules:

Don't throw your money around.

Don't boast about how much better life is in the United States.

Refrain from arguments about whether the Americans were there to "pull Britain's chestnuts out of the fire."

"Please understand," said the guidebook, "the British will welcome you as friends and allies. But remember that crossing the ocean doesn't automatically make you a hero."[5]

And this advice for Americans expecting Britain to resemble a fairy tale from a children's book: Keep an open mind. Because of years at war, the country "may look a little shopworn and grimy to you. The British people are anxious to have you know that you are not seeing their country at its best."

And lastly: "A Briton is the most law-abiding citizen in the world," so said this brochure, "but one should not mistake civility for lack of guts."[6]

Most American troops paid little attention to the brochure and its sage guidance. Common sense worked best. The airborne troops understood the hardships suffered by the British because of the war, and even the hardest soldiers felt sympathy for the local civilians.

Sergeant Wolfe put it this way:

We gradually realized that the scarcity of decent food and drink was not part of a devious British plot to make us feel miserable, but rather the outcome of their own desperate belt-tightening to save enough of the materiel needed for the war.

It made you more understanding to learn that strict British rationing meant that these kids were limited to one candy bar per week and that those five years old or younger had never seen an orange in their lives.

Adjacent to the airfields were small villages or midsized cities that airborne troops visited for entertainment. In the evenings, Colonel Joseph Harkiewicz, a C-47 pilot with the 29th Troop Carrier Command at Folkingham, went to nearby Nottingham. Trucks dropped airmen off at the city's many pubs. His favorite, the Flying Horse Café, made him feel "like he was sitting in someone's home, a cross between a parlor and a dining room."[7]

Beer sold in the pubs had been strictly rationed, sold only for two hours in the afternoon and from seven to ten in the evening. Often the beer ran out before the last call, Len Lebenson recalled. Otherwise, to signify that the beer tap would be shut off, the master sergeant in Headquarters Company, 82nd Division, distinctly remembered hearing a Leicester barkeep yell, "Time, gentleman, time."[8]

American soldiers and young British women, some still in their teens, were encouraged to attend "mixers," or dances. The idea, according to Sergeant Wolfe, "was that most of us were more curious and lonelier than oversexed, and that these needs could be met conventionally and safely through dances." There would be either officers' or enlisted men's dances—never combined. About one hundred young women would be brought onto a base by a motor pool.

On each truck, an officer on "courtesy patrol" would see that nobody got out of line. However, if a soldier wanted only casual sex, that was available, too. In larger cities like London, said Wolfe, "girls would saunter, two by two, in the vicinity of a Red Cross center to play the exciting game of 'pick-up.'" Wolfe and the other soldiers called these women by the British term for prostitutes: "chippies." At the biggest Red Cross hotel of them all, Rainbow Corners, on London's Shaftesbury Avenue near Piccadilly Circus, soldiers could buy condoms along with their newspaper from the street vendors.

Two English women swarmed Colonel John R. Johnson Jr., a C-47 pilot with the 36th Troop Carrier Squadron, while on leave in London. Johnson, who came from a small Kentucky coal mining town and wrote home to his mother regularly, likely had no inkling that he was meeting a pair of these so-called chippies. Having arrived the day before after a two-hour train ride from Cottesmore Royal Air Force Base (set in Rutland, England's smallest county), Johnson set out in the morning for a barber shop to get his haircut. He was strolling aimlessly "on the lookout for a striped and revolving barber pole" when he heard a feminine voice call out, "Hello! Hi, Yank, need some company?"

Startled, since the street where he walked was almost empty, all Johnson could respond was "Huh? What did you say?"

She replied, "Would you like some companionship, tea, or," she paused suggestively, "something?"

Johnson hesitated, still not sure how to respond: "Thanks, but I'm on my way to get a much-needed haircut. Is there a barber shop nearby?"

She answered with a luring voice: "Darling, couldn't that wait just a little while?"

Before Johnson could come up with an answer, another female approached. She stepped between them. A scuffle broke out. The first woman shouted, "Leave him alone! I tell you—I saw him first."

The second woman countered, "Shut up! Go away. Get your own!" As they pushed and slapped each other, ignoring Johnson, he sneaked away. When he found that barber shop and told the barber what had just happened, the barber couldn't keep from laughing.[9]

Prostitutes were readily available; occasionally, a soldier even smuggled one onto base. The Americans called them "Piccadilly commandos" regardless of where they came from. But prostitutes were outnumbered by girls and women looking for dates. Wolfe recalled Americans "getting dirty looks and a few curses from British soldiers when we walked down the street or into a pub with a British girl on our arm. Let me tell you, some of those English soldiers hated our guts."

Private Spencer Wurst of 505th PIR, also on leave in London, couldn't believe how many prostitutes had congregated at Piccadilly Circus. The street was "so thick" with the ladies "that the standing joke was that they put out heavy trip wire so the soldiers couldn't get past."[10]

London's streets also teamed with military police from different Allied armies: American, British, French, and a few other countries that Wurst couldn't easily identify from their uniforms. He heard that plain-clothed policemen were likewise out in force.

None of the lawmen were going after the prostitutes, and that became an accepted wartime practice. Rather, they searched for men absent without leave (AWOL), or deserters. They accosted soldiers, demanding to see their identification, passes, and leave papers. Wurst had to explain who he was, why he was in London, and who gave him authority to be there.[11]

Summing up the overall experience of American and British relations, Wolfe thought that they "were perfectly decent." As an example, Wolfe recalled "a sweet old lady near our Membury base, who lived just beyond our officers' club, and who found out that I loved to drink milk but couldn't stand to drink the stuff made from powdered milk." Occasionally, she brought Wolfe a gift of milk. "It was something I really appreciated, though at the time I remember a couple of qualms about the milk not being pasteurized," he recalled. "But I think of that as an example of the good relations we had with these English neighbors."

12

C-47s

To the American airborne—and, for that matter, the British paratroopers as well—the C-47 was as essential to their job as the parachute itself. In fact, in his memoir, Dwight Eisenhower named the Douglas C-47 troop transport as one of the five pieces of military equipment he regarded as vital in defeating the Germans.[1]

Paratroopers who rode the C-47 into Normandy fondly nicknamed their planes "Gooneybird," "The Doug," "Old Fatso," "Skytrain," "Dakota," or "Skytrooper." The most fitting name, however, was "Workhorse."

Powered by two 1,200-horsepower Pratt and Whitney motors, the C-47 measured sixty-three feet long and weighed more than eighteen thousand pounds. It could hold up to six thousand pounds of cargo and carry a four-man crew and eighteen airborne troops in full combat gear. It had a top speed of 220 miles per hour and a maximum range of 1,500 miles.[2]

The design of this transport was slightly modified from Donald Willis Douglas's brilliant DC-3, the airplane that had revolutionized commercial travel in the early 1930s.

Long before Douglas had conquered the commercial airline industry, this Brooklyn-born, seventeen-year-old son of an assistant bank cashier had seriously considered a naval career. Brooklyn had one of the world's largest navy yards, so naturally Douglas wanted to become a sailor. After he applied and was accepted to the US Naval Academy, he headed down to Annapolis, Maryland, in July 1909.

In that same month, two brothers named Orville and Wilbur Wright demonstrated their flying machine before the army at Fort Myer, across the Potomac River from Washington, not far from Annapolis. The Wright brothers hoped to secure a Signal Corps contract.

Douglas, deeply passionate about airplanes, had received permission to witness the last test flight. On a warm, cloudless day, Douglas stood among a crowd of army officers, their gaze aimed skyward. He watched Orville Wright gracefully handle the box-kite biplane and circle the field twice to gain attitude. Wilbur's younger sibling then pointed the plane south to Alexandria; he flew roundtrip at an average speed of forty-two miles per hour—pretty impressive.

The Army bought the Wright brothers' machine for $30,000.[3]

Douglas was also hooked on that machine, mesmerized by what he had observed that day. Just as quickly, his thoughts of sailing were eclipsed by dreams of flying. In between studying and playing lacrosse, Douglas stayed in his dorm room constructing model planes and then testing them on the academy grounds and the floor of the armory.[4] After three years, Douglas left Annapolis to work as an aeronautical engineer. Only a handful of airplane manufacturers was around, and none took his goal seriously. So Douglas went back to college—this time the Massachusetts Institute of Technology (MIT)—to earn an engineering degree.

With that MIT diploma in his back pocket, his career took off. He stayed at the institute to teach engineering before helping to conceive the Navy's first dirigible for the Connecticut Aircraft Company. Douglas's big break came when Glenn L. Martin, an early aviation pioneer, appointed the twenty-three-year-old as chief engineer in his California plant. Douglas led the engineers who designed a "hydro-airplane" for the government of Holland.[5]

In the midst of World War I, the US Army Signal Corps had enlarged its air force after having purchased the Wright flyer several years back, and the corps had created an Aviation Section to oversee further expansion. Douglas came on as chief engineer.[6]

After the Great War, he briefly returned to Glenn L. Martin before quitting to form his own company. Douglas moved back to California and found office space in the rear of a Los Angeles barber shop. He formed a partnership with financier David Davis and developed an airplane, the

Douglas Cloudster, that could fly coast to coast, nonstop; engine failure, however, doomed the plane from the start.[7]

Davis bailed out, leaving Douglas as sole owner. In July 1921, the Douglas Aircraft Company opened a factory in Santa Monica to compete in the expanding passenger aircraft market. One of the company's early products, a twin-engine DC-1, could reach a speed of 150 miles per house; it had room for twelve passengers and a crew of two plus a flight attendant.

The DC-2 was next off the assembly line. Longer and faster than its predecessor, it could also carry two additional passengers. That was fine for the nonce, but United, Trans World, and American quickly demanded an even larger aircraft.

Douglas responded with the DC-3 in 1935. Bigger and faster than any other plane available, the DC-3 cruised between 165 and 180 miles per hour, had a larger fuselage, and could hold between twenty-four and twenty-eight passengers.

Airlines could also order an optional cargo door for handling air freight. Fresh fruit, vegetables, flowers, even Maine lobsters could reach their customers much faster than being shipped in rail cars and with less chance of spoiling. The DC-3 set the standard for commercial airliner design and became the most successful airplane of its day.[8]

In 1940, when the US government issued a request to industry for a cargo aircraft, Douglas responded with a specially modified DC-3, which had special appeal; its size, speed, and long range were perfect for Hap Arnold and the Army Air Force. In 1941, shortly before the United States entered the war, Arnold approved production of the redesigned DC-3, named the C-47 in a number of variants.[9]

Plush seats intended to keep air passengers comfortable during long-distance voyages were replaced by hard metal bench seats—like the metal trays that soldiers clanked in a mess hall. The fuselage was reinforced to withstand enemy fire, and a navigator's dome was added along with a large cargo "barn door" for loading Jeeps and other heavy equipment.[10]

The Air Corps designated the DC-3 as the C-47 Skytrain.[11] The British also purchased C-47s and named the aircraft Dakota (possibly an acronym for Douglas Aircraft Company Transport Aircraft). The first

C-47s were built at Douglas's Santa Monica factory, which ran around the clock, ceasing production only on major holidays. Every month, hundreds of DC-3s turned into C-47s.

The War Department paid Douglas almost $129,000 for each plane upon delivery. As volume increased, however, the price per plane decreased, so, by the end of the war, a single Skytrain could be purchased for just over $85,000.[12]

An inspector certified each plane, deciding whether it was fit to fly after a pilot put the aircraft through dozens of tests. If any defects were discovered, the planes went to the repair hangar and then gained input through the same series of tests before being signed off, ready for delivery.[13]

Toward the end of 1942, Douglas had outgrown its Santa Monica factory. Besides the C-47, Douglas had contracts to build numerous other military aircraft. The US government's Defense Plant Agency funded another facility, a new, windowless factory near Long Beach Municipal Airport.[14]

As the war pressed on, so did the need for more C-47s. Douglas opened his third factory in Oklahoma City. Encased in double brick walls nearly two miles long, the building had special insulation for air conditioning and cement floors painted white so the overhead fluorescent lights could illuminate above a 55-candlepower level.

At Douglas's Long Beach factory, skilled workers could be found on practically every street corner, but in Oklahoma City, qualified mechanics were hard to find. Douglas adapted to the local labor pool, wrote *Business Week* magazine, by creating "non-confusing simplicity for its green crew." Managers designed the factory to accommodate its Oklahoma workers' lower skill levels by simplifying the machine and assembly process. "Parts bear easily understandable names instead of numbers," the magazine reported. "Work is delivered to the workers by either mechanical conveyers or by stock girls."[15]

On the eve of D-Day in 1944, Troop Carrier Command had more than 1,300 C-47s lined up, ready to carry paratroopers and gliders from the airfields of southern England to the enemy-held positions along the Normandy coast. Douglas had also produced a small number of C-53 troop carriers. It was essentially a C-47 but without the heavier construction necessary for cargo transport, like reinforced floors and double cargo doors. Of the 821 troop carriers that took part in Operation Neptune, only twenty-one were C-53s. The remainder were the workhorse C-47s.[16]

13

Gliders

"Big, slow-moving kites that flew only at the mercy of the wind and air currents."

That's Matthew Ridgway's description of gliders upon seeing the Army's CG-4As for the first time. Certainly, the CGs (cargo gliders) were an unconventional aircraft, but they were the planes that would carry the 82nd and 101st Airbornes' equipment, supplies, and men into Normandy on D-Day.[1]

Gliders can be traced back to the 1880s. Otto Lilienthal, a German mechanical engineer and aviation pioneer, began developing the aircraft after watchng birds glide through the air. Over the course of five years Lilienthal made more than two thousand documented glider flights. On Sunday, August 9, 1896, he took off from a hill fifty miles northwest of Berlin. After flying briefly, the glider hung motionless in midair before plunging to the ground from an altitude of fifty feet. Lilienthal was paralyzed in the crash and died the next day. Supposedly, his last words were "Sacrifices must be made."[2]

Produced by the Waco (formally known as Weaver) Aircraft Company of Troy, Ohio, and its subcontractors, each CG-4A, which cost $18,000, could carry more than a dozen fully equipped troops, plus two crew. Although the planning load was 7,500 pounds, the CG could still take off while bearing up to nine thousand pounds. The glider flew a maximum speed of 150 miles per hour, a normal descent speed of seventy-two miles per hour, and a landing speed of sixty miles per hour.[3] The nose section could swing up to allow Jeeps, 75mm howitzers, or other ordnance and vehicles to fit inside the glider's belly. A Waco glider could hold a pilot, copilot, and thirteen soldiers, or a Jeep or trailer and two soldiers.[4]

Many of the soldiers who flew into combat by glider were assigned to one of the nine glider infantry regiments created by the US Army. Seven of these units were deployed to Europe. The 325th, 327th, and 401st Glider Infantry Regiments arrived on D-Day and the day after to support the paratroopers and remained with their divisons, the 82nd and 101st, for their entire length of service in Normandy. Even though flying in a glider was almost as dangerous as jumping by parachute into combat, the glider troops initially received less pay than paratroopers.[5]

Passengers seated in a Waco CG-4A experienced anything but a comfortable ride. Because of air pockets and turbulence, soldiers were jolted up and down on the wooden seats, and the plane's forceful engines rocked the machine back and forth.[6]

Pilot Donald MacRae, 37th Troop Carrier Squadron, received a bit of protection from his caring ground crew: "Some of the guys found an extra flak jacket for me"—not to wear, but to sit on. "They didn't want anything coming up from underneath the plane to hit anything vital," he remembered.[7]

As with C-47 pilots, glider pilots and passengers nicknamed the CG-4As. They called them the "Flying Coffin" and "Tow Target" in recognition of the plane's flimsy construction—wood, canvas skin, and steel tubing—more like a kid's model balsa wood plane from a kit than a real airplane. The gliders' floors, made of plywood, could be easily penetrated by enemy antiaircraft fire. Gliders, built for one-way travel, were simply easy prey for enemy guns.

Nevertheless, the plane had its admirers, who called the CG-4As "Silent Wings." MacRae couldn't understand why. "It was louder than hell," he complained. Newsman Walter Cronkite, who rode in a Waco a few months after D-Day, seconded MacRae: "It was like sitting inside a bass drum at a Grateful Dead concert," the journalist recorded in his autobiography.[8]

General Bill Lee greatly influenced the incorporation of gliders into the airbornes' arsenals. While in Europe during the 1930s as an observer, Lee, the paratrooper visionary and first commander of the 101st

Airborne, had witnessed German sport-glider training. At that point, gliders had not yet been used in combat, but that changed when Hitler's force employed glider-borne attacks in Belgium and Crete.

Lee also noted that the British were developing glider tactics with the Airspeed Horsa, which carried almost twice as many passengers as the CG-4A would. After returning from abroad, Lee spoke volumes about the gliders. General Hap Arnold listened.[9]

In March 1941, Arnold ordered the Air Corps Experimental Test Center to design a glider, but engineers overseeing the project floundered: "From the beginning the program was plagued with false starts, incorrect judgments, and an overabundance of disorganization," wrote one historian. "Time and money were wasted on a myriad of misguided decisions." One such blunder involved the agonizing discussions over "determining the optimum size of a glider. There was no precedence to go by, but tremendous pressure to get the program off the ground since Arnold wanted quick delivery of the planes."

After winning the initial contract, Waco couldn't keep up with demand. The Air Corps, now renamed the US Army Air Corps, brought on twenty-one companies to keep up production. Many of the gliders were built in Michigan, where large furniture and automotive manufacturers provided ready-made factories and workers.[10]

As the glider's primary designer, Waco had to make production and engineering data available to the other contractors and allow observers from the other builders to visit its plant. Because of a tight labor market, the contract forbade subcontractors to entice employees to leave Waco to join their companies. The US government contract also allowed Waco to charge those companies $250 per glider based on the number of planes each company produced. The quantity ranged from 20 to 230, depending on how many gliders the participating company was expected to produce.[11]

Although not a complex aircraft to assemble, the glider had more than seventy thousand parts. Over fifty subcontractors manufactured glider components. Sometimes the subcontractors shifted over from odd sources. For example, Steinway and Sons, the piano makers, produced wings and tail surfaces; Heinz, the condiments company, refitted its food-processing equipment to make wings and other components instead of mustard and ketchup; Anheuser-Busch Brewery, the St. Louis beer maker, produced in-board wing panels.[12] By 1942, glider production was in full swing, which meant Waco and the other contract builders met their obligations. Soon, hundreds of gliders sat idle while the Army Air Corps faced the more unenviable tasks of (1) finding pilots and (2) training them for combat.

Hooking a glider on to the back of a C-47 was a complicated affair. Before the troop transport carrier and the glider could connect, two poles were placed on the runway, positioned some fifty yards ahead and to the right of the parked glider to allow the tow-plane plenty of clearance as it swooped in for the pick-up. Next, one end of the tow-line would be fixed to the glider's nose and the other end draped over the tops of the poles in a closed loop configuration.

In making its approach to snag the tow-line, the airplane had to drop to an altitude of only twenty feet. Once the line had been snagged by the airplane's trailing hook, a length of cable would be rapidly released from the drum. Tension would then be gently applied to the cable, drawing the tow-line taut almost at once. Coordination between pilots of both aircraft had to be complete, because in a matter of seconds, the glider, as one historian put it, "would be whisked off the ground at about the same speed as an accelerating city bus." "During practice, glider pilots maneuvered their craft to fly higher than the powered airplane to escape the turbulence."

For his part, the glider pilot had to keep the glider from swinging too far to the right during take-off. Failure to maintain a steady position during this critical phase of the operation could cause either the steel cable or the tow-line, or both, to slap into the underside of the tow-ship's elevators, forcing them upward and causing the airplane to stall and crash. [13]

Such precision training totaled about four thousand hours between April and May. By the time D-Day rolled around, the C-47 and glider pilots had little fear of linking their two aircrafts together. What happened after they unhooked over Normandy was questionable.

14

Eisenhower's Parachuting Correspondents

Rarely does a paratrooper earn an obituary in *Variety*, the show business publication, but Barney Oldfield, both a paratrooper and a journalist, became the first to do so: it was headlined "Barney Oldfield, Show Business Journo, dead at 93."[1]

Oldfield died in 2003 after a most remarkable career as not only a journalist but also a publicist in and out of the Army. He was a talent agent, a radio broadcaster, a winner on Groucho Marx's quiz show *You Bet Your Life*, a wisecracker, and publicity stuntman. A philanthropist after he retired, he set up forty scholarships at his alma mater, including one for the student who could cite the most "you know"s in a single broadcast. He also facilitated the burial of Marlene Dietrich's German mother during World War II.

Obviously, Barney Oldfield was not your ordinary paratrooper. He wasn't even your ordinary soldier. Although he grew up in Nebraska, he did not tumble off the turnip truck onto a military parade field.

He was born in Tecumseh, Nebraska, in 1909, the namesake of his uncle, Arthur Barney Oldfield (both preferred their middle name). Uncle Barney was a world-famous race-car driver, the pioneer who had raced an unheard-of sixty miles per hours around a track. Nephew Barney graduated from the University of Nebraska in 1932 with a journalism degree.

He parlayed that degree into writing columns and features for the *Lincoln Star* and the *Lincoln Journal*. His part-time job as a theater usher was followed by a stint reviewing films, and in 1930, he became a correspondent for *Variety*. This "world-champion film reviewer" was hailed in *Ripley's Believe It or Not!* for sitting through more than five hundred films during 1937–1938. During his time as a newspaperman, he interviewed many Hollywood stars, including Clark Gable, Shirley Temple, Doris Day, and Fred Astaire, and Cecil B. DeMille interviewed him on his radio show. He also helped launch champion boxer George Foreman's career.

In late 1940, Oldfield joined the army reserves and then stayed permanently with the rank of captain. First an intelligence officer, he was later placed by the Army with Major General Ben Lear as his publicist during the 1941 Louisiana Maneuvers, a series of US Army exercises held in the area, including Fort Polk, Camp Claiborne, and Camp Livingstone. Looking for excitement beyond what war games could deliver, Oldfield left Lear's staff in March 1942 and joined the paratroopers.[2] During World War II, Oldfield thought and acted like a journalist because he had been a "news hunter-upper," banging out copy on his Remington typewriter. He became a full-time soldier after America entered the war. As a public relations officer (PRO), he said, "I peddle ideas to the scribes, sometimes talking them into trouble, sweating them out."

Lieutenant Colonel Oldfield reinvented the relationship between PROs and war correspondents. Smart, brash, funny, and a master showman, Oldfield shepherded reporters covering the war in Europe as if they were a flock of sheep wandering aimlessly in a vast pasture. Or, as he liked to say, he was like a "prohibition era bootlegger." He hawked stories instead of illegal booze. He graduated from Fort Benning's jump school in Georgia on July 4, 1942. What Oldfield remembered most about the transition from writing press releases to leaping out of perfectly safe airplanes was his final jump. On board a C-47, fifteen thousand feet above the Georgia clay, the jumpmaster barked "Stand by the door!" to Oldfield and the other recruits. First to jump was Lieutenant Leonard Anglin from nearby Lumpkin, Georgia. Oldfield watched Anglin plant his feet and stick his head out the door. Then the jumpmaster approached the trembling soldier. "Swinging the flat of his hand hard up against the underside of Anglin's leg," he yelled, "'Go!'" Out Anglin went.

Oldfield was up next, but the usual broad smile was not quite so sunny above his cleft chin. He also leapt out the door with help from the jumpmaster. Afterward, Oldfield recalled, "I looked up and the canopy was over me like a tent." Touching down, Oldfield "spilled backward and did a complete roll." With that, he had completed his fifth and final jump—earning the right to be called a paratrooper.[3]

Oldfield remained at Benning, where he served as the PRO for Jim Gavin's 505th Parachute Infantry Regiment and started its newspaper, *The Static Line.* Their tight friendship lasted for the rest of their lives.

One day, the colonel in charge of the post's bond drive asked Oldfield to help him stimulate sales of the bonds, even though few GIs had the money or desire to buy them. Oldfied came up with what he thought was a brilliant stunt; Gavin thought so, too.

Oldfield contacted Broadway producer Michael Todd (later to be Elizabeth Taylor's third husband). In 1942, Todd was producing *Star and Garter,* featuring stripper Gypsy Rose Lee. Oldfield asked, and Todd agreed, to send Lee to Benning, where she would stand unclothed before the men. For a fee, the men could affix bonds to her torso, "with the minor denominations located at less strategic spots and the larger denominations affixed to the more obvious spots." Oldfield suggested auctioning bonds to the highest bidders.

Oldfield told Lieutenant Colonel J. D. Rosenberger, the post adjutant, about the plan. "He went through the ceiling," Oldfield said. "'I can't have that woman on these premises,' he said with a growl. 'My wife grew up here in Columbus. Her friends would be horrified if I should host that woman.'" Rosenberger ordered Oldfield to cancel Lee's visit right away.[4] Oldfield was so upset that he told Gavin, "I am going to find a flat rock and get under it."[5]

In 1943, after Gavin and the 505th left for Europe with Ridgway's 82nd, Oldfield transferred to Troop Carrier Command, the Army Air Forces' unit that furnished planes, gliders, pilots, and crews for the airborne. A year later, the chance for Oldfield to go overseas was dangled in front of him by Lieutenant Colonel Jack Redding, former *Chicago Herald-American* reporter, who was talent-hunting in the United States as executive officer of European Theater of Operations (ETO) PRO.

Oldfield's boss, Major General E. G. Chapman, commanding general of Airborne Command, gave Oldfield the nod to go, with a request that he should not forget the airborne and the people in it.

"I promise," Oldfield replied.

Redding came up with the idea of recruiting journalists to cover the coming invasion of Europe, planned for spring 1944. His plan was for reporters to either jump with the paratroopers or fly with the gliders.

Since Oldfield was a parachutist, "although generally acknowledged by all the grads of Ft. Benning's jump school as the poorest specimen to whom the school had given a proficiency certificate," he had the credentials "needed to stall the run of negative reactions" from correspondents. "This called for the convincing of a bunch of professional unbelievers that they could safely pole vault the English Channel by glider or parachute," Oldfield wrote, and "get the best story of the war, live and see it in print—collect bonuses."

Redding based his idea on General Eisenhower's doctrine that the press was an instrument of public opinion with an important military part to play in warfare. Eisenhower regarded war correspondents virtually as his staff officers. "The war correspondents," Eisenhower said of their role, "would be a conduit to the home front for the reassurance of the people who were back there and had to rely on the newspaper and radio. I know of no thing that improves morale for a soldier that sees his own name or the name of his unit in print."

To entice journalists to join the invasion as part of the airborne—despite knowing that the gliders could be impaled on iron spikes and paratroopers could be shot out of the sky or drown in the marshes—Oldfield pitched three angles:

1. Airborne troops were certainly the only new story of the war. They were a novel product of the current conflict, just as fighter and bomber aircraft had been in World War I.
2. Airborne correspondents, up to that time, had never suffered casualties (there had been two or three during Operation Husky, but Oldfield planned to leave this information out).
3. Some four hundred correspondents were accredited with ETO, but only 150 could expect to go with the ground forces on the invasion, and fewer than sixty in the first four days. Airborne was wide open and would take any given number, so correspondents could rest assured they'd be part of D-Day—or before.

Correspondents, Oldfield knew all too well, "don't like unknown quantities," and "they have an awful responsibility to officers, wives, children and barkeeps." Oldfield started recruiting on October 25, 1943, to allow enough time to prepare a team by D-Day, at this point set for some time in spring 1944. Before arriving in London a week later, Oldfield had spent a few days in Washington, where he'd snared his first recruit: Walter McCallum, a golf writer turned military correspondent with the *Evening Star* who wanted to tell the airborne story by glider.

In England, Oldfield went to see Bill Lee at 101st Airborne headquarters. Lee granted Oldfield permission to allow correspondents to take part in the two-week refresher course he'd put his men through at the Chilton-Foliat parachute school on the site of the old Whitlaw Reid estate near Newbury.

What Oldfield learned as he spoke with the war correspondents was that they knew little about the paratroopers, or, as he called them, "three-dimensional warriors." Oldfield would explain that the airborne divisions were composed of infantryman, artillerists, and engineers, who used a different mode of transport to take part "in the caving of Hitler's iron girdle." In the public's imagination, paratroopers, according to Oldfield, were "cocky, boot-wearing, extra-paid, suicidal—raise hell today, and to hell with tomorrow." He needed finesse for "casting of this aerial play against the Axis."

Bill Walton with *Time* magazine was the first correspondent to step forward. A University of Wisconsin graduate, he had been in London for some time, had rubbed elbows with writer Ernest Hemingway and photographer Robert Capa, and later would consort with the Kennedys and Katharine Graham, publisher of the *Washington Post*.

Walton had already seen combat aboard a submarine and on a Liberator during a bombing run in France. Walton passed through the Screaming Eagle course with ease, completing his five qualifying jumps in two days. But he warned Oldfield, "If I die, it will be with your name on my lips, and it won't be complimentary."

The next prospect was forty-year-old *Colliers* photographer, Joe Dearing. He did his five jumps in one day. On the last one, he dented his helmet on a tree and knocked himself out.

With three correspondents joining Oldfield's fold, the word began to spread within the correspondent community. This created an unforeseen problem: female correspondents wanted to take part. The most persistent were Dixie Tighe with the International News Service, Betty Gaskill from *Liberty Magazine*, and Judy Barden of the *New York Sun*. This situation presented Oldfield with a serious quandary. He knew that neither Bill Lee nor the 82nd's Matthew Ridgway would sponsor women in combat.

Oldfield took a well-traveled road to reject their proposals and asked an army medic friend, "Doc, isn't there some physical reason why it isn't practical for women to jump?" The medic managed only that he had once known a professional female parachutist "who used to have queer feminine things happen to her when she jumped—every time." What exactly the medic meant by this statement, Oldfield didn't know or ask.

That reason, though specious and vague, was good enough for Oldfield, but he chickened out when it came time to tell the women. He asked their bosses to break the bad news. After he'd wiped his hands clean of the whole uncomfortable situation, Oldfield heard nothing more about it.

Meanwhile, Oldfield had gathered a few more recruits, including Marshall Yarrow, a British journalist with Reuters; American Robert "Bob" Reuben, also with Reuters; Corporal Phil Bucknell with *Stars and Stripes*; and Corporal John Preston with *Yank Magazine*. Oldfield called the latter trio his "three victims."

Reuben recalled the day they drove down to Chilton-Foliat to enroll in the Army's paratrooper school as a nice, sunny, spring Sunday. Along the way, Reuben also recalled, Oldfield regaled the three with tales "when the chute PRACTICALLY never failed but did" with "gory detail of the few accidents he'd seen." He told "of how miserable parachuting made him feel." Oldfield, said Reuben, "chortled happily at our misery."

Running the school was a quiet Southerner, Lieutenant C. D. Wallace, a "good-natured handsome officer who seemed to have absolutely no nerves," Reuben observed. "He was as casual the moment he jumped out of a plane or later on during combat when [he] took a bead on a German sniper as I am at the boring game of gin rummy."

At parachute school, Reuben, Yarrow, and Bucknell heard lots of stories about parachutists—such as the one about "the paratrooper who was given a folding bicycle jump when he bailed out of the plane." A folding bicycle jump occured when the man's chute didn't open. When "he pulled his emergency and that didn't open either, 'Well, now if that isn't just like the Army,' he said, 'I suppose when I get to the ground the bicycle won't work either.'"

After graduating from the abbreviated jump school, the three joined other recruits in London. They stayed in a little South Kensington apartment to await word on when the invasion force was heading overseas. "It was only a matter of weeks," Reuben guessed, "probably days."

No one really knew.

Not even General Eisenhower.[6]

15

Brereton's 9th Air Force

"The most intimate relationship must exist between the airborne troops and the troop carriers," the 9th Air Force commander, Lieutenant General Lewis Brereton, wrote in his diary on November 2, 1943, seven months before D-Day. This will "promote mutual confidence and knowledge of the many problems involved."

Brereton would have his work cut out for him in restoring faith between the paratroopers and the C-47 pilots after the wayward drops and horrific friendly-fire incident in Sicily during Operation Husky, which had occurred only four months before he took command of 9th Air Force. No one could blame the airborne troops for being more than a little skittish after more than eighty men from Ridgway's All-Americans were killed and another 132 wounded.

A 1911 graduate of the Naval Academy, the "five-foot-six, hard-boiled and relentlessly driven" Brereton figured out right away that he liked the ground better than the water and transferred to the Army. During World War I, he liked being above the trenches better than in them, so he volunteered for the Air Service.[1]

In September 1918, while on a reconnaissance mission during the St. Mihiel offensive, Brereton shot down his first and only enemy plane and was wounded during the fight. His action earned him the Distinguished Service Cross and a promotion to temporary lieutenant colonel. Also in 1918, Brereton joined General Billy Mitchell's staff as his assistant for operations. He helped the general devise plans for dropping infantry by parachute behind enemy lines. The innovative idea went nowhere, but Brereton's career took off.[2]

Between the world wars, Brereton held a variety of instructor, staff, and command posts. The day after attacking Pearl Harbor, the Japanese struck American airfields in the Philippines, where then–Major General Brereton, as commander of the Far East Air Forces, had responsibility for all B-17 "Flying Fortresses." The planes were lined up in tidy rows as though they were "waiting for execution by the Japanese."

After Japanese fighter pilots destroyed most of the fleet, Brereton's "benefactor and long-time friend" Hap Arnold blamed General MacArthur for not ordering the planes evacuated. Arnold sent Brereton to command the US 9th Air Force in Egypt, where he remained until taking the 9th to England in late 1943.

Much like his mentor Billy Mitchell, Brereton earned a reputation within the Army as "cocky, amusing, and highly intelligent," but at the same time "lazy, fond of rich living, attractive women and partying till dawn."[3]

In Ascot, England, a small town in East Berkshire, twenty-five miles west of London, the 9th Air Force set up its headquarters. Close by, some of Brereton's staff officers billeted at Berkshire Country Club, the preferred course for many golf champions.

Planning for Overlord took up most of Brereton's time, which often meant attending meeting and conferences. During one meeting, Bill Lee presented a combined directive and doctrine for airborne operations that he created with Brereton's staff. It set the stage for training between the airborne and the troop carriers to commence in November 1943.

At a conference Leigh-Mallory convened at his London Allied Expeditionary Air Force (AEAF) headquarters, Boy Browning and Montgomery alarmed Brereton by suggesting that all troop carriers should be under one command. Brereton agreed in principle, as long it was an American, knowing that the British would want one of their own officers in this role (probably Browning).

At this point, Leigh-Mallory stepped forward with a logical compromise: the Americans would command their airborne, and the British would do the same with their paratroopers and carrier command.

Now that Brereton hadn't lost any authority to the British, he took a major step in strengthening Troop Carrier Command in February 1944 by bringing Major General Paul Williams from the Mediterranean to command 9th Troop Carrier Command. The Detroit native and Stanford University graduate set up headquarters at Cottesmore, Grantham, in Lincolnshire, a short drive by Jeep to the air bases where his C-47s were training.[4]

Williams had been in the air service since February 1918, although he remained stateside during World War I. In 1942, he played a key role in directing 8th Air Force's strategic bombing of Germany. From there, he went to the Mediterranean and directed the troop carriers in North Africa and Italy. Williams had a depth of experience, but, more important to Brereton and the anxious paratroopers, he intimately knew about the problems in Sicily in 1943, and it was his task to see that they weren't repeated in Normandy.

Under General Williams's guidance, the C-47 pilots and crews were very familiar with their planes and complexity of carrying and dropping paratroopers and gliders.

Training, training, and more training, complained staff sergeant Michael N. Ingrisano Jr. after arriving in Cottesmore, England, in March 1944. Much like other Troop Carrier Groups, Ingrisano's 316th teamed directly with the paratrooper and glider regiments and practiced dropping men and planes over the English countryside.

Aircrews practiced not only dropping paratroopers and towing gliders but also day- and night-flying formation. They also familiarized themselves with instrument flying, radar, radio operations, and basic aircraft orientation through take-offs and landings.

Glider pilots and mechanics were embedded with the troop carriers and were put through their own intensive training that included wide-ranging lectures on topics such as evacuation procedures, enemy aircraft identification, German uniforms and equipment identification, and escape procedures.[5]

For Lieutenant George L. Collins and the crews of the 438th Troop Carrier Group, they would practice "the skills necessary for a near-perfect drop of paratroopers and a near-perfect drop for gliders day after day." Collins, like the other forty-seven pilots, had to fly a CG-4A glider so when it came time to tow one, he'd know what problems a glider pilot behind him had to deal with.[6]

Although there is no substitute for actually flying airborne into combat, a series of large-scale exercises in England was intended to portray what it might be like on D-Day. The exercises were as realistic as possible, other than the fact not a single enemy soldier firing an antiaircraft gun was in sight.

In early March, Taylor's 101st took part in a VII Corps exercise that was code named Beaver, the first real practice for D-Day. At Slapton Sands, the 4th Infantry Division landed from the sea, followed by elements of the 101st, also by landing craft. Next came the parachute and glider battalions, which were motored to the drop zones by trucks. The exercise didn't go particularly well. "Confusion was rife in the transit camps and marshaling areas and continued through the landings," wrote a historian, "but a lot of lessons were learned."[7]

Later that month, on March 23, Brereton attended an 101st Airborne exercise along with Eisenhower, Bradley, and special guest Prime Minister Churchill. Three groups of C-47s gave an excellent demonstration of paratrooper drops, landing their men directly on the drop zone. Before that, gliders skidded to a stop on the landing zone. Much to the relief of the spectators and participants, not one of them crashed.

Eisenhower sat on Churchill's left and Brereton to his right. Churchill was in very good spirits, full of energy and very enthusiastic. The prime minister referred to airborne troops as "the most modern expression of war."

Public Affairs Officer Colonel Barney Oldfield was on hand to shepherd Eisenhower and Churchill around. Churchill came with a large entourage of British officers, as well as his daughter, actress and dancer Sarah Oliver. Oldfield had to keep photographers away from Churchill; the "old boy in the high bowler," as Oldfield called him, turned irritable when they snapped his picture.[8]

War correspondent Frank A. King witnessed the occasion and published a story that ended up in at least three London newspapers. "Hundreds of American soldiers cheering wildly, carrying aloft their national flags and unit emblems," King recorded, "broke from their compact and serried ranks to gather in a great, tight-packed circle around a Jeep, on which stood, bareheaded, the British prime minister, gripping his gold-headed cane as he watched the mass of green-gray men surge in and around him."[9]

When the exercise concluded, American soldiers were invited to gather around Churchill, who addressed them as only one of the world's great orators could.

"It is with feelings of emotion and profound encouragement that I have the honor to review you here today," he told them. "In these weeks that are passing so swiftly, I see gathered here on the English soil these soldiers of our great American ally preparing to strike a blow for a cause which is a greater cause than either of the two countries have fought for."

"Soon," he added, "you will have the opportunity of testifying your faith in all those inspiring phrases of American Constitution, and of striking a blow, which, however it may leave the world, will, as we have determined, make it a better and broader world for all. I thank God you are here, and from the bottom of my heart wish you all good fortune and success."

Afterward, Churchill was taken for a trip around the field. Entering a CG-4A Glider, he said to the crew onboard, "You look very comfortable in here."

Then the prime minister and Eisenhower left in the Supreme Commander's car, carrying the flags of the United States and Great Britain and Churchill's four-star banner. With Ike's pretty *chauffeuse*, Kathleen "Kay" Summersby, a member of the British Mechanised Transport Corps, at the wheel, the paratroopers watched them drive off.

Meanwhile, Ridgway's 82nd spent two and a half months camped in Northern Ireland, just north of Belfast. In mid-February, Ridgway moved the 82nd Division to England so they could be nearer to their D-Day departure points. While in Northern Ireland, the 82nd acquired two more parachute infantry regiments, the 507th and 508th, plus a glider battalion formerly with Colonel Harper's 401st.

In the English Midlands, where Ridgway set up camps, his men could practice with General Williams's Troop Carrier Command, as the 101st had been doing for some weeks. On May 12, a final joint parachute exercise with the two airborne divisions was held. Called Exercise Eagle, it involved 532 C-47s 50th and 53rd Troop Carrier Wings transporting Taylor's men, while 369 C-47s carried Ridgway's paratroopers.[10]

Many of the aircraft had recently landed in England by way of the Southern Atlantic Air Ferry Route, while others had flown to the United Kingdom from the Mediterranean. The pilots who flew the Southern Route touched down no fewer than ten times in nine different countries.

They "could say they had seen four continents, lots of islands, and too, too much ocean." The aircrews could also "show off the gaucho boots bought in Brazil, describe the taste of mangos they ate in British Guiana, and tell about the real dangers from German fighters on the leg of the flight from North Africa to Land's End in England."[11]

Eagle, a carefully scripted night-time exercise, took place in Berkshire (Hungerford-Newbury area) in terrain resembling the drop zones back of Utah Beach. Seventh Corps' General Collins was there that night. "I watched this exercise with keen interest," Collins wrote, "and, I will admit, with some trepidation, as the troopers poured out of the skies and rained down around a group of observers, which I was one."[12]

Ridgway and Taylor's men "encountered stiff resistance from the 'enemy,' actually the US 28th Division." C-47s carried the paratroopers from the same eleven airfields they would use the night before D-Day. The exercise forecast much of what would happen on June 6, 1944.

Two C-47s collided in midair, killing all the crew and occupants of both planes. A handful of C-47s dropped paratroopers nine miles from the drop zones, and other paratroopers crashed through the roofs of houses in the village of Ramsbury. More than four hundred were treated for broken bones, sprained ankles, and lots of minor injuries.

Besides the C-47 crash casualties, none of the paratroopers died while on their way down or on the ground, unlike what would happen on D-Day. Collins said that "it went well and many valuable lessons were learned." At this late stage, that's all Ridgway and Taylor could wish for.[13]

16

The Unbearable Burden of a Conscience

Tuesday, May 30, 1944: "Ike had a tough one today," Captain Harry C. Butcher, Eisenhower's naval aide, recorded in his diary.[1]

Butcher was referring to a visit that day to Eisenhower from Air Chief Marshal Trafford Leigh-Mallory "to protest once more what he termed the futile slaughter of two fine divisions."

Months before, when the Overlord airborne plan had been drawn up, Leigh-Mallory had objected to dropping the American 82nd and 101st Airborne Divisions into enemy-held territory behind Utah Beach. He predicted heavy casualties. Paratroopers and gliders would be shot out of the sky, he insisted.

Eisenhower never brushed off Leigh-Mallory's apprehension. In fact, it fueled his own apprehension. Just a week before the Air Chief's latest visit, he had drafted a secret memorandum in his diary:

In contemplating Airborne operations, which I originally thought would present very little difficulty because of our tremendous preponderance in fighters, we have run into great difficulty because of the almost universal coverage of the European continent by strong flak. When going into areas where gliders cannot land at night, we run into most appalling difficulties and obstacles due to this fire. This is one phase of the operation that still worries me and I am somewhat concerned that the 82nd Division will have a most sticky time of it. I am going to see whether or not special support by fighter bombers cannot be given them.[2]

Leigh-Mallory's forceful argument caught Eisenhower's attention once again, but so did General Omar Bradley's counterargument: without airborne support, the First Army commander advised, the 4th Infantry Division would never make it ashore onto Utah Beach. Eisenhower had sided with Bradley, so as far as Leigh-Mallory was concerned, the matter had been settled. The decision for the SHAEF commander was not easy. As his son John later remarked, Eisenhower "bore the heaviest burden of anyone as the man on whose shoulders the success or failure of the campaign rested."[3]

By the end of May, Ike had assumed "that the only remaining great decision to be faced before D-Day was that of fixing, definitely, the day and hour of the assault"—at least until Leigh-Mallory stirred the airborne question up again.

Still, Eisenhower listened carefully as Leigh-Mallory rehashed the old fight. "We'll lose 50 percent of the paratroopers before they land," he told Eisenhower. He predicted that glider losses would be even worse, around 70 percent. Airborne troops who did make it to the ground would have little "tactical power and the attack would not only result in the sacrifice of many thousands of men, but would be helpless to effect the outcome of the general assault."

"To protect him in case his advice was disregarded," Eisenhower wrote in his postwar memoir, "I instructed the air commander to put his recommendations in a letter and informed him he would have my answer within a few hours. I took the problem to no one else. Professional advice and counsel could do no more." Eisenhower then retired to his quarters at Telegraph Cottage in Bushy Park, on the western outskirts of London near Hampton Court Palace. SHAEF had moved to the site in March 1944, after Eisenhower had found London too distracting.[4]

Eight months before, Eisenhower had had his own doubts about using airborne troops in combat, but not doubt fueled by the Sicily friendly-fire disaster. "I do not belive in the Airborne division," he cabled General Marshall in Washington on September 20, 1943. "I believe that airborne troops should be organized in self-contained units comprising infantry, artillery and special services, all about the strength of a regimental combat team."[5]

Yet Eisenhower soon softened, as the planning for Neptune was well under way and Utah Beach was added to the operation, along with a two-division airborne component. In fact, Eisenhower had to fend off Marshall and General Hap Arnold, who insisted on a more extreme airborne landing around Evreux, some seventy-five miles east of Caen, to capture airfields and threaten Paris. On February 19, 1944, Eisenhower fought back and told Marshall that the airborne had to be used in close support of the amphibious assault. "The resistance to be expected by our landing forces at the beaches is far greater than anything we have yet encountered in the European War."[6]

By his bed, where he would contemplate Leigh-Mallory's case for disbanding the airborne from Neptune, Ike kept a stack of westerns mailed by Mamie to one of his aides, Sergeant Mickey McKeogh. Eisenhower preferred stories with lots of shooting in the plot. Next to the paperbacks waited ashtrays and packs of Marlboros. McKeogh was assigned, among his duties, the ugly job of emptying the ashtrays after they overflowed with butts. Mixed in with the spent Marlboros were "smoldering cigarettes"—Ike would often "light one," McKeogh recalled, "put it down, forget it, and light another." The general wasn't a tidy smoker either—he had a nasty habit of not using ashtrays at all. Instead, Eisenhower would tap off the ashes against a chair, desk, or anything else within reach, believing, according to McKeogh's wisecrack, that "cigarette ashes are good for carpets."

Eisenhower had started his nicotine habit thirty years before at West Point, sneaking smokes since tobacco was prohibited on the academy grounds. After graduation, he was rarely seen without a cigarette perched between his lips. Slowly, his consumption increased to two packs a day. Now, tenser than ever with D-day around the corner, he consumed four packs daily, perhaps more right after Leigh-Mallory left on May 30.

Leigh-Mallory's urgent plea to Eisenhower resulted from fresh intelligence about German troop strength on Utah Beach. On May 24, Bletchley Park intercepts revealed that the 91st *Luftlande-Infantrie* Division (91st Air Landing Division) had arrived on the Cotentin Peninsula, now occupying the same ground designated as the drop zone for Ridgway's paratroopers.[7]

Bletchley Park comprised a stately mansion and grounds where code-breakers, cryptanalysts, and hundreds of other allied staff with varying jobs disseminated wartime intelligence. They worked twenty-four hours a day, seven days a week. They had to: there was a war on.

They worked entirely in secret. The Germans had no idea that teams of highly trained women and men, working in the outskirts of London, knew about the enemy's operational movements almost from the moment the information was distributed.

On her first day of work with the Women's Royal Navy Service, Patricia Steadman was made to sign the Official Secrets Acts. She had to promise to say nothing about her work to anyone. Steadman and other new recruits were met by an "impressive gentleman . . . who proceeded to put the fear of God into us by saying that once through the gates . . . we would hear, see and learn of things that must never be divulged."[8]

Only in the mid-1970s, when wartime information was declassified, were citizens alerted to the essential war work that went on in BP, as it was known. These activities have more recently been captured in books and on film. In 2012, for example, British television offered a fictionalized mystery series, set in 1952, of women in *The Bletchley Circle*. In 2014, *The Imitation Game* told the story of Alan Turing, Joan Clarke, and their brilliant associates, exploiting the forerunners to modern computers to break the German codes.

Designated "Ultra" or "Ultra Secret," and encrypted on the Enigma machines employed by the Nazi government and all its military branches, the intelligence generated at Bletchley Park had to be a closely guarded secret to ultimately make the difference it did.

Bletchley's origins as the Government Code and Cypher School (GC&CS) can be traced to 1919. The school not only advised the British government on the use of its own cyphers and security codes but also taught how to decrypt cypher communications used by foreign powers. GC&CS operated out of the Secret Intelligence Service (SIS) headquarters in London, across from the St. James's Park tube station.

In 1938, with Hitler on the rise and, thus, the potential for another war, the British government decided it best to move GC&CS out of London lest the city become a target of aerial bombardment. The SIS chief secured a deal to purchase a nineteenth-century mansion known as Bletchley Park and its fifty acres. Fifty miles northwest of London, the site's main attraction was a nearby railroad, linking the site not only with London but also with Oxford and Cambridge, where the colleges afforded an ample source of "brain power."[9]

During World War II, intercepted German messages came to Bletchley's brain power from Y-Stations, where wireless operators sat at banks of receivers, scanning the airwaves for enemy transactions. Twenty Y-Stations throughout England intercepted messages from Enigma, encryption machines brought into German army service in 1932.

Enigma passed on code by cable or wireless using Morse code or by Lorenz, which were non-Morse teleprinter intercepts. Bletchley workers dubbed the Lorenz message traffic as FISH. Enigma-encrypted messages could be sent in any form but were typically sent using hand-speed Morse. The Lorenz cipher machine could be attached to a regular teleprinter and would encrypt the resulting message automatically.[10]

On May 24, a series of intercepted JELLYFISH (the code name for FISH messages sent between Berlin and Paris) revealed that the German 91st Division had entered the Cotentin Peninsula and established head-quarters at Chateau Haut, north of Carentan. The division now joined two other outfits already in Normandy in the area of Utah Beach: the German 709th Infantry Division staffed the east and north coasts, while the German 243rd Infantry Division maintained vigil on the west and across the base of the peninsula.

Bletchley had been tracking the 91st since its formation in January 1944. The division had been organized to take part in Tanne, a March 1944 operation to capture islands in the Gulf of Finland. The attack never took place, and Hitler's generals transferred the 91st to the west. In April, the division arrived in Strasbourg, France, and then gradually moved by rail to Normandy, arriving around May 11, 1944.[11]

Two of the division's Grenadier Regiments occupied a position around Pont-l'Abbé in Brittany and the 6th Paratrooper Regiment south of Carentan. Although understrength, the regiment remained dangerous, staffed with many veteran troops who had fought in Italy and on the Eastern Front.[12]

Like all FISH messages, the ones concerning the 91st Division would be disseminated in two of Bletchley's buildings, Huts 3 and 6. The two huts partnered to play a crucial role in providing intelligence for planning Overlord. Hut 6 processed only Enigma traffic, while Hut 3 did the intelligence analysis of both Enigma messages from Hut 6 and FISH traffic sent to them by the "Testery," the code-breaking team created by Major Ralph Tester, tasked with breaking the most high-level German code.

First, the raw data were sent to Hut 6, where cryptanalysts in a "watch" of army and air force Enigma worked in a cold, damp room roughly twenty-five square feet. A watch consisted of twelve or fourteen women or men, both service personnel and civilians, who received and reviewed the intercepts. The watch sat on wooden chairs in front of a plain wooden semicircular table, about fifteen feet long and two and a half feet wide, with a brown fiberboard top. Although the room's one window was blacked out, a fluorescent light hanging from the ceiling provided enough illumination to enable staff to read. Air and military advisers who worked with each watch were usually RAF and army officers. Their job was to guide the civilian watch keepers on military and technical details.[13]

The deciphered material from Hut 6 was then sent to Hut 3 by way of deciphered messages. By 1944, both huts had moved into Block D, and messages were moved by conveyer belt. The duty officer put the messages in order of priority, making sure the most important ones were dealt with first. If the duty officer deemed the message urgent, "he'd place it on the little shelf atop the partition," one historian wrote, "very much in the manner of a short-order cook setting out dishes for a waiter to pick up."

Once the messages reached Hut 3, they were translated, and "any rough German texts were edited and turned into complete sentences in English." Furthermore, Hut 3 had to determine the value of each message. If determined to have immediate value, the decrypted message had to be rushed to commanders in the field.[14]

Messages ordering the 91st Division to Normandy certainly rose to this level of importance.

On May 26, 1944, two days after the messages were received at Bletchley, General Omar Bradley convened a meeting at his First Army headquarters in Bristol, a three-hour car ride from London. Bradley had the use of an English country home, complete with ballrooms, green-houses, and stables. Before he'd arrived in October 1943, Bradley learned that the mansion "had been tentatively earmarked as a home for wayward girls." And "when the first American army truck rolled into its drive, the neighbors were said to have shrugged with resignation, if not relief."[15]

The meeting took place a short distance from Bradley's palatial surroundings, in a "dingy, windowless war room," at nearby Clifton. Generals Collins, Ridgway, and Taylor, Field Marshal Montgomery, and Air Marshal Leigh-Mallory met in the room crowded with crates, as Bradley's staff had already began packing equipment for the invasion.

> *We hurriedly revised the plan. The 101st would stick by its original mission, but the 82nd would now drop north of the 101st, within striking distance of Utah Beach. General Collins scaled down the original plan. Now, Ridgway's paratroopers would secure both banks of the Merderet River to hold the bridges south and west of Sainte-Mère-Église.*
>
> *Additionally, the 82nd would seize the crossroads at Sainte-Mère-Église and guard against counterattack from the northwest. Then, with available forces, the 82nd would try to expand west to stop any German reinforcements from entering the area.*[16]

However, the 101st's drop zones remained the same. Taylor's paratroopers would secure the Utah Beach exits and, at the same time, protect the southern flank of the invasion by holding the roads and rail bridge over the Douve River north of Carentan.

Although seemingly enthusiastic about the plan, Ridgway later commented that "the drop was a great gamble, we admitted. The whole great operation was a desperate gamble.... Both General Bradley and I argued strongly that these were risks that we would have to take, and we were willing to take them. General Bradley and I argued that despite the hazards, which we recognized clearly, the divisions would carry out the missions assigned to them."

Returning to 82nd Division headquarters, Ridgway shared the outcome of the meeting with General James Gavin, his assistant division commander. Gavin's direct response to Ridgway is unknown, but his diary records that he "worried that the new drop looks like a snafu, confusion and indiscriminate fighting galore." He predicted that "it will be several days until any semblance of organization or tactical integrity comes out of the mess."

Over dinner on May 30, Bradley confidently reassured Gavin that the Americans would "swamp the Germans." Still, the All-Americans' assistant commander remained unconvinced, according to his diary. "It is difficult to fully share this optimism although one really wants to."[17]

Leigh-Malory left the Bristol meeting still unconvinced. On May 27, he met with Air Marshal Arthur Tedder, Bradley, and others, telling them, "If you do this operation, you are throwing away two airborne divisions." Bradley, still stubbornly holding to his position, responded flatly that he "would not land on the Utah Beach without support of the 82nd Airborne." Montgomery's chief of staff, Major-General Sir Francis ("Freddie") de Guingand, also in attendance, supported Bradley, as did Tedder.

Two days later, on May 30, Leigh-Mallory went right to Ike to gripe about the new plan. Leigh-Mallory pointed out that 915 aircraft (96 of them with gliders in tow) would have to fly from west to east across the Cotentin Peninsula at lower than one thousand feet—under a full moon and over known enemy concentrations.

This journey would take three hours, at the end of which, Leigh-Mallory said, he doubted whether 50 percent of the parachutists or 30 percent of the gliders' loads would be effective for use against the enemy.[18]

Both convincing arguments put Ike in a tough spot. He later wrote, "It would be difficult to conceive of a more soul-wracking problem." He weighed his decision—his, the only one that mattered. "If my technical expert was correct, the planned operation was worse than stubborn folly. ...If he was right, it appeared that the attack on Utah Beach was probably hopeless, and this meant that the whole operation suddenly acquired a degree of risk, even foolhardiness, that presaged a gigantic failure, possible Allied defeat in Europe. I would carry to my grave the unbearable burden of a conscience justly accusing me of indifference to the lives of thousands of Americans, and of a stupid, blind sacrifice of thousands of the flower of America's sons."[19]

Ike thought Leigh-Mallory "earnestly sincere and noted for personal courage." He had given Ike, "as was his duty, his frank convictions." Finally, after much self-debate, Eisenhower realized that Leigh-Mallory's "estimate was just an estimate, nothing more." Giving the question no more thought, Ike "was encouraged to persist in the belief that Leigh-Mallory was wrong." Keeping his promise, Eisenhower telephoned the air marshal that the attack would go as planned and that this decision would be confirmed at once in writing.[20]

Bradley did not learn of Leigh-Mallory's last-minute appeal until much later. When reflecting on those tense couple of days, Bradley felt comfortable that "Eisenhower's choice, however, had not been one between Utah and Caen. Either the airborne went in on Utah or we could not land on that beach. And in the most portentous invasion of the war, Ike could never have shelved Utah Beach without chancing defeat."[21]

17

"A Rendezvous with Destiny"

It was a typical winter day in England: damp, cold, and cloudy. General Lee rode by Jeep from his 101st headquarters just north of Newburg, accompanied by Lieutenant Colonel Joseph H. Harper, a bookish career officer who studied agriculture at the University of Delaware and now commanded the 401st Glider Infantry. They were headed to the regimental training camp in Reading, England, where the 401st was scheduled to participate in a field exercise that morning, February 5, 1944.

Harper's driver parked the Jeep, and the two men followed a regimental battalion into the woods. They hadn't walked very far when General Lee said, "Bud, I can't go any farther, I have a terrible pain in my chest."

Harper, who knew Lee's history of heart trouble had begun in 1941, walked Lee back to the road and flagged down a two-and-a-half-ton truck driving by. At the 302nd Field Hospital, Lee's doctors diagnosed a serious heart attack.[1]

The Army wanted to send Lee back in the United States, where he could receive better treatment at Walter Reed. Lee refused to go, convinced he'd quickly be back with the 101st. General Omar Bradley had even promised Lee that he'd hold his command for him.

But William Carey Lee never left the hospital. His doctors medicated him with morphine and oxygen, and the treatment made him feel better. He wrote his wife Dava back in Dunn, North Carolina, that he could "dangle his legs off the side of the bed," but he "still had to use the bed pan."[2] A second heart attack in March ended his career. Lee finally accepted the fact that he needed to be evacuated back to Washington.

Back in August 1942, at Camp Clairborne, Louisiana, when the 101st had been organized, Lee had stood before thousands of troops. Those were the men who now, two years later, called themselves the Screaming Eagles. He prophesied to them.

Their division, he had declared, "has not a history, but a rendezvous with destiny." He reminded his men that the 101st badge depicted a defiant eagle—a Screaming Eagle. "This is a fitting emblem for a division," Lee assured them, "that will crush its enemies by felling them like a thunderbolt from the skies."[3]

Unfortunately, Lee would not be with his beloved paratroopers, dropping from the skies into Normandy when this prophecy came true.[4]

The question was who would fill Lee's legendary paratrooper's boots. Don Pratt was a possibility. While Lee received treatment in England, Eisenhower had placed assistant division commander Brigadier General Don Pratt temporarily in command of the Screaming Eagles. A Missouri native like Maxwell Taylor, Pratt had been in the army since World War I but had never served overseas. During the period before World War II— again like Taylor, and also like Ridgway—Pratt spent much of his career training other units and attending school, going overseas only once. In August 1942, he joined the 101st as Lee's assistant.[5]

Now that Lee wouldn't be coming back and D-Day was fewer than three months away, Eisenhower had to select a permanent replacement. Pratt assumed that he would stay on to lead them to Normandy, but there is no indication that Ike even considered this option. Another possibility, Brigadier General Anthony McAuliffe, the 101st artillery commander, had a fine pedigree as a graduate of West Point, Leavenworth's Command and General Staff College, and the Army War College. None of Pratt's or McAuliffe's credentials mattered, however, because Eisenhower chose Maxwell Taylor to lead the 101st into Normandy.

Although Taylor served as Ridgway's chief of staff and assistant, he had actually been listed as the division's artillery commander. Jim Gavin had received a well-deserved promotion from colonel to brigadier general, and he was on the rolls as assistant commander. Ridgway appointed Colonel Ralph P. Eaton, known as "Doc" because he had served as a stretcher-bearer on the Western Front during World War I, as his new chief of staff.[6]

Ridgway's friendship with Taylor had much to do with the selection because Ridgway recommended him to Eisenhower. Taylor's strong resúmé, however, would have given him the edge over any potential competitors—had there been any. His most recent exploits—the daring mission to Rome and participation in the Allied attempt to establish a puppet Italian government—were lauded by Eisenhower and Chief of Staff Marshall, who approved Taylor's appointment.[7]

Many years later, Eisenhower recalled Taylor's "personal adventure" into Rome as one of the more spectacular moments of his time in Europe. "The risks he ran were greater than I asked any other agent or emissary to undertake during the war," Eisenhower wrote. "He carried weighty responsibilities and discharged them with unerring judgment, and every minute was in imminent danger of discovery and death."[8]

Prior to the "personal adventure," Eisenhower had barely known Taylor. In 1941, a week after Pearl Harbor, Taylor met Eisenhower for the first time. Ike had just been called back from Fort Sam Houston, Texas, been made brigadier general, and been appointed to head the War Plans Division. Taylor took him from Marshall's office to the White House to see President Franklin Roosevelt. It's unknown whether Eisenhower and Taylor talked much that day, or whether Ike formed any opinion of the junior officer.

Colonel James Gavin, the 505th commander, also had no real opinion about Taylor—other than he was jealous of him. Gavin had been a paratrooper longer and had jumped into combat in Sicily; yet Taylor outranked him, and it didn't seem fair. When Gavin learned from Ridgway that Taylor would replace General Lee, Gavin's only real concern was that he "would at last feel like and actually be the assistant commanding general." He also hoped that sooner rather than later Ridgway would advance to corps commander, so that he (Gavin) might become division commander.[9]

Taking command of the 101st meant that Taylor succeeded Lee as airborne representative on the Overlord planning committee. For the next few months, until the lead-up to D-Day, Taylor spent much of his time in London attending meetings with VII Corps commander Lieutenant General J. Lawton Collins and 1st Army's General Omar Bradley.

Otherwise, he worked the Screaming Eagles hard in their southern England training camps, putting them through rigorous exercises to simulate what they should expect in Normandy after jumping.

Taylor brought to the 101st an ethos of leadership that he drilled into his men. Although he was division commander, "it was not enough for soldiers to be technicians at arms, a true professional soldier required training in history, economics and international affairs and language, no less exacting than a civilian-clothed diplomat."[10]

In demonstrating his own capability of leading from the front on the battlefield in Normandy, Taylor proved these words weren't one bit hollow. He could "be hard as nails," the Reuters war correspondent observed; yet Taylor was also very "matter of fact," his granddaughter said, "capable of sentiment, but at the same time pragmatic."[11]

After witnessing a day of intense fighting during the Normandy campaign during which a number of his men had been killed or badly wounded, Taylor sat down with some of his staff and, without prompting, reflected on the character of those men.

"There are real heroes," he explained, "the guys who know there's an important job to do even though it means death: they know it's worth more than their life and they do the job—and get killed. Then there's the foolish hero—he takes chances he shouldn't. He risks his neck when he shouldn't. And he gets killed when he shouldn't. The third kind of guy that gets killed is someone whose luck runs out—just an ordinary guy doing his job like you or me. But when his time comes, when a shell falls or a bomb drops, well, his luck runs out and his time is up."[12]

Throughout the remainder of his career in the military and into civilian life, Taylor showed this same character.

18

Pathfinders

Captain Frank Lillyman jumped forty-seven times in practice—always with a cigar clenched in his teeth.

On June 6, 1944, when parachuting into combat for the first time, Lillyman kept up his tradition: he dropped into battle with a fully lit stogie. "It was just a pet superstition," he tried to explain when asked about his peculiar habit. "I never got burned but once when I swallowed the end of one."[1]

Lillyman loved cigars so much that his weekly ration included twelve supplemented by a fresh supply sent by Jane, his wife, in Syracuse, New York.

Frank Lillyman Jr. became a legend of D-Day, but not because of his unusual smoking habit. Specially trained as the lead pathfinder for General Maxwell Taylor's Screaming Eagles, Lillyman, twenty-nine, was the first American soldier in Normandy. He landed at 12:15 a.m. in a field near the village of Saint Germain de Varreville.

Lean-faced at 140 pounds, Lillyman came from military stock. His father, Frank Sr., was, according to his son, an "honest to goodness Soldier of Fortune." At one time or another, Frank Sr. served in the Argentine navy, the Brazilian cavalry, and the US Navy. He ended his career in the Army, retiring in 1940 as a major.

After Pearl Harbor, Frank Jr. left his job as a cub reporter for a couple of Binghamton, New York, newspapers, "writing sports, high school news and helping out election nights," to follow his father into the army. In 1943, Lillyman volunteered to become a paratrooper, a decision that Dad, the "old horse cavalryman," didn't approve of.[2]

Lillyman helped pioneer a new assignment of the airborne divisions called pathfinders. Jim Gavin created it, in part as a reaction to the troubling jumps in Sicily when paratroopers were scattered apart from their appointed landing sites. Troop Carrier pilot Colonel Joel L. Crouch led in the creation of a professional training unit at Biscari Airfield in Sicily. His objective: developing "specially trained pathfinder units, consisting of experienced pilots and reliable paratroopers, who could land about 20 minutes before the main assault."

Within the 82nd and 101st Airborne divisions, 380 paratroopers were designated as pathfinders. Twenty-one aircraft carried the pathfinder teams, preceding the eight hundred aircraft of the main body of American paratroopers.

General Ridgway assigned Captain John Norton, the 505th's operations officer, to work with Crouch. For the operation, Crouch created three pathfinder teams within the 82nd Airborne: each consisted of one officer and nine enlisted men, with about nine other troopers to stand guard as electronic gear and lights were laid down on the drop, or landing, zone.[3]

The most important piece of equipment pathfinders carried was a top-secret Eureka radio transponder, developed by Telecommunications Research Establishment (TRE), a British organization that also devised radar equipment for the Royal Air Force (RAF). Placed in a compact container called a leg pack, a Eureka set weighed around twenty pounds. One man jumped with the leg pack, but on the ground, another paratrooper helped set up the equipment and provided cover from the enemy.[4]

The Eureka radio transponder emitted a series of electronic pulses that could be detected by Troop Carrier planes loaded with a Rebecca receiver. General Boy Browning chose the name "Rebecca" in tribute to his wife, Daphne du Maurier, whose 1938 novel of that name is her most successful work. To help guide C-47s at night, pathfinders were also issued Holophane lights. Each regiment's lights, which shone in a different color, were laid out in the form of a T.[5]

During the second week of September 1943, the first major operation using pathfinders took place in Salerno, Italy. On the night of

September 14, 2,100 men from the 505th, including its commander, Colonel Gavin, boarded C-47s in Sicily. A short time later, Gavin's plane approached the drop zone, but from the C-47's door, he didn't see an illuminated T. Not until he jumped from the plane and began floating to earth did he glimpse the glowing light. Gavin's biographer wrote of the Italian landing, "The drop on Salerno would be remembered by surviving troopers of the 505th as the easiest jump of the war."

Operation Neptune's planners hoped to replicate this success for Overlord.

In early 1944, Colonel Crouch set up a Pathfinder School in England to train pilots at North Witham, an airfield in Lincolnshire. Known among the Troop Carrier community as "Colonel Joe," Crouch had worked as a high school principal in Hanna, North Dakota, before the war. He left to join the Army Air Corps for a few years; afterward, he left active duty and moved to Riverside, California, to become a United Airlines pilot, ferrying passengers between Los Angeles and Seattle.

On the first day of pathfinder class, Crouch spent only fifteen minutes with the group. To him, they were volunteers. "Not only had they volunteered for the Army Air Corps, or for the airborne, but I made sure they had a way out of our operation if they wanted it." Consequently, Crouch told them, "I can't tell you where we are going, when we are going, or exactly what we are going to do when we get there." But he promised them it would be interesting. It would also help the Allied cause—and, according to one, "probably we would have some fun."[6]

About six months later, Crouch guided the C-47 that carried Lillyman and the other pathfinders in his stick out of North Witham Airfield. *New York Journal-American* reporter Lorelle Hearst, wife of William Hearst Jr., whose corporation owned the two merged newspapers, wrote about Crouch right after D-Day. She referred to him as "the spearhead of the spearhead of the spearhead" for his role in carrying the first airborne troops to Normandy.

Through the closed door separating the cockpit from the plane's main cabin, Crouch and his copilot, twenty-two-year-old Captain Vito S. Pedone—"a laughing, dark-haired boy"—could hear the pathfinders singing all the way to France. He knew a chorus when he heard it, for

Pedone had studied music before joining the military. "When I was growing up in New York in the 1930s," he explained years later, "the only choice I had for education, being a minority, was to be a gangster, a priest or a musician—in that order."[7]

When Crouch reached Normandy and neared what he thought was Drop Zone A (the village of Saint Martin de Varreville), he alerted the jumpmaster to hook up. As the first out the door, Lillyman reached French soil before anyone else. Out of the seventeen pathfinders in his stick, only seven fell close to where he'd been dropped. In the darkness, Lillyman could see what looked like other paratroopers, but he couldn't be absolutely certain. He grabbed his cricket and clicked it once—a challenge. Much to his relief, he heard a double click in reply.

Lillyman gathered together the men from his stick. Only then did he realize that Crouch had actually placed them a mile away from the drop zone. Lillyman had to improvise because in fewer than thirty minutes, the main force of paratroopers would arrive—not enough time to reach the correct drop zone.

Seeing a church some one hundred yards away gave Lillyman the idea of placing a Eureka in its steeple. One of his men knocked on the church door. The priest who answered was relieved to see Americans, not Germans. After speaking French to the padre, the pathfinders placed the Eureka in the church and went on their way to avoid confrontation with the enemy, who could be heard nearby.

Lillyman had his men place another Eureka in tree branches by the road and lay out lights in a T in a field by the church. The pathfinders finished their work in the nick of time. A few minutes before 1 a.m., Lillyman could hear planeloads of paratroopers approaching. He ordered his men, "Turn on the lights!"

Back home in Syracuse, Jane Lillyman didn't know about her husband's dangerous mission, but she had an inkling he was about so do something big, and soon. In the last letter she'd received from him, dated May 19, Frank told Jane, "When the newspapers and radios blare out the news, remember that your pappy led the way." Previous mail from him, although cut up by censors, hinted that he was a pathfinder, so when the time came, he would be "jumping in advance" of other paratroopers.[8]

Moments after Lillyman landed and his men set about laying their equipment, the results of 101st's pathfinder teams elsewhere on the Cotentin Peninsula were mixed. Poor visibility from thick cloud cover, along with heavy German resistance, prevented all but one of the other pathfinder teams from reaching their targets. One stick dropped directly on enemy positions, while another planeload of pathfinders ended up in the English Channel.[9] Several paratroopers from a three-stick team that jumped into Drop Zone D near Angoville-au-Plain were, in Lillyman's words, in a "helluva mess, either killed or captured."[10]

Ridgway's 82nd Division pathfinders departed one hour after Lilllyman's teams. Before they left, Gavin told one group, "When you land in Normandy, you will have only one friend: God."[11]

For the most part, the 82nd's pathfinders enjoyed better success than the 101st Airborne's teams. Two groups, one landing near Drop Zone O (Sainte Mère Églisle) and another dropping into Drop Zone T (about a mile from the La Fière Causeway), set up their equipment quickly and accurately.

Not so for a team assigned to Drop Zone N, by the village of Picauville. It ended up a mile southeast of the drop zone. Quickly recovering, the men were guided by compasses and maps toward the direction of Drop Zone N, but Germans blocked the way. Instead, the team assembled the Eureka beacon and two amber lights on the spot, and, as one historian wrote, "They hoped for the best."

Unfortunately, this patchwork scenario became all too familiar for most of the paratroopers on D-Day.[12]

On the morning of June 6, 1944, war correspondent Wright Bryant delivered the first account of the paratroopers dropping into Normandy. (ATLANTA HISTORY CENTER)

"Father of the Airborne," Brigadier General William "Bill" Lee. (208-PU-116N)

Right: Major General Matthew Ridgway jumped with his 82nd Airborne Division on D-Day and led them in combat during the Normandy campaign.
(111-SC-144517)

Below: Major General Maxwell Taylor took over command of the 101st Airborne Division in March 1944 and jumped into combat for the first time on D-Day.
(111-SC-PP-195369)

General Omar Bradley with his wife at the Pentagon the day he was sworn in as chief of staff. (HARRY S. TRUMAN LIBRARY)

Father Francis Sampson, the 101st Airborne's "Paratrooper Padre," prays for soldiers killed in Carentan. (111-SC-190490)

Above: Demonstrating
the wind machine at
Fort Benning's Parachute
Training School.
(111-SC-188260)

Right: Learning the
art of jumping at Fort
Benning's Parachute
Training School.
(111-SC-188261)

Men released from the top of Parachute Tower while training at Fort Benning's Parachute Training School. (111-SC-188263)

Colonel James "Slim Jim" Gavin commanded the 505th Parachute Infantry Regiment prior to being promoted to assistant commander of the 82nd and the rank of brigadier general seven months before the division left for Normandy. (111-SC_272024)

General Dwight D. Eisenhower, commander of Operation Overlord. (286-MP-PAR-01853)

On the evening of June 5, 1944, American paratroopers receive final instructions before boarding their C-47. (111-SC-377579)

Glider men make last-minute preparations before being towed by a C-47 to Normandy. (342-FH-3A-15169)

American glider troops in England demonstrate how to load a Jeep onto a Horsa glider. (111-SC_293754)

Press officer Colonel Barney Oldfield sits in front of his typewriter surrounded by a team of war correspondents. (NEBRASKA HISTORY CENTER)

Reuters war correspondent Bob Reuben jumped with General Maxwell Taylor into Normandy and remained with his division for most of the campaign. (REUTERS NEWS AGENCY)

Lieutenant General Lewis Brereton commanded 9th Air Force, which included the Troop Carrier Command that dropped the paratroopers over Normandy on D-Day. (111-SC-164131)

Brigadier General Paul L. Williams headed Troop Carrier Command and was responsible for the C-47s and gliders that transported men and equipment of the 82nd and 101st Airborne Divisions. (111-SC-187924)

Prime Minister Winston Churchill shakes hands with 101st Airborne assistant commanding general Don Pratt as General Dwight D. Eisenhower and Major General Maxwell Taylor look on with approval. (111-SC-314393)

Prime Minister Winston Churchill, General Eisenhower, General Maxwell Taylor, General Don Pratt, and a British naval officer inspect installations in the 101st Airborne training areas in England. (111-SC-209284)

A Waco CG-4A glider makes a practice flight over England in preparation for D-Day. (208-AA-39-5-3)

On the evening of June 5, 1944, an American paratrooper makes final parachute adjustments before boarding his C-47. (111-SC-377586)

Signal Corps photographer Lieutenant Leo S. Moore snapped this iconic image of General Dwight D. Eisenhower giving last-minute good wishes to paratroopers from the 101st Airborne at Greenham Common Airfield. (111-SC-190270)

On the night of June 5, 1944, a heavily weighed-down paratrooper boards a C-47. (111-190367)

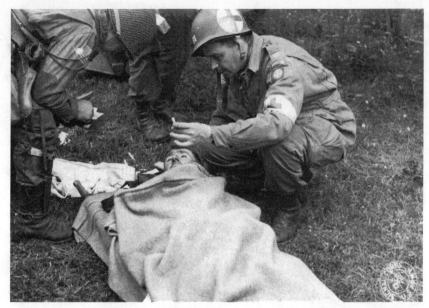

An 82nd Airborne medic hands a lit cigarette to a wounded soldier on the Normandy battlefield. (111-SC-190289)

A wrecked American glider lies in a Normandy orchard. (111-SC-320878)

Fully equipped glider troops wait outside their Waco CG-4A glider just before D-Day. (342-FH-3A-15198)

Paratroopers from the 101st Airborne meet some local girls from Sainte-Marie-du-Mont. (111-SC-190294)

Paratroopers of the 101st Airborne walk along a hedgerow-lined road in Sainte-Marie-du-Mont. (111-SC-320873)

Paratroopers from the 101st Airborne move warily through a field in Carentan, France, passing men from their division killed by German snipers. (111-SC-190347)

19

Readying the Skytrains

Two-year-old John Cornish awoke a little after eleven at night, jarred by the nearby roaring of 1,200-horse-power Pratt and Whitney airplane engines, the squealing of Jeep and truck brakes, and talk that was as loud as a football crowd. The date was June 5, 1944.

John, a chubby-cheeked, fair-haired little boy, had gotten used to hearing commotion from Upottery, the RAF airfield where American C-47 and glider pilots and their crews from 439th Troop Carrier Group, 50th Troop Carrier Wing, had been stationed since February.

His family's stone house was one of only ten in Smeatharpe. The small village in the East Devon countryside stood on the same road as the airfield, only a short distance away. During the day, John often saw the C-47s flying above the village, some towing Waco CG-4A or British Horsa gliders.

The Americans aroused envy in the villagers. Because of wartime restrictions, Smeatharpe residents had comparatively little to eat—most food was rationed or homegrown. Oil lamps provided light, and water was drawn from a well. Down the road at Upottery, villagers regularly saw trucks hauling in loads of food for GIs. *They* never went thirsty, and *they* turned the lights on whenever they wanted.

The American airmen, however, were friendly. Their pockets bulged with British currency, which the Yanks spent freely at the King's Arms Pub. They spread around their wealth at the village hall at social functions run by John's mother, Mary, a member of the Women's Volunteer Service.

Each day, John tottered into his family's flower and vegetable garden by the road. He waited, as patiently as a toddler can manage, for the

Americans to walk by on their way to the village. The men stopped, said hello, and bent down to pat John's head and maybe, just maybe, present him with a chocolate bar.

At the end of May, John stopped seeing the Americans. They'd vanished, but he could still hear their activity, so he knew they hadn't left Upottery. He simply had no idea that they had been restricted from leaving the airfield due to the impending invasion.

A week later, on the night of June 5, the sky was still light because of British Double Summer Time, a rejiggering of the clock that added an hour to daylight-saving time. John stood with his mum in the garden. She held tightly to his little hand as they listened to the Troop Transports rolling down the runway at intervals of twenty seconds. The planes' engines were "whining and popping" as the pilots lifted the nearly twenty-thousand-pound C-47s (aka Gooney Birds) skyward.

John was too young, of course, to understand the significance of that night. Many years passed before his parents regaled their son with the story that he had witnessed the invasion of Hitler's Fortress Europe.[1]

Before the C-47s left Upottery and other airfields in southern England for Normandy, Troop Carrier Command quartermasters issued combat crews protective flak jackets, but they were designed to cover only the torso. Leather leggings and steel helmets provided further protection. Pilots and copilots wore goggles to guard their eyes from glass shards if a shell shattered the windshields. They wore chest parachutes should they need to bail from a burning plane.

Radio operators, crew chiefs, and navigators, however, were issued seat parachutes, and many of these crews elected not to wear the chutes. "Why bother?" they argued, for the C-47s, upon reaching Normandy, were to drop the paratroopers at low altitude. To these men, that distance made their chutes nearly useless.

Flight crews also carried escape kits, gas masks, and firearms. A canteen of drinking water was attached to the ammunition belt. At their waists, officers wore a holstered, standard-issue .45-caliber pistol, while enlisted men carried an M-1 carbine. None of these arms were intended to be fired from a flying aircraft but were to be deployed if crews were forced down into enemy territory.

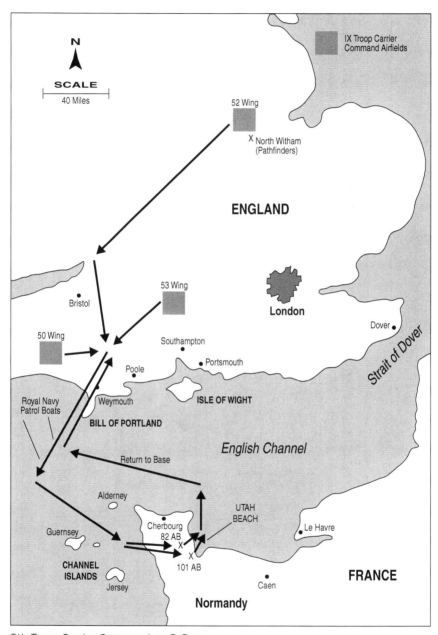

N

SCALE
40 Miles

IX Troop Carrier
Command Airfields

52 Wing

X North Witham
(Pathfinders)

ENGLAND

Bristol

53 Wing

London

Dover

Strait of Dover

50 Wing

Southampton

Portsmouth

Poole

Royal Navy
Patrol Boats

Weymouth

ISLE OF WIGHT

BILL OF PORTLAND

English Channel

Return to Base

Alderney

UTAH
BEACH

Guernsey

Cherbourg
82 AB
X

Le Havre

CHANNEL
ISLANDS

X
101 AB

FRANCE

Jersey

Caen

Normandy

9th Troop Carrier Command on D-Day

Creature comfort had been addressed during the early formation of Troop Carrier Command: crew chiefs had devised a tube to be used for urination during flight. Staff Sergeant Ingrisano Jr. described the clever set-up of the "relief" tube:

> *A cone-like nozzle at the end of a black flexible rubber tube was positioned below the pilot's seat, which meant that every time a crew member, other than the pilot, needed to use the tube, the pilot would have to relinquish his seat to the user.*

Engineers solved that problem by drilling a hole in the bulkhead behind the pilot. The rubber tube was pulled through, and the cone reattached. It was held in place in a snap clamp attached to the bulkhead.

The exterior of the C-47s was given a makeover right before D-Day. The brown-gray camouflaged transports received so-called "war paint," echoing the face paint and the Mohawk hair styles the men had borrowed from Native Americans. Each plane was painted with five alternating, foot-wide stripes—three white and two black—on each wing, on the fuselage between the door and tail section, and just forward of the US star. All aircraft, including gliders, was similarly marked, thus easing recognition as friend or foe by Allied ground forces.

One day, Ingrisano saw Brooklyn-born artist Ogden M. Pleissner sketching the newly painted gliders. Pleissner had joined the Army Air Force in 1942 as a war correspondent assigned to *Life* magazine. In April 1944, Pleissner's war artistry was exhibited at the National Gallery of Art in Washington, DC. First Lady Eleanor Roosevelt attended that exhibition, and she "was very impressed" by the works by Pleissner and other war artists. "I hope there will be many more such paintings for us to see in the future," she told the *Washington Post*.[2]

In addition to a paint job, each plane was chalked with a number that could easily be erased from mission to mission. The number identified the sequence in which the planes would take off on a particular mission. Numbering also helped airborne troops find the aircraft or glider to which they were assigned.

Still, Ingrisano worried. Even with all the preparations to ready the planes for Normandy, he fretted that unarmed C-47 Skytrains, developed for the military from civilian aircraft, were vulnerable to a direct hit. The planes weren't equipped with self-sealing tanks or extra armor. The engines and Para packs attached to the bottom of the plane, right below the cockpit, also lacked armor plating. "A direct hit," Ingrisano said, expressing his fear, "almost certainly meant the plane would blow apart since the packs were often stuffed with extra ammunition and other explosive materials."

Despite Ingrisano's concern, which was certainly shared by others, no changes were made. In fact, there wasn't much left to do in the immediate days before the invasion other than preparing the planes for Neptune, so air crews had significant downtime. They spent some time listening to music on German radio, even though broadcasters Axis Sally (both Mildred Elizabeth Gillars and Rita Zucca used this nickname) and Lord Ha Ha (the *nom de guerre* for William Joyce) frequently interrupted the entertainment with Nazi war propaganda.

Of the two, Lord Ha Ha truly scared the crew of 316th. He not only specifically mentioned the 316th in his broadcasts but also cited individuals by name, adding "how pitiful and heart rending it would be when their parents received fearful telegrams that their sons had been sent to be slaughtered in action."[3]

Despite projected heavy losses among the air crews and paratroopers, optimism ran high. Colonel Charles H. Young, commander of the 439th Troop Carrier Command, described emotions on the eve of D-Day: "More than anything else, we wanted a chance to perform our duty and do the job we had been trained to do for so long."[4]

20

The Paratrooper Generals Make
Final Preparations

On May 28, Major General Maxwell Taylor set off to visit the seventeen marshaling areas from Wales to southern England. He traveled like an evangelist, preaching the word to congregations in different towns. His troops were sealed into those gated encampments before heading to Normandy on June 5, 1944.

At each location, his Jeep became his pulpit. Taylor stood on top of his vehicle, "trying to communicate to the men his feeling of the historic significance of the drama in which we were key actors," he wrote in his memoir. "We will someday feel pride in telling our children and grandchildren that we had been in Normandy on D-Day."

After delivering his final pep talk on June 4, Taylor stared at the "bright-eyed attention of the men" of the 101st, "their visible eagerness to get on with the hazardous business which seemed to hold no terrors for them." The self-deprecating Taylor wondered how much his words had touched the men, recognizing that "Henry V had said it much better on St. Crispin's Day."

The Paratrooper Padre, as Father Francis Sampson called himself, could not have agreed more with Taylor. At a secret location where the 501st PIR were holed up, Sampson heard Taylor's last pep talk. He found it uninspiring.

After graduating from Fort Benning's Jump School, Sampson had been placed by the Army in the 501st training at Camp Macknall, North Carolina, under the command of Colonel Howard ("Jumpy" or "Skeets")

Johnson. The son of a Maryland boat manufacturer, Johnson had a reputation as forceful and domineering, and before he left for Macknall, Sampson had been warned that Johnson was also the "toughest, roughest, noisiest officer to ever hit the silk"—that is, to parachute. Maxwell Taylor called Johnson "tough, very, very tough."

He had been impressed that Johnson, after two years at the Naval Academy, where he had been an All-American collegiate boxer, left Annapolis to take a commission in the Army. Although Normandy would claim Johnson's first combat jump, he had scored more than one hundred practice jumps before D-Day. Working his men brutally hard, Johnson made it known to Taylor that "he wanted the 501st to win the war all by itself."[1]

The day Father Sampson arrived at Macknall, Johnson ordered him into his office. Nervously, Sampson walked in. There, the colonel stood up from behind his desk to greet the chaplain. Johnson wore a tailored jump suit. He held a long knife in his hand. Sampson was, of course, put off by the weapon, only inches from potentially ripping a hole in his chaplain's uniform or, worse, in his gullet. To Sampson's relief, Johnson explained the weapon: each day he practiced knife throwing.

Johnson began: "Tell me why you joined the paratroops." "Well, sir, they asked for volunteers at chaplains' school" was all Sampson could stutter.

"You're a Catholic priest, aren't you?" Johnson followed up. "I assume you know your religious business. . . . You fellas always do."

Before Sampson could respond, Johnson kept talking. "I'm not a Catholic, but I think you can do a lot for my boys. They need a priest. I like your business of confession. I'm not a Protestant either, but I believe in God and I believe in Jesus."

Johnson then told Sampson to keep his "fingers on the pulse of the regiment," to monitor its morale, and to report back any issues right away. "I want you to be with the men all of the time. You'll march and jump when they do."

Sampson stood up and said, "I'll do my best, sir"—more words than he had spoken during the entire meeting. In leaving, he saluted Johnson, who came back with the most vigorous salute Sampson had ever seen.

Taylor's speech to the 101st on June 4 earned Father Sampson's criticism, and he accused Taylor of losing "contact with the average soldier's mentality" and, thus, using hyperbolic and romantic expressions like "glorious mission" and telling paratroopers they would be "making history."

"The average soldier," Sampson would learn from experience, "sees nothing glorious in killing a farmer's son, mechanic, school boy, or a laboring man, even if those individuals happen to be in the German Army." In fact, Sampson believed, "high-brow phrases such as 'glorious mission' and 'making history' irritated the average American soldier."[2]

After Taylor finished and received tepid applause, Johnson spoke. Sampson judged that Johnson had been preparing this talk since the war began, practicing it for weeks, making Taylor just a warm-up to the main attraction.

Unlike Taylor, Johnson could reach the heart of each man. He had his audience in the grasp of his hand as his voice grew louder and emotional. He reached to grab his long knife from his jump boots. It wouldn't budge. Johnson finally freed it from its sheath, raised the blade above his head, and screamed, "I swear to you that before the dawn of another day this knife will be stuck in the foulest Nazi belly in France! Are you with me?"

"We're with you!" the 101st responded in unison, amid loud applause. Then "Let's get 'em! Good hunting!"[3]

Next on his speaking circuit, Taylor met with General Bradley at his (Bradley's) Bristol headquarters. The First Army leader wanted his corps and division commanders to brief him regarding their "scheme and maneuver" for Normandy. Bradley, an "old school teacher from West Point and the Infantry School, personally conducted the generals."

Each commander stood before the operations map in the front of the room with a pointer to show Bradley exactly where the unit or units under his command would land or come ashore. When Taylor had his turn, he discovered that "Bradley knew as much about what my battalions were supposed to do as I did." Taylor sat back down, wondering "whether he had made a passing mark for the day." After the last officer gave his presentation, Bradley, a man of few words, said only "Good luck, men."[4]

In his memoir, Matthew Ridgway never mentioned this meeting with Bradley, but he certainly would have been there at the Bristol headquarters. Nevertheless, as the invasion date grew closer, Ridgway remained as busy as Taylor. He, too, visited his men, by either car or airplane, in the far-flung camps of southern England. He also made two practice parachute jumps, both without injury. Although his staff thought his intention was to enter Normandy with them by glider, Ridgway insisted that he would jump along with his paratroopers.

According to his aide, Captain Arthur Kroos, Ridgway "never really seriously considered going in by glider." The general contacted General Williams at Troop Carrier Command to request "the best pilot, the best navigator, the best crew. I want no screw-ups on this thing." Whether Ridgway shared his desire to jump with Taylor is unknown; also unknown is when the 101st commander elected to jump alongside his troops.[5]

While "making his rounds," a high fever drained Ridgway. He became very weak. A doctor diagnosed his condition as recurrence of malaria, which he had first contracted in the 1920s while on a Latin American mission. The malaria had returned before, but this current bout hit so much harder than before that it threatened to keep Ridgway from going to Normandy. Ridgway ceased his rigid schedule and returned to his headquarters in Leicester, England, to stay in bed for the next few days.[6]

Ridgway survived the malaria outbreak and readied himself for D-Day physically—but not emotionally. As division commander, he had executed an exceptional job because he had left his men "inspired with enthusiasm by his presence and impressive appearance" during his visits in the marshaling areas. War correspondent Bill Walton said the 82nd Division commander general looked like a "Roman Emperor."

Yet, he would write later, he had never taken time "for introspection, for troubling thoughts of what fate might hold in store for me." This brave warrior, whom some called "Iron Tits," was as vulnerable as any soldier about to enter combat.

After recuperating, and just a few days before boarding a C-47 with some thirteen thousand other paratroopers, Ridgway remembered thinking heavily about "what fate might have in store for me." A deeply spiritual man, Ridgway believed his fate was in the hands of the Almighty. Many years after D-Day, Ridgway reflected on being in "darkness, after you have gone to bed, when you are not the commander, with stars on your shoulders, but just one man, alone with your God in the dark, your thoughts inevitably turn inward, and out of whatever resources of the spirit you possess, you prepare yourself as best you may for whatever test may lie ahead."[7]

Those same thoughts were on the minds of every soldier in the Allied armies who would soon face the same test in Normandy.

21

Delay

For the past thirty-six hours, Major General Maxwell Taylor had been a nervous wreck—just like all the soldiers, sailors, and airmen who would take part in Operation Overlord.

The invasion he had finally embarked on was supposed to have launched the previous night, but early on Sunday, June 4, General Eisenhower instructed his SHAEF staff to send a coded message alerting all army commanders that D-Day would be postponed from June 5 to June 6, 1944.

Eisenhower based his decision on the weather. He and his Overlord staff gathered in a conference room, the former library, at Southwick House in Portsmouth, a small seaport village on England's southern coast. On June 3, meteorologist J. M. Stagg forecast unfavorable conditions for June 5. The Royal Air Force group captain predicted that it would be cloudy, stormy, and windy. Seas would be too rough for landing craft and the sky too cloudy for flying.

The following morning, June 4, the group convened once more. Eisenhower sat down at the table after a muddy walk in the rain from his "Circus Wagon" and lit a cigarette—the first of many that morning.

The trailer where he slept, ate, and worked lay hidden in a copse by Southwick House outside Portsmouth, England.[1] The Lockheed Overseas Corporation, based in Northern Ireland, had built the trailer from designs by one of its engineers and architects, G. V. Russell, who had created some of Hollywood's most lavish nightclubs before the war.

The Circus Wagon was one of three windowless, sixty-foot trailers amid other smaller units on the house's grounds. Eisenhower's unit, among the most elaborate of the portable structures, contained a bunk, kitchenette, shower, and chemical toilet. Like the other trailers, his had air conditioning, a portable power unit, radio equipment, and outlets for telephones.[2]

This morning Stagg, the tall, no-nonsense naval officer, normally described by an aide as 6'2" (of which 6'1" was all gloom), had a reason to be cheerful. A few more hours of rain, he predicted, would be followed by three days of clearer skies and lighter winds. If the forecast held, this small window meant D-Day could launch on June 6.[3]

With Overlord delayed by a day, Taylor worried about how this change would impact the momentum that had been building among his men. For eight days, the paratroopers had been cooling their heels in marshaling areas by airfields. Men, quartered in hangars, slept on cots and were attended by quartermaster units specifically designated for this job.

All personnel were sealed within their area by barbed wire. Strict guard and counterintelligence measures were in place. Security was so tight that only a few liaison parties were permitted to enter, and no one else could leave. All letters were deposited in a box for mailing after the invasion.

Wright Bryan, the war correspondent who would make history by delivering the first invasion broadcast on the morning of D-Day, filled the deposit box in his marshaling area with letters, including one to his wife and children back in Atlanta. He wrote them on June 5 and intended for them to be read should he not survive the war. "I'm not eager to write this letter, but I think I should," he told them. Although Bryan didn't specifically say he would be going into action that night, he did hint:

The time is coming, though when that time will be, I do not know, for me personally to face some of the hazards of war. I've tried to be mindful of my responsibilities to you and the children, and of the fact that a dead correspondent could not do my employers or the war effort any good.

In closing, he admitted that "no doubt I shall be plenty frightened. The Army says that those who claim they aren't afraid are either liars or fools." He added, "All this is merely an adventure to reassure you that I am doing nothing for the sake of silly adventure and that I keep always in mind you and our precious three, whom I love more than life itself."[4]

For a little more than a week at the seven different marshaling airfields in southern England, the ones where Taylor visited and gave pep talks, the 101st paratroopers stood over sand tables, maps, and aerial photographs set up in large tents to prepare them for what they should expect after dropping into Normandy.

Each man had to learn not only his own mission but also those of the other men in his stick. More than a few probably reread sections from Field Manual 3 (FM 3J), "Tactics and Techniques of Airborne Troops." Published two years before and not updated to include the lessons learned in Sicily and Italy, FM 3 served as the paratroopers' bible and told them just about everything they needed to know about preparing for combat: "Order and Information from Higher Headquarters," "Information of Enemy, Maps and Aerial Photographs," and "How to Treat Civilians in Occupied Territory," among other helpful tips.[5]

William Sturgis, a private in 101st Airborne Signal Company, wrote his father before heading to Normandy that "we had drilled into us every detail of our phase of the landing. We had to draw the road networks by memory." That wasn't all. Sturgis and the other paratroopers had "to know flight direction, the terrain, what is expected from the civilians, every tiny detail."

Prior to D-Day, press officer Colonel Barney Oldfield called Jim Gavin, whom he had remained friendly with after they'd served together in the 505th PIR at Fort Benning. Oldfield told Gavin that Eisenhower planned to visit a division the night before the invasion launched and "wanted to know if the 82nd should be the one for him to see."

Gavin responded immediately with the "assurance there was no other division with the record of the 82nd and that he should see it by all means." Then Gavin posed the question to Ridgway, and they talked it over. The division commander was lukewarm about the idea of having a bunch of press swarming around the division area as his men prepared for the biggest day in their military careers and, for many, the most unforgettable day of their lives.

Gavin called Oldfield to stress that "the important thing was to have one of the airborne divisions remembered in history as the one Eisenhower saw." They decided that Eisenhower would go the 101st's marshaling areas.[6] After a sleepless night, Taylor learned the following morning that Eisenhower and his British aide, Lieutenant Colonel Jimmy Gault, a pre-war investment banker and now a member of the Scots Guards, were coming to see his men off. Whether he believed that the general's visit would distract the men is unknown.

Driven by Kay Summersby, on the afternoon of June 5, Eisenhower and Gault departed SHAEF headquarters at Portsmouth. Ike wanted to personally send off Taylor's paratroopers, his Screaming Eagles. Their marshaling fields were all within a few miles of each other, so, depending on how much time he spent at each one, he might be able to visit all six.[7]

Taylor then turned his attention to his own well-being: What would he do during the unexpected downtime? It so happened that an old army friend, Colonel Frank "Froggie" Reed, had been sent from London to witness the takeoff that night. Before the war, Reed and Taylor had played a great deal of squash together, so Taylor suggested a match on a court not far from his command post at the Royal Air Force's Greenham Common.

Things did not go Taylor's way, to his dismay: "When we got into action, I was surprised to discover that Froggie knew a lot more about the English version of squash than I did." Taylor ramped up his racquet skills to avoid "a first-class licking." Then, in midswing, he heard an "audible pop," followed by a sharp pain shooting up his leg. Taylor had pulled a tendon and immediately limped off the court. By evening, he could hardly walk.

Ridgway also learned by coded message that D-Day would have to wait a little bit. Ridgway returned to his quarters in Leicester for the night, and the next day, June 5, he went back to Spanhoe. To burn off nervous energy, he played softball with some of his men. While taking a swing at the ball, a jolt in his back reminded Ridgway of an injury incurred when playing baseball with Omar Bradley at Fort Benning the previous year. Fearing another attack might occur that would keep him from the "Great Adventure," Ridgway dropped his bat and walked off the field.

On the evening before D-Day, as he sat in his quarters for the last time for many weeks, Ridgway picked up a photograph of himself and jotted a few lines on the bottom to the men of the 82nd in the event that death awaited him:

To the members of the 82nd Airborne Division, with everlasting affection and appreciation of life shared with them in the service of our country. May their incomparable courage, fidelity, soldierly conduct and fighting spirit ever keep for this Division a place second to none in our Army.

Reflecting on that moment, Ridgway wrote, "It was no literary composition, I know. But it expresses my feelings."

With his "soul at peace," his "heart light and spirits almost gay," around ten that evening, Ridgway boarded his plane. He carried a hand grenade taped to his right chest harness balanced on the other side of his chest by a first-aid kit. This became a distinctive feature of his uniform throughout not just the Normandy campaign but also the remainder of the war. From afar, the first-aid kit could be mistaken for another grenade. Because of this get-up—and "Ridgway's intense and steely battlefield demeanor"—some GIs referred to the general as "Old Iron Tits."[8]

Eisenhower's chauffeuse, Kay Summersby, drove his entourage to Greenham Common around six. Eisenhower's first order of business was an early dinner with Taylor at Taylor's headquarters' mess.

As Eisenhower, Taylor, and their staffs dined privately, paratroopers also ate their final meals. Menus varied, depending on the marshaling area, but all of the men enjoyed a high-calorie feast of steak, fried chicken or pork chops, white bread, ice cream, and coffee. Afterward, they marched back to the hangars to secure their equipment and prepare for battle.

The long list of equipment, either issued or brought along for comfort, included a small brass compass small enough to fit in a paratrooper's anus, a map of France printed on a hanky-sized piece of silk, and a small steel file. Battle preparations included bullets, birds, and bills. Weapons were inspected and oiled. Pigeons were issued in small crates with strict orders to the men to use the birds only if all other means of communications back to England failed. English pounds were exchanged for French francs; one thousand francs were placed in rubberized fabric container escape kits and entrusted to each company commander to pay guides.

Furthermore, flight manifests were checked and delivered to commanders. For the colossal undertaking on which the airborne soldiers were about to embark, a typical paratrooper was issued a map of the entire Cotentin peninsula and a specially prepared night map of the drop zone and immediate vicinity. Phosphorescent discs were issued for individual identification or night recognition.

Metal "crickets," children's novelty toys, were distributed for "challenging"—that is, verifying friend or foe during the paratroopers' assembly on the ground: one click signaled the challenge and two clicks the reply. Passwords for the first five days were memorized. Parachutes were issued, fitted, and checked. A typical paratrooper wore a jumpsuit, helmet, boots, gloves, main parachute, and a reserve parachute. He also wore a "Mae West vest," a life preserver that looked like a buxom woman when the front air pockets ballooned completely.

Small arms—like a rifle, a carbine, a .45-caliber pistol, ammunition, and grenades—were issued to each man, along with containers for rifles or carbines, sacks for machine-gun belts, and ammunition. Some paratroopers chose to arm themselves additionally with a trench knife, jackknife, hunting knife, and machete.

They also brought one blanket, one raincoat, one change of socks and underwear, and two cartons of cigarettes. Messages from Generals Eisenhower and Montgomery and from the regimental commanders were given to each jumpmaster to be read after takeoff. Motion-sickness pills were handed out.[9]

After equipment was issued, the men lined up outside the hangars while bands played military marches or struck familiar tunes like "Over There" (George M. Cohan's 1917 song, popular in both world wars) or "Paper Doll" (in 1943, the Mills Brothers sang Johnny Black's lyrics from 1915). Trucks arrived to take the men to the planes, but before they left, Division Headquarters Parachute Echelon Major Paul A. Danahy went around to each stick to give a pep talk. "Men, for God's sake, be careful," he advised. "We all know the German soldier for what he is. He is full of tricks. Be cautious, fight fairly; give no quarter—expect none. I'll see you in France."

Standing by the C-47s, the paratroopers tried on their parachutes one last time, made necessary adjustments, and then took them off. Each stick was subjected to a final briefing on various subjects: time of departure, time of flight, course to be flown, and handling emergencies.

The men listened only halfway. Some thought this exercise would turn into practice; the "show" would be postponed like the previous day's—or, worse, called off completely. While they awaited orders to board, more trucks came, carrying thick bundles containing radios, engineer equipment, heavy weapons, and ammunition. Rations and medical supplies were loaded onto racks underneath the planes. When that space was stuffed, the remaining bundles filled cabins. These items were to be thrown out with the first man to jump.

Meanwhile, Eisenhower slowly made his rounds. At the Greenham Common marshaling field, he nearly tore his trousers trying to reach a group of paratroopers gathered by their plane. Those men turned out to be Company E, 502nd Parachute Infantry, the soldiers later immortalized as the Band of Brothers in a book and television miniseries.

Lieutenant Leo S. Moore followed closely behind Eisenhower at each stop that evening. Before joining the Army in 1942, Moore had worked in Hollywood as a film studio projectionist and amateur photographer. He was assigned to the Signal Corps as a cameraman to take photos at VIP events.

On one such assignment, Ike's considerate, professional nature rose to the fore. Moore attempted to photograph Eisenhower pinning an award on a soldier's chest. Just as the ceremony closed, Moore snapped the shutter. "No picture. The flash was a dud," Moore reported later of the moment.

"Hold it a minute," Moore asked the SHAEF commander.

"You do your job, and I'll do mine," the general responded.

"That's what I am trying to do, Sir," Moore replied.

Eisenhower, recognizing that Moore had lost the shot due to no fault of his own, re-created the moment for him.

Moore's own professionalism paid off because, when D-Day neared, opportunities to photograph Eisenhower increased. The general was asked whether he had a preference as to the photographer assigned to cover his activities. Ike remembered the cameraman "who at least knew what he wanted." Moore earned the assignment to cover the general for the remainder of the war. [10]

The Army Signal Corps photographer snapped Eisenhower speaking directly to Lieutenant Wally Strobel, a jumpmaster in the company. The resulting shot became one of the most iconic images from D-Day—if not all of World War II. Behind Strobel stood a half dozen or so paratroopers, their freakish hair and faces painted green to look like fierce camouflage. The paint amused the SHAEF commander. Ike turned to Taylor to whisper, in jest, "They might not scare the Germans, but they would certainly scare me."

In the photograph, Eisenhower, wearing his signature "Ike" jacket, a waist-length blouson, and service cap (the kind with a brim), buried his hands deep in his pant pockets. He likely asked Strobel, "Where are you from, soldier? What did you do in civilian life?" because he posed the same questions to every paratrooper. Yet Eisenhower had a way of speaking to these heroes-in-the-making that made them feel as though he took a personal interest in their welfare. And he did. From the look on Eisenhower's face on his rounds, Taylor believed the "supreme commander found an almost personal responsibility for the fate of these men."

One of the many paratroopers Eisenhower spoke with believed the commander found comfort in engaging with the troops: "I honestly think it was his morale that improved by being with us." Ike smiled whenever he was told, "Don't worry, General. We'll take care of this thing for you."

Indeed. Eisenhower recalled his experience that day: "I found the men in fine fettle, many of them joshingly admonishing me that I had no cause for worry."

Eisenhower stopped in front of Private Sturgis and asked the usual: "Where you from?"

"Atlanta, Sir," Sturgis replied.

"Swell town—Atlanta. Well, good luck," Eisenhower responded and moved on to the next soldier.

"Wasn't much of a conversation," Sturgis told his father later, "but it sure felt swell—imagine a guy like that walking around seeing us off. It was a damned nice thing."

Eisenhower took his time speaking either individually or to groups of men. For that reason, he covered only three airfields on his rounds. After shaking Taylor's hand for the last time before they met up again weeks later in France, Ike wasn't ready just yet to head back to Portsmouth. He stuck around to watch as each plane was loaded with men and equipment. Then he stayed to watch the planes take off.

Boarding went fairly quickly. Equipment and parachutes added another 150 pounds to each man, so they had to be helped aboard the planes. Private Bob Noody from Company F, 506th PIR, tipped the scales at more than 250 pounds: he jumped with his M-1 rifle, a bazooka, three rockets, land mines, and fifty-nine feet of bundled rope that would lower his leg bag.[11]

Major General Taylor was the last soldier to enter his plane. Major Laurence Legere not only helped Taylor into his parachute but also aided him in deciding which extra equipment to take. Besides an emergency parachute, Taylor carried a pistol, jump knife, hand grenades, field rations, canteen, first-aid kit, gas mask, and maps. And one more thing: a leg bag in which he had stored a bottle of Irish whiskey.

When everything was in place, a "brawny sergeant" proceeded to tighten the straps on the general's parachute to the point that Taylor found it hard to breathe. The sergeant, careful not to aggravate Taylor's newly bum leg, lifted him onto the plane.

Besides the pilot, the most important crew member was the jump-master, the specially selected and trained paratrooper responsible for confirming that the men in his stick were accounted for and properly equipped. He also reminded the men of the exit procedure: when the plane reached a landing zone, the jumpmaster would signal the men to stand up, hook up, and jump out. He was always the first man out.

The assistant jumpmaster, or "push-out man," was always the last out. If a paratrooper was hit by ground fire while still near the plane, the assistant's task was to hook the man to a static line and literally push that wounded warrior out the door. The theory behind this shove was that an injured man had a better chance of survival if treated on the ground than if he had to fly back to England. And, the thinking went, if he recovered, he could be put into action right away. Captain Charles W. Lusher, a chaplain with the 438th Troop Carrier Command, went down the long line of C-47s, stopping to offer a word of encouragement to each paratrooper. As the men headed to the planes, Lusher spoke to each man. They exchanged few words, he said, "just a clasp of hands, and a deep look into each other's eyes. I could only promise to pray."

He added, "Most of these boys had never killed a man and I shuddered to think of the thoughts that must be in their minds. Frankly I didn't know what to say for my gospel is of Jesus, Prince of Peace." Inside the planes, Chaplain Lusher tried to touch each paratrooper's hands or pat each man on the head. However, before he left one of the C-47s, he missed a paratrooper. Still, the boy wanted this benedictory moment with the chaplain, so he asked Lusher for the blessing: "Lay your hand on my head," the younger man implored the clergyman. "I did," the chaplain later recorded, "and no one laughed."

Ike refused to leave Greenham Common until the last plane had left.

The valedictory experience proved to be emotional for the fifty-four-year-old Army veteran. He stood the whole time in silence, watching one plane after another take off, tears rolling down his cheeks. Eisenhower slowly walked back to his Jeep, where Summersby and Gault awaited their general.

22

The Paratrooper Generals Take Off

On June 5, 1944, around 11:30 a.m., Lieutenant Colonel George M. McNeese, the pilot who took Major General Taylor to Normandy, gunned the engines of his C-47. The plane hurtled down the runway at Greenham Common Airfield, southeast of Newbury, England.

"We were off on what was to be our greatest adventure," Taylor recalled. "To me it was a moment of release to be off after so many months of laborious preparations. I was content in the feeling that I could think of nothing which would have been left undone to shore success."

The last plane was Taylor's. The atmosphere on board the C-47 "was strangely quiet" once it was aloft. Some of the men in Taylor's stick dozed on and off, feeling the effect of air-sickness pills. Taylor himself was too anxious about his first combat jump to sit or sleep; instead, he stood by the open doorway for the entire flight. Those still awake stared straight ahead, lost in their own thoughts.

Taylor's plane rendezvoused with other Screaming Eagle C-47s over the channel a half-hour later. Although it was now dark out "with a faint moon showing," Taylor recalled the view out the open door of the plane: "I felt that I could touch the sparkling waves of the channel so close below."

The 101st planes circled over the area waiting for Ridgway's serials, which were due to arrive at any moment from the fields in central England. By the time both airborne divisions linked up in the sky, there were a total of eight hundred transport planes in the formation flying toward France carrying about thirteen thousand parachutists.

The pilots decreased altitude and flew in a very low and tight V formation to "keep below the vision of German radars on the French coast." The planes flew across the channel by way of an air corridor between the islands of Guernsey and Jersey on the west and the Cherbourg Peninsula on the east. Then they turned eastward across the basin of the peninsula to their drop zones. When the planes approached the Channel Islands, Taylor could see from his post by the door "a gray wall to the southeast where the Cherbourg Peninsula should be." It was an unexpected band of fog, "the enemy of the airman." Because all pilots were operating under strict radio silence, the pathfinders flying the same route shortly before couldn't report this problem to those who followed.

Needing to stay in formation, the pilots had no choice but to fly directly into the fog bank. It was so thick that Taylor vividly recalled not being able to see "planes flying on our wingtips."

To avoid collision, the pilots instinctively broke up the formation: some veered right and others went left, and almost all of them increased their altitudes. Having lost all sense of time while in the fog bank, the planes were now over the Cherbourg Peninsula.

McNeese had turned on the hook-up signal, and jumpmaster Legere ordered the stick to stand in the aisle and attach the static line of their parachutes to the overhead wire that would trip the opening device on their chutes as they jumped. By now, German antiaircraft guns had awakened, and flak was spraying all around and hitting the planes. Men were anxious to bail out. In some cases, air-sickness pills had worn off, and men puked into their helmets or directly onto the floor, creating a slippery mess.

Before dropping, the jumpmaster quickly checked every man's equipment as they impatiently waited for the green jump sign to flash. The paratroopers were so packed together that Taylor was almost riding on Legere's back. Suddenly the fog broke, and out the door, patches of ground and the Meredert River appeared.

By the time the plane entered the landing area, the fog had all but cleared. For Taylor, looking out the doorway one last time, it was a sight to behold: "the sky ablaze with rockets, burning aircraft on the ground and antiaircraft fire rising on all sides." Taylor didn't have much time to stare at the spectacle; McNeese turned on the green jump light, and out went Legere, and then Taylor and the rest of the stick, all shouting "Bill Lee," in honor of the former division commander, instead of "Geronimo," the traditional war cry of the parachutists.

As Taylor's plane flew away, he "was left floating to earth in a comparative quiet, broken only by an occasional burst of small-arms fire on the ground." Since the paratroopers had jumped from only around five hundred feet, it shortened the drop time to the ground but exposed the men like floating ducks to the enemy gunners. Taylor, like the other paratroopers, had little time to try to select a landing point.

At the last moment, a gust of air caused Taylor to drift away from the rest of his stick. Only "by a mighty tug on the shroud lines" and sheer luck was Taylor able to escape becoming entangled on the top of a tall tree. At last, he reached the Normandy soil. Taylor came down "with a bang" in a small field close by one of the famous Normandy hedgerows surrounding the countryside. In many places, these hedges consisted of rows of trees planted on earth, banks of which, combined with the trees, presented daunting obstacles to military operations. Unlike the Screaming Eagles commander, many of the parachutists that morning found themselves suspended from one of those tall trees from which you could only hope to lower yourself by a rope before you were discovered by German riflemen.

Taylor struggled to get out of his parachute and expected that some of his men would appear to help. But when he looked around, not a single American soldier was in sight, "only a circle of curious Norman cows, who eyed me disapprovingly I thought, as if resenting the intrusion into their pasture." Taylor continued struggling to remove his chute when he heard German guns open up in the next field.

This sound energized Taylor to move even faster to free himself from the chute. "In the wet morning grass," he recalled, "it was a terrible job to unbuckle the many snaps while gun fire was a short distance away." He finally gave up and used his parachute knife to cut his way out. He then unwillingly abandoned his leg bag and its contents, including the coveted bottle of Irish whiskey. In the dark and quiet night, he started out with a pistol in one hand and identification cricket in the other. His hope was to find his troops, a lonely division commander who had lost (or at least misplaced) his division.

Moving in the shadow of the hedgerow, he "became aware of the smell of freshly turned earth and soon came upon some newly dug trenches," a clear sign the Germans were probably nearby. Taylor proceeded with caution, creeping along a hedgerow to the end of the field. "There I heard someone just around the corner and turned my head towards the sound."

Taylor drew his pistol from its holster, grasping the .45 Colt good and tight while pointing his gun at the shadow, and was ready to pull the trigger when he heard the "welcome sound of a cricket." He quickly responded in kind and jumped around the corner: there in the dim moonlight was the first American soldier to greet him, "a sight of martial beauty." The paratrooper stood before Taylor, "bareheaded, rifle in hand, bayonet fixed and apparently ready for anything."

The relieved division commander and soldier embraced in silence and took off together to look for other parachutists who were now beginning to appear in the darkness. Taylor knew that time wasn't on their side. Only about one hour was left in which to assemble the troops before daylight came.

But it took much longer than he had hoped to gather all his men who survived the drop into Normandy. Taylor had expected three battalions (about three hundred men in each battalion) of parachute infantry to have arrived in the area before he landed, but at this moment he realized that his men were scattered in all directions and that only a few men from the battalions were where they should be.[1]

A similar fate awaited Major General Ridgway and his men.

Brigadier General Paul L. Williams, operations commander of IX Troop Carrier Command, selected the aircraft and aircrew for Ridgway's plane. Pilot Chester A. Baucke and his five crew members equipped the plane with a Rebecca radar and navigator. Because of a shortage of planes to carry the airborne to Normandy, most were loaded to capacity with sticks of around eighteen paratroopers, plus the crew. On Ridgway's plane, there were only eleven men: six officers and five enlisted men. For the most part, they all served in one capacity or another as Ridgway's attendants. Ridgway later caught some grief from jealous officers who flew on crowded planes who believed that he should have been accompanied by a larger stick.

The loading at Spanhoe was interrupted by a freak accident that left eight paratroopers killed instantly, one who lingered before dying, and seven others badly wounded. One of the dead paratroopers had accidentally exploded a powerful antitank Gammon grenade in his pocket, which activated other ammunition and set fire to the plane. At 10:45 p.m., about thirty minutes after Taylor's 101st left England, Ridgway's 82nd took off with about 6,400 men. The All-Americans were divided into three parachute regiments and were joined by fifty-two Waco gliders towed by an equal number of C-47s that left later from Ramsbury in southern England.

Ridgway's plane was part of the V grouping, or serial, of the 505th Regiment. Their destination was Drop Zone O, which lay between Sainte-Mère-Église and the Merderet River. After dropping, their principal missions, which were revised over the previous week after the Germans reinforced the original drop zone, were to capture Sainte-Mère-Église, hold the two bridges over the Meredert, one at La Fière and the other at Chef-du-Pont, and establish a blocking line north and northeast of Sainte-Mère-Église at the towns of Neuville-au-Plain and Beuzeville-au-Plain. At the same time, Ridgway's men would link up eastward with the 101st, which at this point should be concentrated between Sainte-Mère-Église and Utah Beach and southward toward Carentan.

Ridgway's pathfinders were already on the ground; in fact, they reached Normandy ten minutes early and had greater success in placing the lights and radars than the Screaming Eagles had experienced around the same time. As the formation containing Ridgway's plane flew over the channel, it was a calm trip, but that suddenly changed when they reached the western shore of the Cotentin Peninsula. There, the pilots encountered the same turbulent clouds that had impacted Taylor's planes. Ridgway vividly recalled what happened next: "The plane began to yaw and plunge, and in my mind's eye I could see other pilots, fighting to hold course, knowing how great was the danger of collision in the air." To adjust, many planes climbed above the clouds to about 1,500 feet and increased speed to about 150 miles per hour.

Baucke kept calm. As his plane, with Ridgway on board, approached the designated LZ, the Rebecca picked up a strong signal from the Eureka on Drop Zone O. The pilot Baucke then saw the lighted T, made a few minor adjustments, descended to six hundred feet, and decreased speed to 120 miles per hour. Right over the target, Baucke turned on the green jump light and rang the bail-out bell. Jumpmaster Dean Garber, already standing in the doorway, shouted, "Let's go!" He leaped into the pitch-black night. Seconds later, Ridgway, making his fifth jump, followed. After catching a brief glimpse of Garber floating earthbound, Ridgway felt his chute snap open, "the most comforting of all sights," though he could see nothing in the darkness. "I was alone in the sky," he remembered years later, as though it had just happened, and the "descent was fast."

Before Ridgway knew it, he hit "a nice, soft, grassy field," but hard. Just like he was taught over and over again, he rolled to keep from breaking a limb, released the air from his canopy, and yanked off his harness. Ridgway nervously reached for his .45 pistol, but it slipped from his grasp and tumbled onto the grass. In the darkness, he pawed around for the weapon when he sensed a nearby movement.

Ridgway called out the password ("Flash") and anticipated the response ("Thunder"), but there was only silence. To his great relief, Ridgway realized the movement was from a cow. "I could've kissed her," he recalled, because it meant the pasture was not mined or booby-trapped.

Still alone, and for the moment safe, Ridgway had to figure out where to find the rest of his stick. With his pistol securely in hand, he carefully moved from the pasture, which was surrounded by hedgerows, but it was hard to get his bearings. The 82nd commander seemed to revel in the moment: "I felt a great exhilaration of being here alone in the dark on this greatest of adventures."

Like every paratrooper who jumped into Normandy that day, Ridgway felt overwhelmed by the experience. "By now, all over the countryside around us the Germans were beginning to rouse and shoot," he recalled. "The finest fireworks display I ever saw was going on around me. Rockets and tracers were streaking through the air and big explosions were going off everywhere." He caught another movement in the shadows of the hedgerow, whipped out his pistol, turned around, and spoke the password out loud. This time, he received the proper countersign. It was company commander Captain William Follmer, who was hobbling around in agony with a broken right hip.

Ridgway, pistol at the ready, left Follmer behind for the medics and moved along the hedgerows to try to locate the division command post.

After walking a short distance, he encountered 2nd Battalion, 505th PIR commander Benjamin H. Vandervoort's intelligence officer, who brought him to Vandervoort's command post.

Vandervoort was ailing, having broken his right ankle. With his boot tightly laced and using his rifle as a crutch, he hobbled over to Ridgway, and the two of them looked at maps by flashlight. Ridgway set up his command post northwest of Sainte-Mère-Église in an orchard, along with a paltry staff of eleven officers and men.[2]

German troops from the 91st Division were close by: Ridgway figured some were only five hundred yards from his CP. Had the enemy known this, Ridgway would have been easily killed or captured.[3]

23

Scattered in Streams and Cow Pastures

At 2:44 a.m., June 6, 1944, D-Day, IX Troop Carrier Command's C-47 troop transports dropped the final stick. That load of paratroopers in one aircraft was the last group of the more than thirteen thousand 82nd and 101st paratroopers who flew to Normandy that day, highlighted forever in history by its military shorthand designation of D-Day.

About six hours earlier, all over southern England, General Paul Williams's Troop Carrier Command armada of 821 C-47s prepared to take off for Normandy a little more than two hours later.

In their briefings, the pilots and crews learned where the drop zones were located and which paratrooper sticks would be dropped over them.

Mission Albany included almost seven thousand paratroopers from Taylor's 101st Airborne, loaded on to 432 C-47s, flying to three drop zones, including DZ A, located north of Turqueville and Audouville-la-Hubert. There, the 502nd Parachute Infantry Regiment (PIR) would seize causeways 3 and 4.

The 1st and 2nd Battalions of the 506th PIR and the 3rd Battalion of the 501st PIR were to land at DZ C, located north of Hiesville, with the mission of seizing causeways 1 and 2. Lastly, DZ D, south of Vierville, was dedicated to the 1st and 2nd Battalions of the 501st PIR and the 3rd Battalion of the 506th PIR. These paratroopers were tasked with seizing Saint-Côme-du-Mont and bridges over the Douve River. The total area of all the Albany drop zones totaled about twenty-four square miles.[1]

An hour after Albany, Mission Boston commenced with 320 C-47s carrying 6,420 of Ridgway's paratroopers to three drop zones. DZ N was situated north of Pont-l'Abbé and Picauville, where the 508th PIR had to destroy two bridges on the Douve River at Pont-l'Abbé and Beuzeville-la-Bastille while controlling the western edge of the Merderet River. DZ O, west of Route 13, was to facilitate the capture of Sainte-Mère-Église by the 505th PIR, while DZ T was assigned to the 507th PIR, which placed the regiment north of Amfreville so it could hold the northwest approaches of the La Fière Bridge.[2]

From the briefings, the pilots and crews went directly to their planes, grouped into three Troop Carrier Wings: 50th, 52nd, and 53rd. Within each wing were Troop Carrier Groups, further divided into Troop Carrier Squadrons. Each paratrooper infantry regiment took off on board three to four aircraft formations called serials, which contained anywhere from thirty-six to fifty-four C-47s.

When Sergeant Martin Wolfe walked up to his plane the first time, he noticed paratroopers who had blackened their faces for the coming assault. The jumpmasters had the men stand up and strap on all their extremely heavy equipment.

Fully loaded down, the men weighed around 150 pounds. Crews had to help push some of them up the stairs into the plane. Before the paratroopers boarded, some gave away their British money, figuring it was "something of no value to them . . . in France."

Once the planes took off, the serials rendezvoused twenty miles east over Birmingham, England. Despite the huge number of planes in the air and the potential danger of collision in the darkness, the planes formed a perfect V-of-Vs as they joined the rest of the airborne armada.

From this point, the serials of that wing would fly sixty miles southwest to the head of the Severn Estuary. From there, they flew south another sixty miles to the Command Assembly Point, code named ELKO, where naval vessels equipped with navigational aids would signal the planes that they were over the correct location.

Next, the pilots veered their planes south-southwest to the command departure point called Flatbush, which is at the tip of a sandy cape called Portland Bill. At this point, the planes flew straight over the channel for fifty-seven miles before reaching navigational point Hoboken, which consisted of British Motor Tanker (MT) boats.[3]

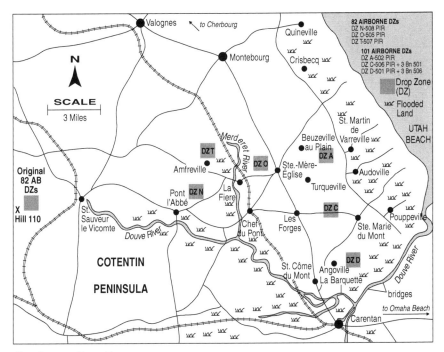

Paratrooper Drop Zones

From there, they made a ninety-degree turn to the left and flew another fifty-four miles between Alderney and Guernsey, just far enough out of range of the German antiaircraft fire on both islands. Lastly, they would reach Peoria on the west coast of the Cotentin Peninsula north of the towns of Carteret and Barnesvillle.

"As we turned southeast from our corridor over the Channel and toward Normandy," Sergeant Martin Wolfe recalled, "the feeling grew that this monstrously complicated operation was clicking along perfectly. This feeling was strengthened when we saw that the antiaircraft fire from the German-held Channel Islands (Guernsey and Jersey) was falling short—as we had been told it would."

Within a few minutes, the planes reached the western coastline. Here, "disaster loomed up." The C-47s "slammed headlong" into a dense cloud bank. "Nothing had prepared us for this," Wolfe still grumbled many years later. "The weather briefing had not foreseen it; our flight over

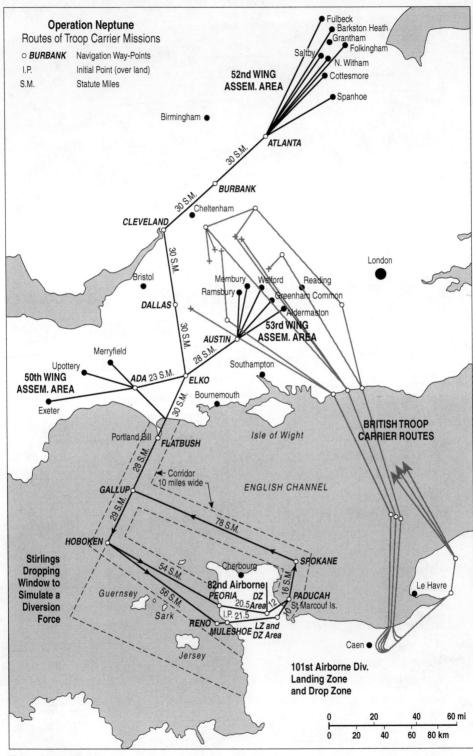

Troop Carrier Routes

the Channel had encountered only scattered clouds. The cloud bank was thicker in some spots than others. For some of us it was so thick that it was as if we had suddenly stopped flying through air and were now flying through grayish soup."

A half-hour or so before, the pathfinders had also flown through these same clouds. Because strict radio silence had been imposed on all the pilots, they had no warning they would fly into almost zero visibility.

Out of the clouds in a matter of minutes, although it must have seemed much longer to the confused pilots, landmarks such a town, river, or railroad came into view. But this didn't mean that the pilots were out of trouble. Many found that the "Eureka-Rebecca" radar beacons, designed to guide individual planes to the correct DZ, were not working.

A few planes had been equipped with the more sophisticated "GEE" radar location device, but their crews could not make sense of their readings.

Pathfinders, as the pilots learned later, had not been given enough time to get down on the ground, find the right locations, and set up their holophane T lights and radar beacons. This meant many of the pilots and navigators tried to recognize some landmarks in the darkness, praying that the paratroopers had a reasonable chance of jumping into the DZ.

In spite of that, pilots illuminated the red light at the door, signaling four minutes to go! The paratrooper jumpmaster yelled out, "Stand up! Hook up! Sound off for equipment check!" The troopers yelled back, in sequence from the rear, "Sixteen OK! Fifteen OK! Fourteen OK!" all the way up to the first in line.

Then the jumpmaster screamed, "STAND IN THE DOOR!" and "the troopers squeezed forward against each other, their right hands on the shoulders of the man in front." The jumpmaster on board Sergeant Wolfe's plane yelled, "ARE WE READY? ARE WE FUCKING-A READY!?"[4]

No one answered. They stood silently by the door waiting for the light to change from red to green. A crew chief aboard one of the C-47s that dropped some of Ridgway's paratroopers believed "it must have been a kind of momentary relief to the paratroopers, as they went out the jump door, heading for uncertain but presumably solid ground beneath."

No matter when a trooper jumped, whether with the First Division sticks alongside commanders Ridgway and Taylor or from the last C-47, scores of airborne were scattered from the drop zones and assembly points. Many of the men who weren't shot out of the sky or killed in plane crashes ended up in cattle pastures or in water, thinking only of surviving and connecting with other paratroopers.

Here, then, is a selection of their stories of D-Day:

Chaplain Francis Sampson plopped directly into the middle of a deep stream. Quick thinking saved him from drowning. Sampson grabbed his knife to cut off his bags and Mass kit, which contained a chalice to hold the wine and a paten to hold the host; however, the parachute still hugged his torso. Before he could swim to shore, the strong wind that caught his still-open canopy blew him downstream about hundred yards into shallow water. "I lay there a few minutes exhausted," Sampson recalled, "securely pinned down by equipment as if I had been in a straitjacket."

Regretting that he had removed his Mass kit, the tools of his trade as a chaplain, Sampson came ashore and crawled back to the spot where he'd dropped it in the stream. He dove under the water, searching frantically. After five or six dives, he recovered the kit—"by sheer luck," he proclaimed.

German machine-gun and mortar fire rang all around him. Alone in the darkness, not one single other American paratrooper in sight, Sampson waded through the swampy ground, looking for the pathfinder beacon lights at the drop zone where he hoped men from his stick had assembled. He couldn't find the lights; later, he heard that they had been shot out as soon as they were turned on and that the pathfinders placing them were either killed or wounded.

After a short while, Sampson spotted his assistant, still struggling to remove his chute. Hiding by a hedgerow, the two men were joined by two other Americans. However, their choice of cover proved dangerous. Eighty yards in front of them, a C-47 crashed and burst into flames, throwing blazing pieces of metal over their heads. A little farther away, two other planes plummeted to the ground.[5]

The three destroyed C-47s were among twenty-one that were shot down by the Germans or crashed due to mechanical issues. A stick from Easy Company, 507th Parachute Infantry Regiment, perished before they could vacate their plane.

At seven minutes past midnight, thirty-two-year-old Lieutenant Guy Remington, a descendent of the family that invented the typewriter, jumped into Normandy with the 501st PIR. Remington, the second man from his stick out the door, attracted enemy fire right away as "the black Normandy pastures tilted and turned far beneath" him.

German machine guns and 45mm antiaircraft tracers turned the sky yellow, then green, blue, and red. Remington described his descent as being "pitched down through a wild Fourth of July." Above his head, he saw flaming transports fast approaching the ground. One of the C-47s spiraled to Earth with a trooper hooked to the tailpiece by his burning parachute. Remington may have witnessed the same destroyed transports that Sampson and his party saw.

Remington landed against a hedgerow in a small garden behind the rear of enemy barracks. His own chute and uniform were riddled by bullets. Tracers had burned four holes in his pant legs, and both breast pockets were torn off. Miraculously, he was uninjured.[6]

Bob Bearden with the 507th PIR hit the ground "in a matter of seconds, alone and right in the middle of a pasture within a few miles of the intended T Drop Zone." Bearden headed toward the sound of small-arms fire, hoping his fellow 82nd Airborne paratroopers were besting the Germans, and not the other way around.

With another paratrooper from his division, the two stumbled upon a farmhouse with a Dutch door split in two horizontally. Bearden, his tommy gun pointed straight ahead, knocked on the closed door. The other paratrooper remained in the yard, covering Bearden with his M-1 rifle.

After what seemed like forever to Bearden, the top half of the door opened. A pretty, young French girl appeared, her eyes blazing with terror. Bearden understood her fear because all she could see of him was a helmet, a gun, and hand grenades hanging from his uniform jacket—"everything,"

Bearden summarized, "that symbolized bad times for people who had been under Nazi authority for some time."

However, American soldiers preparing for D-Day had been instructed to suspect the French because intelligence claimed that many were collaborators and thus protected by the Germans.[7]

Bearden turned sideways to show the girl the American flag sewn on the upper section of his jumpsuit jacket's sleeve. She smiled, walked back into the room, and "faded into the darkened house."

"Papa, Papa," Bearden heard her whisper. An old, graying man appeared at the half-open door. He, too, stared at the American soldier. He said nothing. Nor did Bearden. He knew little French, so he stood at the door dumbly. Then he shrugged his shoulders as if to say, "I don't know what the hell I'm doing here," and walked toward the other soldier, stopping once to wave to the father and daughter.[8]

Near Sainte-Mère-Église, a sixteen-year-old French girl watched as a "paratrooper fell right in the garden in front of her house. He landed in a row of garden peas, breaking the stakes." Abruptly, the American opened the front door without knocking. The girl never forgot him. She wrote years later of the encounter, "His face blackened, head covered with a khaki net helmet, entered. It was a sight worthy of Dante, this black man from the sky."

The paratrooper raised his machine gun and, with a gesture, told the family not to move. He walked around the house, opening drawers of the furniture to look everywhere. Satisfied there were no Germans hiding in the house, he softly approached the petrified family. With a warm smile, he handed out cigarettes to the girl's father. The chewing gum he handed to the children was something they'd never had before.

Major Philip Gage, the son of a brigadier general, jumped with the 501st PIR, landing smoothly in a field near Carentan.

Three hundred yards in the distance, he saw silhouettes and stopped. Wondering whether they were "friend or foe," Gage pulled from his pocket a metal cricket, the children's toy that had become so helpful to men of war. He clicked it twice. Receiving no response, he decided to risk heading forward. "It was like being in a cemetery at midnight," Gage remembered, "alone and frightened, wondering whether the tombstones would suddenly move."

The decision to approach the silhouettes almost ended his life. Two men came toward him, stopping twenty feet away. When they spoke in German, Gage drew his pistol and fired. He missed, and they returned fire. One bullet tore through Gage's diaphragm; another shattered his right arm just above his hand. Suddenly, Gage's hand "was on fire," and his "belly burned with a lesser pain." Too weak to tear open his first-aid packet, he thought, "I'm going to die." Nearby, in a pasture, a cow chewed her cud, oblivious to Gage's predicament.

The Germans hovered over him and searched his pockets; then they placed Gage on a two-wheeled cart. He fell off, so they roughly hauled him back up on the cart. Much like the cow, the enemy soldiers cared little for his well-being. They took Gage to a church converted into a German field hospital. A doctor gave him two morphine pills and wrapped a tourniquet around his arm. In the afternoon, Gage was operated on; when he awoke, he saw his hand had been amputated at the wrist. However, he rather quickly adjusted: He recorded this in his diary a month after being wounded, "I almost forgot I ever had a right hand. I swept half the ward after lunch and supper."

Precisely six years after pitching a no-hitter against the Orlando Senators, twenty-five-year-old Forrest "Lefty" Brewer jumped into Normandy at 2:20 a.m. with the 508th PIR, 82nd Division. For three seasons, the athletic, 6'1" Brewer had pitched for the St. Augustine Saints, a minor league team. In 1941, the Washington Senators invited him to compete for a slot on their spring roster. But the Army wanted him, too, so he put his baseball career on hold. Instead of pitching in the Major Leagues, Brewer went to Camp Blanding, Florida, for basic training, and a year later, he volunteered to become a paratrooper.

On the afternoon of June 6, Brewer led a squad of men from the 508th along a causeway near La Fière Manor. The heavily fortified chateau, a key D-Day objective for the 82nd Division, stood on the left bank of the Merderet River.

After his regiment secured the area early in the day and opened one of the Utah Beach exits, the Americans—including the baseball player—fled for cover under a vicious German counterattack with tanks and artillery. A machine-gun blast hit Lefty Brewer in the back—he fell face down in the river, dead. He was buried temporarily in Normandy; in 1947, Brewer's remains were sent home to his family in Jacksonville, Florida.[9]

The 501st PIR's Sam Gibbons, a captain from Tampa, Florida, heard his parachute "open with a loud crack—reflecting the added weight of combat equipment." Only thirty-five to forty seconds later, he'd dropped from his C-47 into Normandy.

Twenty-four-year-old Gibbons landed at 1:26 a.m., six miles farther into German territory than he had planned. By himself in a large, grassy field, Gibbons crawled slowly on his stomach toward a hedgerow. He couldn't see anyone. All he heard was German gunfire behind him.

With no Americans in sight, he "began to wonder whether the whole mission had been aborted and he just hadn't gotten the signal." Moments later, though, Gibbons "saw a helmet silhouetted against the sky." An American helmet? Instinctively, he clicked his cricket once, and a response came back with two clicks. "I felt a thousand years younger," he later wrote, "and both of us moved forward so we could touch each other."

The two paratroopers found a paved road where a bunch of other parachutists from mixed units had gathered. As dawn came, the party had a better sense about where they should head—Saint Côme-du-Mont. There, General Taylor's troops were heavily engaged.[10] The paratroopers continued to walk along a paved road for an hour; then Gibbons called for a halt. He gathered the men to his side and pulled out the two cans of Schlitz beer that he had tucked inside his gas mask. They drank deeply and left the empty cans in the middle of the road "as a monument to the first cans of Schlitz consumed in France."[11]After the war, Gibbons served in the Florida state house and senate for ten years, and then in the US House of Representatives for thirty-four years: a total of forty-four years of public service.

Eight miles from Sainte-Mère-Église, First Lieutenant James M. Irvin, 505th PIR, 82nd Division, rallied thirty of his men together to lead them toward the battalion command post. Immediately, Germans surrounded them. Wounded by mortar fire, Irvin was lying in a ditch when the Germans captured him and took him to a hospital for ten days and then to a POW camp south of Saint Lô.

Three weeks after D-Day, Irvin and other captured officers were bussed to another camp. He decided to escape en route. The bus's windows were blacked out. Guards were in the front; to distract them, the officers began to sing. One held the door open so it wouldn't bang, and Irvin and two others jumped out as the bus kept going. Using a map and compass from an escape kit, the party headed to the Brittany Peninsula and to eventual repatriation behind Allied lines. Along the way, French farmers fed them and gave them a place to sleep and civilian clothes.[12]

German troops captured Private Arthur Mullins of the 502nd PIR, 101st Airborne and six other paratroopers two miles west of Saint-Martin-de-Varreville.

A "polite, English-speaking" German officer interrogated the group but gave up after they refused to reveal their unit, the name of their commanding officer, and the objectives of the invasion. The Nazi locked the Americans in a room. For three days, they subsisted on a half loaf of bread and a sip of water once or twice a day. Eventually, Mullins was placed with three hundred other American POWs. During a prisoner count on a road between two hedges, Mullins decided to make a break for it. He "zigzagged" through the crowd and then took out two German guards by practicing the judo he'd learned in paratrooper school.[13]

Private Spencer Wurst received a new pair of jump boots in 1943, whereupon he proclaimed himself one of the "Army's Top Dogs." He jumped on June 6, "an hour and fifty-one minutes after midnight." Now a squad leader in the 82nd's 505th PIR, he, like many other paratroopers, tumbled into a Normandy field shared by cows and edged by hedgerows.

Wurst could make out a large spire pointed at the horizon and flames glowing in the darkness not far from where he landed. The sight turned

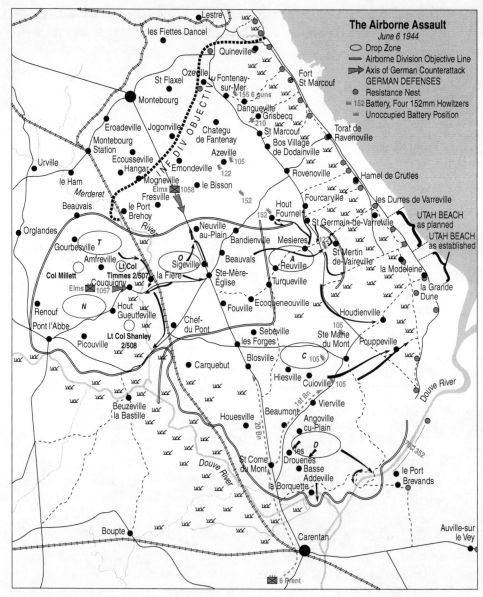

Airborne Assault

out to be Sainte-Mère-Église, ablaze from a fire that had broken out shortly before the paratroopers arrived. Even though his back, hips, and joints were sore from a hard landing, Wurst ached his way toward a "green star-cluster flare," a sign that someone among his battalion had found the assembly location.

When Wurst reached the other paratroopers, he discovered they were a mixed bag of All-Americans and Screaming Eagles, a common occurrence the morning of June 6, with men scattered from one end of the Cotentin Peninsula to the other. [14]

By dawn, the vast majority of wayward paratroopers had assembled with their units. Now led by Ridgway and Taylor and their subordinate commanders, the paratroopers spent the remainder of D-Day surging forward to clear the enemy so that the amphibious troops could come safely ashore.

24

The All-Americans on D-Day

Ridgway's All-Americans were in for a tough D-Day.

The 82nd Airborne had been tasked with two major objectives once it landed. First and most significant was establishing a defensive base in the town of Sainte-Mère-Église. The second was organizing bridgeheads over the Merderet River at La Fière and Chef-du-Pont. Both missions proved equally difficult and couldn't be accomplished in a single day.[1]

Lieutenant Colonel Edward C. Krause, commander of 3rd Battalion, 505th PIR, drew the task of taking Sainte-Mère-Église. After capturing the town, Krause would set up roadblocks to the south and east. Nicknamed "Cannonball," Krause had a reputation for his fiery temper and tough-taking demeanor. At the drop of a hat, Krause would go on a tirade against some unlucky paratrooper.[2]

Around eleven at night on June 5, about three hours before Krause and his men headed for the town, a fire broke out at the home of Julia Pommier, just across from the Sainte-Mère-Église church in the town center.

Mayor Alexandre Renaud, a proud French Army veteran who saw action at Verdun during the Great War, and the fire brigade were called to help. The Germans issued a partial lifting of the curfew, and a human chain was formed to bring in buckets of water. They tried in vain to extinguish the flames, which were beginning to spread to a nearby barn.

The blaze was still going strong when a C-47 Troop Carrier dropped a stick of paratroopers over the town around one in the morning on June 6, and more American airborne would follow. The town square was in total chaos as the civilians hurried back to their homes. The German soldiers garrisoned at Sainte-Mère-Église killed several paratroopers as they hit the ground and then, after exchanging sporadic fire, withdrew to their command post in Fauville, two kilometers away.[3]

Within forty-five minutes, 180 men had gathered around Lieutenant Colonel Krause, who split them into two companies and gave a brief explanation of what would come next. One man in the group looked far different from everyone else. He dressed in civilian clothes, spoke French, and was drunk.

Lieutenant William F. Mastrangelo, one of the officers who rounded up troopers for Krause, had found the inebriated Frenchman wandering the road. Fearful that he might be a German collaborator, Mastrangelo brought him at gunpoint to the battalion commander.

The civilian offered to lead Krause's band toward the town from the northwest, but Krause was reluctant to rely on him. Despite his condition, the Frenchman verified Krause's location and provided the Americans with useful intelligence. He revealed that Sainte-Mère-Église was held by a small garrison and that most of the German troops were on the roads leading into the town.

Krause placed him at the front of the pack with several paratroopers to ensure that he didn't run away and alert the Germans. The Americans proceeded forward but strayed from the trail he suggested. He had led them correctly, however, and within thirty minutes they were on the outskirts of Sainte-Mère-Église.

Krause sent his men directly into the town. Since it was still dark out, he ordered his soldiers to attack using only bayonets and grenades. That way, the men would know the direction of German fire. The paratroopers spread out, clearing the major roads that intersected at the square. As the drunk Frenchman had promised, the town had been held by only a small garrison of Germans.

Krause's men made quick work of the meager force, killing ten Germans and taking thirty prisoners. Around 4:30 a.m., the lieutenant colonel raised an American flag to signal that Sainte-Mère-Église had been taken, the first town liberated in Normandy. By 9:30 a.m., it had been cleared of Germans. Now with 360 men, Krause had bagged only about

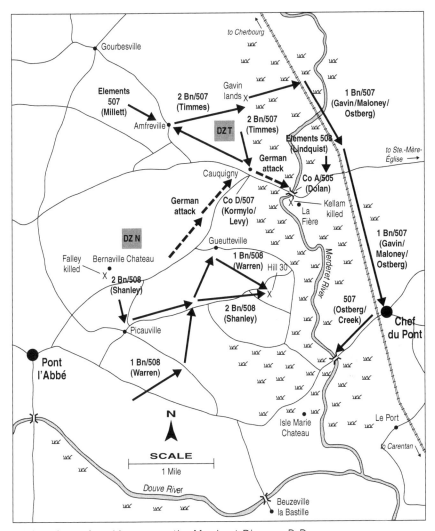

All-Americans Attacking across the Merderet River on D-Day

thirty enemy prisoners and killed ten. The remainder of the Germans, caught off-guard by the attack, retreated southward.[4]

Although badly limping with a broken ankle, Lieutenant Colonel Vandervoort set out with men from his 2nd Battalion toward Neuville-au-Plain, but an hour later, the 505th PIR commander, Colonel William

Ekman, ordered Vandervoort to stop his advance. Ekman had not heard from Krause, even though Krause had sent out runners to let him know that Sainte-Mère-Église had fallen. Ekman, however, never received the news but waited another two hours before turning Vandervoort around and sending him back to Sainte-Mère-Église.

Physically, Vandervoort was having a tough time getting around on his busted ankle. On the way to Neuville-au-Plain, Vandervoort had noticed two sergeants pulling a collapsible aluminum cart, so he requested a ride. One of the sergeants flippantly told him that "they hadn't come all the way to Normandy to pull any damn colonel around." Vandervoort recalled later, "I persuaded them otherwise."[5]

Vandervoort finally arrived in Sainte-Mère-Église and conferred with Krause, who was ailing from shrapnel wounds in his thigh. They agreed to divide up the town, with Vandervoort's men securing the eastern and northern ends, while Krause took responsibility for the south and west.

Krause's paratroopers took the brunt of the fighting that afternoon at the hands of the 795th Georgian Battalion supported by tanks and self-propelled guns. His men held off the first German counterattack, but the enemy kept coming. Krause's men guarding the southern outpost could hear trucks rumbling toward them.

Krause sent Captain Harold D. Swingler and eighty-four men from Company I to try and cut off the German convoy before it reached Sainte-Mère-Église. For two hours, Swingler's men fought so tenaciously against the German unit, twice the size of Company I, that the German commander thought he was outnumbered and withdrew his men to Hill 20 south of town. Several members of Company I were killed in the attack, including Swingler.

At Neuville-au-Plain, Lieutenant Turner B. Turnbull also had a tough fight. After moving his platoon of forty-two men unopposed through town, he placed them on high ground to the north. Before they could get into position, a full-strength company of Germans from the 91st *Luftlande* Division attacked. Although outnumbered five to one, Turnbull's men, equipped with Browning automatic weapons, bazookas, and two 57mm antitank guns, fought the Germans to a draw after eight hours of fighting.

Eventually, the stronger German force turned Lieutenant Turnbull's flank. Vandervoort sent a platoon to cover Turnbull as he withdrew in the late afternoon. Of the forty-two men he went into battle with, only sixteen remained. Turnbull's stand above Neuville-au-Plain had kept a large enemy force to the north, providing Krause and Vandervoort time to hold off the Germans attacking from the south. The next day, June 7, Lieutenant Turnbull was also added to the casualty list when German artillery killed him as he led an attack outside of Sainte-Mère-Église.[6]

After Krause repulsed the German attack at Sainte-Mère-Église, he went on the offensive. He sent eighty men from his battalion against the enemy's western flank, and the results were almost disastrous. The company commander got lost among the zigzagging hedgerows, turned east in the wrong place, and ended up ahead of the German position. As a result, Company I attacked a German convoy with Gammon grenades (improvised hand-thrown bombs).

The convoy was wiped out with such ferocity that it convinced the German forces immediately south of Sainte-Mère-Église to withdraw, believing the American presence was much stronger than they thought. Toward the end of the day, Krause could safely report that the town was no longer under serious threat. German snipers were flushed out of buildings, and after dark the few small-scale enemy efforts to probe Sainte-Mère-Église from the north were easily turned back.

Around four in the morning, Mission Detroit, composed of fifty-two Waco gliders, reached Normandy in support of Ridgway's 82nd Airborne. Twenty-three of them made it to LZO, near Sainte-Mère-Église, including two that landed in the town; the others landed close by, and some crashed into hedgerows like the glider crash that had killed General Pratt. Private Tony DeMayo, 2nd Battalion, 505th PIR, witnessed the glider landings, such as they were. "One crash after another as they hit the so-called hedgerows." DeMayo recalled. "It was just like crumbling wooden match-boxes in your hand."[7]

Because of the violent landings, only half of the equipment sent over was operational. Only eleven out of twenty-two Jeeps, for example, could be driven. The others needed to be repaired or had to be scrapped. Of the sixteen 57mm guns on board the gliders, only eight were useable. Three

soldiers were killed and another twenty-two wounded, including Ridgway's chief of staff, Colonel Ralph "Doc" Eaton, who broke three ribs and
badly bruised both legs.[8]

That same night, Mission Elmira took 100 C-47s, a mix of Wacos
and Horsas, with two field artillery battalions and 75mm and 105mm
howitzers, plus forty-eight tons of ammunition and supplies, from Membury, Welford, and Greenham Common airfields at 8:40 p.m. As the
glider armada reached LZ O about eleven, German guns opened up, and
casualties were high. Fifty-six Horsas and eight Wacos were destroyed.
Ten pilots and twenty-nine soldiers died; another 135 suffered wounds.[9]

Six hours before Elmira, Task Force C, known as "Howell Force,"
came ashore on Utah Beach. Named for Brigadier General George P.
Howell Jr., who served alongside Jim Gavin as a second assistant division commander, the task force included troops, tank, artillery, and badly
needed supplies for Ridgway's men. Colonel Edson D. Raff led ninety
troopers from F Company, 2nd Battalion, 401st Glider Regiment, along
with Sherman tanks and armored cars.

Following 8th Infantry Regiment, "Task Force Raff," as it was known,
made it to the small village of Les Forges, due south of Hill 20. The 8th
Infantry commander stopped at the village and refused to go any farther.
Raff begged him to continue to the hill and clear it of Germans before the
gliders came in, but infantry orders said to stay put. Raff tried to attack
the Germans on the high ground with his Shermans and armored cars,
but they were no match for the enemy firepower.

Three tanks and one car were obliterated after rolling only three hundred yards. Raff then sent the glider troops forward with the remaining
Shermans firing in support. The troopers made it to within five hundred
yards of Hill 20 when the gliders started to appear overhead. Raff pulled
the men back and tried to divert the gliders from the landing zone, but it
was too late.

Private Spencer F. Wurst from 1st Battalion, 505th PIR, never forgot the "terrific beating" the gliders took on that morning. Years later,
he wrote, "It was one of the sickening things I remembered." He saw
the flimsy planes crash into hedgerows. Wings were torn off, equipment
smashed, and crews mangled among the carnage of metal and wood.

Wurst's platoon leader spotted a soldier standing on a hedgerow at one end of the LZ, also watching the gliders come in. Worried that this lone figure would give away the American position, Sergeant "Little Joe" Holcomb told Wurst, "Go tell that asshole to get down and take cover." Wurst shouted the message, or words to that effect, at the unknown paratrooper. Then, as the paratrooper turned around, Wurst saw two stars on his uniform. It was Ridgway. In the future, Wurst took great care in whom he chewed out.[10]

Wurst shouldn't have been too surprised to see Ridgway there. Throughout the day, he spent little time at his command post and, instead, sought to be where the action occurred. In his memoir, he wrote, "There was little I could do during that first day toward exercising division control. I could only be where the fighting seemed the hottest, to exercise whatever personal influence I could on the battalion commanders."[11]

Poor communications with his men, as well as the infantry of 4th Divison on Utah Beach, hampered Ridgway throughout the day. There were few walkie-talkies or radios on hand that hadn't fallen into the rivers or marshes, so unless the regiments made contact by runner, commanders had little idea where other units were located. Not until nine that evening did Ridgway have access to a working radio. He called down to the beach and requested medical supplies, ammunition, and tank support.[12]

Even though the day had been tough going for the All-Americans, Ridgway wasn't rattled. "Few American generals in World War II would experience such a hellish nightmare," one of Ridgway's biographers wrote. "And yet Ridgway, according to many who were present, did not once falter, did not yield to pessimisim, doubt, or fear, or if he did, he gave no outward sign of it."[13]

Nowhere was the fighting more hellish on D-Day than at the La Fière and Chef-du-Pont bridges over the Merderet River.

Lieutenant John J. "Red Dog" Dolan, commander of Company A, 1st Battalion, 505th PIR, led the attack on the La Fière Bridge, "a smallish stone affair and little more than a large culvert." On the other side of the river, the 507th and 508th PIRs would support Dolan by securing the Merderet's west bank, but both regiments landed poorly. They were supposed to drop north of Amfreville and Picauville, but pathfinders marking those DZs ran into heavy enemy resistance.[14]

As a result, many of the paratroopers overshot the target and landed in flooded marshland along the Merderet. Aerial photographs taken of the area showed grassy swampland but did not reveal the widely flooded terrain created when the Germans shut off the La Barguette lock. Grass had grown so tall and thick out of the water that from the sky, the area resembled a prairie. Heavily weighed-down paratroopers sank in water sometimes seven feet deep.

Initially, the Americans found it easy to reach the La Fière Bridge. Once the men regrouped from the poor landings, they followed a railroad line, which was known to be the only one in the Merderet valley. Lieutenant Dolan moved carefully toward La Fière, and when he was about seven hundred yards away, he halted his platoon at the edge of an open field. He sent three scouts from his unit to probe for Germans, but when the paratroopers approached the wood line, German machine gunners and snipers opened fire. All three were killed.

Dolan now had a sense of what he was up against and split his force by sending some troopers toward the Germans to get a better sense of their direction, while the others flanked the enemy. The German firepower was overwhelming, however, and Dolan's unit got pinned down for over an hour.[15]

Among the first soldiers to arrive at La Fière was a group led by Captain F. V. Schwartzwalder with men from the 507th PIR. Once his men reached the bridge at dawn, they met opposition. From an orchard near a group of houses east of the bridge, Germans poured mortar and small-arms fire into Schwartzwalder's men. Several efforts to quiet the attack by storming the houses resulted only in more casualties.

Three other paratrooper units joined in the fray: Company A from 505th PIR and one hundred men from 507th and 508th PIRs led by the commander of 508th, Colonel Roy Lindquist. They were soon joined by thirty men from under Lieutenant John H. Wisner, the 507th Regiment's intelligence officer. Wisner reconnoitered to the north, where he met a group of three hundred soldiers heading to the fight.

Some of them had been collected by General Gavin, who dropped near the bridge. Others were picked up by Lieutenant Colonel Arthur Maloney and Lieutenant Colonel Edwin J. Ostberg. This group of men proceeded to where the fighting seemed the heaviest, on the west bank of the river.

When Gavin arrived, he learned that the effort to approach the bridge had stalled. Still, he didn't think the enemy strength was significant. More paratroopers drifted in, and by midmorning there were between five hundred and six hundred men by the bridge. Gavin elected to take seventy-five men and Colonel Ostberg from the force to try to cross the Merderet at Chef-du-Pont, which he had been told was undefended. Colonel Lindquist was left in charge of the La Fière.

At noon, Lindquist ordered an all-out attack. His battalion led the way, and, in short order, it destroyed the enemy positions. Captain Schwartzwalder's men were the first to cross the causeway, where they made contact with fifty men from Colonel Charles J. Timmes's 2nd Battalion, 507th PIR. Other paratroopers were entrenched a short distance away in the village of Canquigny, but that area wasn't entirely safe since German troops still held the ground south and east.

La Fière Bridge had been in American possession only for little over an hour when the Germans counterattacked with artillery and small-arms fire. Schwartzwalder had taken his battalion to Amfreville, leaving the secured bridgehead vulnerable. Company B, 508th PIR, had been sent as reinforcements across the causeway, but it met a stronger enemy force head-on and was forced south along the river. Casualties were heavy. The men who survived the attack swam back to the east bank as German bullets pinged the water.

To make matters worse, the enemy not only recovered the bridge but also cut off Colonel Timmes's men, including Captain Schwartzwalder's force. Timmes organized the 120 men in an orchard near Amfreville, and they would remain isolated there for another two days.

General Gavin learned of the dire situation at La Fière and came back from Chef-du-Pont in the late afternoon. He found ammunition low and medical aid lacking. Gavin ordered Colonel Maloney to also return with his entire force but keep one platoon at Chef-du-Pont. Before Maloney arrived, the Germans attacked the east bank of the river for the second time, inflicting heavy casualties on 1st Battalion, 505th PIR. At about ten that evening, Maloney appeared with two hundred men and moved them to the 505th PIR line.

At Chef-du-Pont, the situation wasn't much better. Colonel Ostberg and seventy-five men attacked the German positions and drove them from the town and the eastern approaches to the bridge, but they didn't go away entirely. Dug in on the causeways and left bank of the Merderet, they refused to let Ostberg's men cross the bridge. Colonel Maloney, General Gavin, and the seventy-five reinforcements weren't able to break the stalemate.

Because Gavin and then Maloney returned to La Fière, only Captain Roy Creek's platoon of thirty-four men remained at Chef-du-Pont. A German field gun fired on Creek's men, and he was quickly down to only twenty troopers. On the east bank of the river, he could see between seventy-five to one hundred Germans forming in a group of buildings to Creek's left rear. Creek called in for reinforcements, but before more men could arrive, help came from a 57mm antitank gun and ammunition brought in by glider that morning.

Around 4 p.m., two German Renault tanks advanced toward the La Fière Bridge. Paratroopers, armed with two bazookas positioned on both sides of the road, opened fire and destroyed one of them. They then fired at the second tank and also knocked it out of action. A third German tank approached the bridge, but by now the bazooka teams were out of ammunition.[16]

Major Francis Caesar Augustus Kellam, 1st Battalion, 505th PIR commander, ran toward the bridge with a bag of rockets for the bazookas, followed by his operations officer, Captain Dale S. Roysden. A German artillery barrage struck both Kellam and Roysden: Kellam was killed right away, while Roysden, rendered unconscious from a concussion, died the next day. In honor of the deceased major, La Fière would also be known as "Kellam's Bridge."[17]

Sporadic fighting continued throughout the afternoon, but nothing of real consequence came from it. General Ridgway called the clash at La

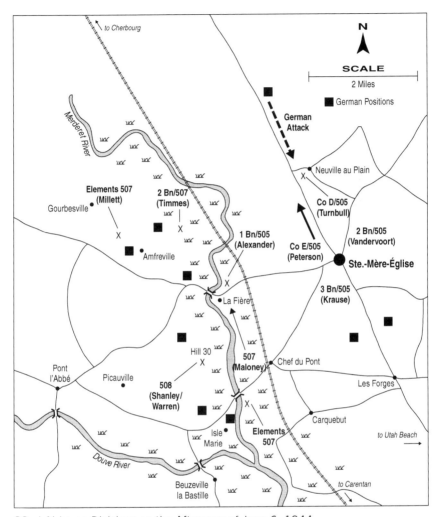

82nd Airborne Divisions on the Afternoon of June 6, 1944

Fière "as hot a single battle as any US troops had at any time during the war in Europe," and it resumed the next morning.[18]

That night, Gavin and Ridgway had an unfortunate encounter that caused a rift between them that didn't entirely heal during or after the war. Gavin had just turned in after a hard fight at La Fière, an objective Ridgway insisted should have been taken that day, when he was shaken from a sound sleep and told that the 82nd Division commander wanted to see him right away.

Guided by the light of a full moon, Gavin walked seven miles with another officer toward Ridgway's command post near Sainte-Mère-Église. When they finally reached Ridgway, who was curled up in a cargo chute, Gavin went over to him and shook his shoulder and woke him up. Although half-asleep, Ridgway glared at Gavin and told him that he had nothing for him and didn't need him. Gavin later guessed that "a zealous staff officer, thinking it might be a good idea to get a firsthand report on the situation along the Merderet River, had sent the message in the name of General Ridgway." Despite Ridgway's well-deserved reputation for his fairness and the well-being of his men, he also had a spiteful side.[19]

At the end of D-Day, practically all of Ridgway's forces were engaged in a small triangle area that encompassed La Fière, Sainte-Mère-Église, and Chef-du-Pont. Of the three, Sainte-Mère-Église was most secure. Seizing the Merderet Bridge crossings required more time. Casualties had been heavy, although the exact number of killed or wounded was unclear. After a short rest, the men would engage in another day of hard fighting.

25

The Screaming Eagles on D-Day

After his warm embrace with the bare-headed paratrooper, Major General Maxwell Taylor rushed to assemble his men so they could move out.[1] Before departing from England to land in Normandy, Taylor reminded his paratroopers, "Hit the ground running toward the enemy."[2]

On the morning of June 6, that's precisely what they did, and Taylor was right with them.

At first light, Taylor gathered together ninety paratroopers. Among them stood his chief of staff, Colonel Gerald Higgins; jumpmaster Major Larry Legere; artillery commander Brigidier General Anthony McAuliffe; Lieutenant Colonel Julian J. Ewell, commander of 3rd Battalion, 501st PIR; and Reuters war correspondent Bob Reuben. Taylor recalled that his group "ranged in rank from general to private and, in skills, from radio operators, cooks, clerks, and military police," as well as riflemen, engineers, and artillerymen.

Officers were in plentiful supply, but few combat troops gathered to do the heavy lifting. This imbalance of men led Taylor to say later, "Never were so few led by so many."[3]

As the party moved out in the darkness, no one in the group could be certain where they were. All those hours intently studying maps in England could not prevent them from becoming disoriented. It soon became clear, however, that they had landed between Sainte-Marie-du-Mont and Vierville, west of the road that linked these two villages. When there was enough light to see straight ahead and to the northeast, Taylor glimpsed the church spire of Sainte-Marie-du-Mont. "I know the shape of that one," he said. "We're right where we belong."[4]

Taylor sent Colonel Thomas I. Sherbourne from McAuliffe's staff and a small detachment westward to Hiesville to establish a division command post. Moving on with the others, Taylor led the mission to capture the exit to the southernmost causeway. Lieutenant Colonel Julian Ewell was placed in command of the column, with orders "to move on to Pouppeville, occupy, and hold it," to ensure that 4th Division could move over the causeway. Taylor, Higgins, and McAuliffe attached themselves to Ewell's column to supervise the objective.[5]

Turning eastward, Taylor, Legere, and Reuben approached a farmhouse, where the farmer and his wife answered the door. In perfect French, Taylor introduced the three of them as "American invasion soldiers who landed during the night." The general then asked the Frenchman where the nearest German soldiers were located. He responded, "Sainte-Marie-du-Mont."

Then Taylor asked about the poles (Rommel's "asparagus") planted in one field but not in the others. The farmer replied that "the Germans told us farmers to pole all our fields by June 15. My cow never liked that west field, so I poled it first." Before Taylor left, the farmer asked him to wait a moment. The Frenchman went back into this house and returned holding a World War I rifle ammunition clip. He handed it to Taylor with this request: *"Allez me tuer un Boche"* ("Go kill me a German").[6]

Continuing eastward, Taylor could see the 4th Division landing on Utah Beach. "We were the privileged spectators," Taylor remembered, "of the greatest military show of history." Taylor wished in retrospect that he could have stayed longer to watch the landing craft come ashore, the naval vessels pound the beach, and the scores of fighters and bombers fly overhead.

But he needed to move. Taylor split the group into columns of two, with patrols walking ahead and on the flank. More paratroopers joined the caravan as it progressed. Late in the morning, outside of Pouppeville, the band of soldiers encountered its first Germans. Taylor halted the column on the outskirts, and Ewell organized the attack on the town. Heading Bob Reuben's column was Virgil Danforth, an ace marksman. Every time the Germans fired in Danforth's direction, the former baker estimated where the shot came from and picked off the enemy soldier.

Every time. One of Danforth's casualties "had his whole head cleaned out like a pumpkin," Bob Reuben wrote of the first war he had seen.[7]

Ewell's men encountered resistance, so it took about two hours to clear each house of snipers. Taylor and McAuliffe were itching to get into the fight, but that would not have been wise, so they watched from a safe distance. By noon, the village had been mopped up. Ewell's group took forty prisoners and suffered about twenty casualties.

Major Larry Legere was among the wounded. He had been exchanging fire with snipers and moved closer to throw a hand grenade. A rifle bullet hit his trenching shovel and ricocheted into his leg. The impact spun him around, and he "skidded into the dirt." Another paratrooper summoned a medic, the large Red Cross insignia on his arm, and hurried across the road to help Legere. As the medic knelt down to cut Legere's pants leg, a German bullet hit him in the head. "It was a bitter medicine to take," Reuben reported, "and we had to leave Larry there untended until we cleared that section of the village."[8]

By early afternoon, Pouppeville was occupied, and 4th Division had broken out of the beach. Concerned about "a collision" between his paratroopers and the infantry, Taylor sent a patrol to greet the infantry to update them on the military situation. The advance guard of the 8th Infantry headed toward the paratroopers, who cheered them on. Taylor recognized it as a historic moment, "the long-planned junction of the air and seaborne assaults on Hitler's Fortress Europe."

Using a 4th Division radio, Taylor "conveyed the welcome news" to General Omar Bradley, offshore on the *Augusta*. The First Army commander, having not yet heard from Ridgway, inquired whether General Collins had. "Nope," Collins replied, "but I'm not worried about Matt. The 82nd can take care of itself."[9]

Taylor turned his "little column" around to start back toward the division command post at Hiesville. He had a hard time keeping up with the group because the tendon injury he'd incurred from the pre-D-Day squash game was troubling him. They made it to Hiesveille before dark, where Colonel Sherbourne had set up the command post in a farmhouse surrounded by a high stone wall, "constructed so solidly as to constitute a formidable redoubt." Across an open field, Taylor had a clear view of the lock over the Douve at la Barquette, where Colonel Howard "Jumpy" Johnson's 501st was engaged much of the day, as well as of the city of Carentan, the Screaming Eagles' next major objective.[10] That evening, Taylor went to work with Chief of Staff Higgins to assess what the rest of the division had accomplished earlier in the day.

Taylor's Screaming Eagles had an ambitious day awaiting them. Attacking forces would be deployed by battalion in an effort to open the causeways leading to Utah Beach so that 4th Division could move inland at a rapid pace. On paper, a battalion meant about seven hundred officers and men, but with erratic drops that morning, commanders were lucky if they could muster 150 paratroopers.

Colonel George Van Horn Mosely's 502nd PIR, along with the detached 377th Parachute Field Artillery Battalion, would try to secure the two northern beach exists. The regiment was to drop immediately west of beach Exits 3 and 4. Mosely broke his leg when he landed, so some of his troopers dragged him by wheelbarrow to division headers in Hiesville. General Taylor replaced him with the regiment's second in command, Lieutenant Colonel John H. "Iron Mike" Michaelis.[11]

Lieutenant Colonel Robert Cole proved to be one of the Screaming Eagles' top battalion commanders. The San Antonio native and West Point graduate led seventy-five men from his 3rd Battalion, 502nd PIR (plus stray paratroopers from other units) toward the German coastal battery at Saint-Martin-de-Varreville. When they arrived, Cole saw that guns had been removed and the fortification abandoned, most likely due to preinvasion Allied bombing.

Cole moved on to the next objective, Exit 3 on the western side of the Audouville-la-Hubert causeway. His battalion reached the spot around 7:30 a.m. and found the German forces abandoning the position. Cole's men killed between fifty and seventy-five Germans as they fled the beach.

The 1st Battalion of the 502nd PIR, led by Lieutenant Colonel Patrick Cassidy, had landed within a mile of his drop zone at Germain-de-Varreville. Cassidy steered a group from his unit toward a cluster of stone buildings at Mézières, designated "WXYZ" on the field order map, that were serving as a garrison for the German coastal battery at Saint-Martin-de-Varreville.

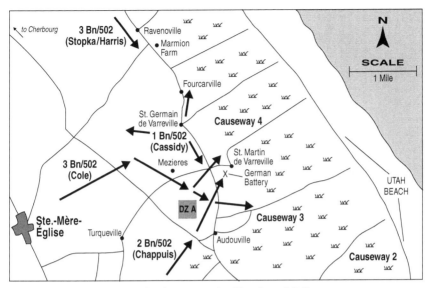

502nd Parachute Infantry Regiment on the Morning of D-Day

Cassidy's men secured the crossroads outside of Mézières and learned that the two exits were open. Another forty-five men from the battalion had joined Cassidy's outfit, so he sent them north to create a defensive perimeter near Foucarville. Cassidy maintained a small body of men near the crossroads to discourage a penetration of the beach from the west, and he sent another group of paratroopers to the eastern side of Mézières to mop up any remaining Germans. A team under command of West Virginia coal miner Staff Sergeant Harrison Summers killed or captured about 150 Germans in a series of small fights.

As the fighting died down, the 502nd regimental commander, Lieutenant Colonel John Michaelis, showed up with two hundred men, allowing the rest of Cassidy's men at the crossroads to follow the other paratroopers to the Foucarville area. Cassidy led the force west to link up with a battalion of the 82nd Airborne expected to drop near Sainte-Mère-Église. On the way, some of his troops tangled with Germans around the village of Foucarville for the remainder of D-Day, while the rest of Cassidy's battalion held the northern perimeter unopposed.

Two battalions of Lieutenant Colonel Robert Sink's 506th PIR were charged with securing the southern sector. Sink's second battalion commander, Lieutenant Colonel Robert Strayer, collected around two hundred men at 3:30 a.m. and, moving south at a rapid pace, captured the area behind Exit 2 at Houdierville.

Brécourt Manor stood between the village of Sainte-Marie-du-Mont and the English Channel. In its fields, No. 6 Battery of the German 90th Artillery Regiment placed four 105mm howitzers in a line hidden by hedgerows, linked by trenches, and protected by machine-gun nests. On D-Day, the guns fired into Exit 2 at Utah Beach leading to the village, disrupting the unloading of men and supplies.

First Lieutenant Richard Winters had taken charge of E ("Easy") Company of the 2nd Battalion, 506th PIR, after the C-47 carrying many of the headquarters staff had crashed into a hedge and blown apart. The 2nd Battalion's operation officer, Captain Clarence Hester, requested that Winters attack the battery. Around 8:30 a.m., Winters and twelve men from E Company and other units went to work. Winters's men snuck toward the first machine-gun nest, while the other paratroopers fired to distract the enemy. As the Americans sneaked closer to the nest, they lobbed grenades and silenced the machine guns. After disabling the first gun position, Winters and the rest of his team used the trenches as covered approaches to attack the remaining guns in turn.

Soldiers destroyed each gun by placing a block of TNT down the barrel and using German stick grenades to ignite the charges. After the four guns were destroyed, Winters's team came under heavy machine-gun fire from Brécourt Manor, and they withdrew. Four American paratroopers were killed and two wounded; fifteen German soldiers were killed and many more were wounded or taken prisoner. Lieutenant Winters received the Distinguished Service Cross for his actions.

On D-Day morning, Colonel Howard Johnson, the knife-throwing 501st PIR commander, had a full slate of tasks ahead of him once he landed in Normandy. Two of his battalions were ordered to seize the locks at La Barquette, which the Germans used to control flooding of the Merderet and Douve valleys. They then had to blow up the bridges on the main highway and the railroad running north from Carentan to Cherbourg. Finally, if time allowed, they were to hold the village of Saint-Côme-du-Mont.

Before any of the three jobs could be accomplished, however, Johnson had to get out of his C-47. When the pilot flipped on the green light, Johnson and the other paratroopers in his stick headed toward the door, where a bundle had slid, blocking the exit. The "fire-eating extrovert" colonel struggled for a bit before the doorway was clear, and then out he went—thirty seconds late.

Tracer bullets, "spouting up like a Roman Candle," whistled past him. Johnson realized that, in battling the bundle in the door, he had inadvertently pulled his reserve parachute cord. He cut the chute away with his jump knife. Once on the ground, Johnson took immediate fire from a German rifleman a mere twenty yards away. Johnson drew his .45 pistol and fired back two shots. Johnson sliced off his harness and rolled a few times until he reached cover under a hedge and bank. He was lucky: because of the delayed jump, he had landed smack in the middle of the drop zone instead of overshooting it like so many others had done.[12]

He got up and headed south, managing to avoid a large building garrisoned by troops from the German 1058th. Along the way, he gathered 150 men from his drop zone and set off to seize the locks at La Barquette before the Germans opened up the flood gates along the Douve River.

But Johnson and his men needn't have worried. Much to their surprise, La Barquette's locks had been left undefended. Johnson had his men dug in on an embankment and the higher ground to the north. They were fired on by Germans positioned on to the south, but they did little harm.

Around the same time, a patrol arrived with word that Johnson's operations officer, Major R. J. Allen, was tangling with a German force a mile away at Basse Addeville. Johnson headed fifty men in that direction. He reached Basse Addeville at 9 a.m. and found Major Allen with a hundred men. Johnson wanted Allen to withdraw to La Barquette with him, but Allen refused to leave his wounded behind.

While Johnson and Allen argued heatedly, Lieutenant Colonel Ballard radioed Johnson to say his 2nd Battalion of 250 men was heavily engaged at les Droueries, a sizeable farm about a thousand yards to the northwest. Johnson requested that Ballard leave his position to concentrate on La Barquette. He also refused, and Johnson backed off. He returned to the lock where he remained for the night with 250 men.[13]

Meanwhile, a thousand yards northeast of Culoville, where Colonel Sink had established his 506th PIR command post, about seventy men from his regiment and paratroopers from Ridgway's 82nd ran into a previously unknown battery at Holdy. The enemy defenses were too strong for the small group, and reinforcements were requested.

Sink sent between seventy and eighty additional men from his 1st Battalion under Captain Lloyd E. Patch of Headquarters Company and Captain Knut H. Raudstein of Company C. When the Germans saw a larger force approaching, they withdrew to some gun emplacements. Rockets fired down on them, and Patch and Raudstein moved the infantry in from two sides and captured the position.

Late in the morning, Sink became restless and worried. He had yet to hear a peep from 3rd Battalion commander Lieutenant Colonel Robert Lee Wolverton. Not until later on would Sink learn that Wolverton, West Point class of 1938, had landed in an apple tree near Saint-Côme-du-Mont. Dangling helplessly, Wolverton had died trying to free himself. When American soldiers eventually recovered his body, they counted about 150 bullet and bayonet wounds. It seems that ruthless German soldiers had used Wolverton for target practice.[14]

Since a soldier had just driven a Jeep to Sink's Culoville headquarters, Sink told his operations officer, Major H. H. Hannah, that they would go "take a look," so they set out on patrol toward Saint-Côme-du-Mont, where 3rd Battalion was supposed to drop. Both officers were lightly armed, with two grenades attached to their torsos and .45 Colts holstered around their hips. Their driver had a carbine across his lap.

A mile past Vierville, they approached a large German horse park. A sentry standing in front of the main gate raised his rifle at the Jeep. Sink and Hannah shot the German before he could discharge his weapon. Suddenly, teams of Germans leaped from the ditches on both sides of the road. Outgunned, Sink and Hannah fired at will with their Colts, while the driver aimed the carbine from his lap. This was enough firepower to send the Germans either into retreat or back to the ditches, and Sink ordered the driver to turn around and go back.

After they made it back safely to Culoville, Sink realized that his and Hannah's grenades still hung from their chests. We "found that we hadn't had sense enough to take off those grenades and toss them amongst those horses and men." Sink thought later that "it would have been so easy and the confusion that would have caused would have been out of this world." He concluded that they simply "forgot that we had them on."[15]

As the battle continued, about forty to fifty additional paratroopers were brought up to Holdy by a lieutenant with the 502nd PIR. Captain Patch placed the lieutenant in charge of the four German 105mm guns and gathered up his own force to attack Sainte Marie-du-Mont from the west. Only about sixty enemy soldiers from the 191st Artillery Regiment held the town.

The small band of Germans put up strong resistance and held the town against Patch's men, but by early afternoon, two battalions from the 8th Infantry Regiment, supported by Sherman tanks from the 70th Tank Battalion, had liberated Sainte-Marie-du-Mont.

Taylor expected the first glider reinforcement operation, code named Chicago, to arrive around four in the morning and provide the 101st Airborne with more men, medical supplies, and heavy equipment for the paratroopers already on the ground.

Assistant division commander Brigadier General Don Pratt flew in the lead glider. The idea of being transported to Normandy in a "Flying Coffin" made Pratt very nervous. Originally, he had planned to land on Utah Beach by landing craft with some of the 101st reserve troops, but he talked Major General Taylor into letting him fly so he could arrive earlier in the day.

Two days before the invasion launched, General Maxwell Taylor visited Pratt in his quarters and threw his cap onto Pratt's bunk.

Known to be superstitious, Pratt ordered, "Don't do that," swiping the cap off the bed. "Don't you know it's unlucky?"[16]

Pratt did not know how unlucky that nonchalant gesture would be.

At 1:10 a.m. on June 6, 1944, Colonel William B. Whitacre rolled his C-47 down the runway at Aldermaston airfield west of London, towing the "Fighting Falcon," a Waco CG-4A glider piloted by Lieutenant

Colonel Michael C. Murphy. Second Lieutenant John M. Butler served as copilot. Two passengers were on board: General Pratt and his aide-de-camp, First Lieutenant John L. May.

Brigadier General Pratt's personal Jeep was strapped in behind Murphy and Butler; it was loaded down with command radio equipment and several extra five-gallon cans of gasoline. Pratt sat on a parachute in the passenger's seat of his vehicle. Before take-off, he read last-minute dispatches by flashlight. Pratt sat slightly higher than May, who took the small jump-seat behind the Jeep. The briefcase in May's lap held top-secret documents and maps.

As Colonel Whitacre lifted off, the tow-line jerked the "Fighting Falcon." Pratt, who was already uneasy about going up in a glider, reached over to squeeze John May's hand. "He was like a little kid," May later told war correspondent Bob Reuben.

Shortly after 4 a.m., just west of the landing zone near the village of Hiesville, where General Taylor had his command post, Colonel Whitacre turned on the green light in the glider's astrodome, a transparent dome fitted in the cabin roof of an aircraft to allow the use of a sextant during astro-navigation, signaling to Murphy to release the tow-cable. Murphy hit the release knob, saying later that it was such a relief because his and Butler's arms and legs ached from trying to keep the aircraft stable after a two-and-a-half-hour ride.

At just 450 feet above the Normandy countryside, Murphy began his descent. In the moonlight, he could make out the LZ, about a thousand feet long and bordered by tree-studded hedgerows. The loaded glider touched down, going about 80 miles per hour on the first third of the LZ. He stomped on the brakes to push the glider up on its nose skid, but the glider kept going. It slid on the dew-covered pasture grass for several hundred feet before smashing into the hedgerow.

Colonel Murphy and Lieutenant May survived the crash. Murphy ended up hanging half in and half out of the plane with his torso still restrained by the seat belt. Both of his legs were broken and his left knee severely injured. Lieutenant May sensed that the glider would hit the hedgerow, so he pressed his body tightly against the seat of the Jeep to absorb the blow. He walked away only bruised and badly cut up.[17]

The others were not so lucky. Copilot Butler's body fell to the floor of the mangled glider. General Pratt, however, remained strapped in the passenger seat of the Jeep, his head, covered by his steel helmet, resting on his chest. He likely suffered whiplash and died from a broken neck.[18] Maxwell Taylor, who said the division "paid a heavy price" with Pratt's death, had him buried in a temporary cemetery with other glider passengers who died on D-Day. The "Fighting Falcon" and its mission that day became legendary.

A chaplain conducted a simple service, without even flowers, as a group of German soldiers on burial duty stood at attention. Pratt, wrapped in a parachute and wearing his jump boots, was placed in the ground without a coffin. Reporter Bob Reuben, noting that "the battle of the day wasn't far from the field" where Pratt was laid to rest, added solemnly, "The guns of General Pratt's boys, fighting close at hand, were all the salute he needed."[19] After the war, Pratt's widow Betty, who received the Purple Heart on her husband's behalf, had his remains shipped to Arlington Cemetery outside Washington, DC.

Sympathy letters filled Betty Pratt's mailbox. One came from Bill Lee, still recovering at his Dunn, North Carolina, home from two heart attacks. He assured Mrs. Pratt that her husband "died a soldier's death—as he would have preferred."

General Eisenhower sent his condolences two days later, telling Pratt's widow that Don Pratt was "a gallant officer and valuable officer—we could not afford to lose him." "Please remember," Eisenhower added, "with just pride, that he made the final sacrifice for his country and for a noble cause and did so unflinchingly."[20]

Even though only six of the gliders from Operation Chicago landed directly on LZ E, fifteen others came down a short distance away. Most of the equipment delivered was in working order. Besides Pratt and Butler, three other glider passengers were killed, seventeen were wounded, and seven were unaccounted for.

That night, there were two more glider operations: Keokuk and Elmira. Named for a city in Iowa, Keokuk resupplied the 101st Airborne. At 6:30 p.m., thirty-two C-47s left Aldermaston Field with thirty-two Horsas in tow carrying nineteen tons of equipment, forty vehicles, six howitzers, and 157 men. For Keokuk, the first daytime glider mission for D-Day's Neptune, the pilots expected to have an easier time landing in LZ E by Hiesville. Glider pilots who'd landed earlier in the day were helped by pathfinders clearing the fields and chopping down trees.

Pathfinders also laid down green smoke and a yellow T panel. Because German troops hadn't been cleared from a surrounding high ground, prep work to help guide the glider into the landing zone had only partially helped. Fourteen men were killed and thirty wounded by enemy fire.

On the evening of June 6, Major General Taylor and chief of staff Colonel Higgins walked the short distance from their stone farmhouse in Hiesville to Colonel Bob Sink's command post at Coulaville.

It was not exactly the safest place for the division commander to be. Twice during the afternoon, Sink came under attack by small bands of Germans. It took his headquarter's forces and even the "walking wounded" to repel the enemy infiltrations.[21]

Sink long had a reputation as one of Taylor's toughest officers and didn't seem concerned about the enemy threat. Back in Camp Toccoa, Georgia, where the 506th trained before deployment to England, Sink pushed his men so hard that one wrote home to his mother and complained about his commanding officer. She, in turn, contacted her congressman, who paid a visit to Sink.

After a chewing out by the congressman, Sink called his men together and threatened that "the next guy who has a Congressman talk to me will wish they were dead." Private Jim "Pee Wee" Martin witnessed the tirade, but he and most of the other paratroopers in the 506th grew to appreciate Sink, especially when they fought under his command at Normandy. "He didn't coddle us," Martin remembered. "He made men out of boys."[22]

During the conference at Coulaville, fortunately, Taylor didn't come under fire when he, Sink, and Higgins discussed the next morning's attack plan, which included the main road and bridges north of Carentan. Taylor would have to accomplish that objective at half-strength. By the end of D-Day, of the 6,600 men who had dropped into Normandy that morning, about 3,500 were reported missing, almost 200 had been killed in action, and 537 were listed as wounded.[23]

26

The Airborne Angels of Mercy

"Angels of Mercy."

That's what Private Tom Mulligan called the medical personnel attached to the airborne divisions.

They saved his life on D-Day.

Mulligan landed nowhere near his drop zone by the village of Valognes, about three in the morning on June 6. Immediately, he and two other troopers from a field artillery battalion of the 101st Airborne Division were attacked by a squad of Germans.

Enemy fire hit Mulligan in the face and stomach. For a day, he lay in a field, German guns pointed at him the whole time. After finally being taken to a POW enclosure, he encountered his battalion surgeon, Captain Felix Adams. That same morning, Adams had dropped into the backyard of a German command post, and he, too, was immediately captured. He spent the day treating wounded POWs. Adams saw that Mulligan was in rough shape. Adams had no anesthesia, so he told Mulligan "to get loaded but good." He successfully removed one of the bullets. Adams, Mulligan would later recall, was "truly [my] Angel of Mercy."

Airborne medical personnel like Captain Adams not only were skillfully trained in treating wounded soldiers but also had earned their boots and wings at Fort Benning like other 82nd and 101st paratroopers.

On D-Day, many of them jumped from C-47s. Eight doctors and corpsmen from the 307th Medical Company dropped alongside General Ridgway. Throughout the day, more surgeons and medics came to Normandy by glider; others arrived by landing craft onto Utah Beach. No matter how they arrived in Normandy, however, their mission was the same: set up aid stations and hospitals and prepare for the onslaught of paratrooper casualties.[1]

Colonel Paul Hayes, a graduate of the Army's Medical School at Walter Reed and VII Corps chief surgeon, commanded the medical personnel at Utah. Hayes ensured that they had extra supplies and equipment—"either carried on their persons, parachuted down in special containers, or packed in glider-borne vehicles."

The 101st hauled large quantities of blankets and two thousand units of plasma. A couple of gliders carried the division's field artillery and were crammed with large-caliber guns and soldiers assigned to operate them, as well as two complete sets of aid-station equipment.

Private Mulligan's ordeal echoed that of many airborne medical personnel. Colonel Hayes estimated that 50 percent of the medical officers attached to Ridgway's 82nd Division "were unaccounted for during the first seventy-two hours of combat," while about 20 percent of the 101st medical personnel were casualties during the entire Normandy campaign, most of them killed, wounded, or taken prisoner in the first days.

Throughout June 6, countless individual acts of heroism by paratroopers aided their wounded comrades. Lieutenant Colonel Patrick J. Cassidy and surgeon Captain Frank Choy from the 1st Battalion, 502nd PIR, 101st, acquired a small cart and found a horse to pull it. They handed it over to a dental technician within the battalion to drive it.

"All day long," according to a battalion report, "this boy drove up and down the roads, exposing himself to sniper fire, working like a Trojan, to bring in the wounded and the parachutists who had been hurt on the jump; his energy saved countless lives."[2]

Regardless of whether a medic was actually a licensed physician, wounded soldiers in dire need of treatment referred to all medical personnel as "Doc." Prior to the war, Private Henry "Mouse" Rapp, a medic in the 501st PIR, had worked in a pet hospital. He had quit high school his sophomore year to become an acrobat in a carnival. Then he switched to tumbling with the Pantages Circuit, a vaudeville act. Finally, he moved up to master of ceremonies in a Chicago burlesque theater. None of Rapp's prior jobs qualified him to treat battlefield casualties, but his "screwball" antics in the unit made him quite popular.[3]

Like Rapp, Private Cledis Whitaker's antebellum life did not presage his war work as a medic. Whitaker had farmed and worked construction in Kentucky's rural Floyd County before becoming a medic with the 326th Medical Company. Walker arrived in one of the first gliders into Normandy. His plane and another one landed safely in a field, but three more gliders carrying medics, doctors, and equipment crashed. For two hours after landing, Whitaker and other medics cared for the crash victims, the medics oblivious to enemy soldiers surrounding them. Forcing the Americans to remove their boots but allowing them to keep their socks, the Germans marched the prisoners for the rest of the day and throughout the night to waiting trucks.

Driven to a temporary POW camp near the Orne River, Whitaker survived mainly on grass cooked in water—not all that appetizing, but he had to eat something. Later, the Germans supplemented his diet with a half-cup of milk per day. Not until five or six days after landing, when the Germans sent Whitaker to Stalag 221 in Brittany, France, did he receive a pair of wooden shoes to wear.[4]

Medics weren't the only "angels of mercy" on this battlefield on this day: they served side by side with Army chaplains. Father Ignatius Maternowski, a Catholic priest from Holyoke, Massachusetts, jumped with the 508th PIR, 82nd Division. He landed into the hamlet of Guetteville, about five miles west of Sainte-Mère-Église. It seemed only natural that he teamed up with a medic to establish an aid station at a café/grocery store. Maternowski treated badly wounded paratroopers whom he had discovered in a downed glider. They were treated in the small hospital, but a German counterattack in Guetteville made it dangerous for them to remain.

So Maternowski took action. Wearing a Red Cross arm band as well as his chaplain insignia, his helmet attached to his belt, he crossed over enemy lines to meet with a German medical officer. Maternowski proposed that the two sides set up a joint hospital in a house on the edge of town.

The Germans agreed to consider the offer and walked with the chaplain to assess the area; afterward, Maternowski escorted him back to his command post. When the chaplain walked toward the American lines, a German sniper bullet struck Maternowski in the back, killing him instantly.

His lifeless body lay in the road; heavy fighting made recovery too dangerous. After three days, a 90th Division infantry unit removed Maternowski's remains. He was buried temporarily at Utah Beach and now lies eternally in a cemetery near his Massachusetts hometown.[5]

Another perfect example of chaplain heroism was Father Francis Sampson. After he and his assistant dodged crashed and burning C-47s, they walked along the side of a road, concealed in the thick hedgerows, in hopes of finding other men from the 501st PIR. They soon stumbled upon a half dozen paratroopers running down the road ditch. Although not from Sampson's regiment, they pointed in the direction to a farmhouse where they could find other soldiers from the 501st.

Inside the three-room farmhouse, there were about twenty-five wounded paratroopers, as well as the French farmer, his wife, and young daughter. Sampson, his assistant, and a medic helped another chaplain dispense first aid for most of the day until the house was struck by a German mortar round, killing the French woman and her child. "The poor farmer nearly went out of his head," Sampson remembered.

By 6 p.m., the situation in the house grew dire. Patients were getting worse, and Sampson decided it best to set out and find a doctor. About a mile down the road, he ran into an American patrol engaged in a firefight. They pointed him toward a regimental aid station. To reach it safely, Sampson left the road and headed into a deep swamp. "It was filthy and cold," he recalled, "but afforded good cover."

As he reached the aid station, the fight grew in intensity, with the Germans gaining the upper hand. The officer in command chose to withdraw to higher ground and take the walking wounded with him. The soldiers too injured to move would have to stay behind. Chaplain Sampson chose to stay back with them. He made a white flag from a sheet and hung it out the door, hoping the Germans would show him and the wounded some mercy.

For two days, Sampson single-handedly cared for the wounded as German shells pelted the house. During a four-hour artillery barrage that left the structure barely standing, Sampson still managed to administer plasma and other aid. At one point, as three shells penetrated the building, Sampson threw his body over the wounded to protect them. Sampson could count himself among the wounded when a tracer bullet inflicted a second-degree burn. He ignored the pain and continued to unselfishly treat his patients.

On the morning of the third day, the Germans left the area, and an evacuation party arrived and took the wounded to a division hospital. Instead of going with them to have his burn treated, Sampson returned to the hospital he had left three days before and continued to provide physical and spiritual aid to the injured paratroopers who had yet to be evacuated. For his "courage, heroism, and fortitude," Sampson was awarded the Distinguished Service Cross.[6]

Throughout D-Day and for the next few days, treating the wounded was hampered by significant loss of medical equipment. "Equipment losses were equally heavy," Colonel Hayes wrote in his summary. "The 101st recovered only 30 percent of its air-dropped supply containers." He later concluded that it was a mistake to drop so much materiel in the early hours when the surgeons did not yet need it and darkness made it almost impossible to find.

During the first few hours of D-Day, medical officers and men who found their way to battalion assembly areas set up "rough-and-ready aid stations," usually near their unit's command posts. At these stations, "surgeons improvised, scavenging for supplies, seizing farm wagons and captured enemy vehicles to transport wounded."[7] Medics set up aid stations at churches, along roadsides, and in open fields, but they preferred farmhouses or, even better, large chateaux.[8]

An advance element of the 101st's 326th Airborne Medical Company, led by Major Albert J. Crandall, parachuted in with the infantry. They improvised a small hospital in a French farmhouse, Chateau Colombierre, near Hiesville, where, earlier, General Taylor had established his division's command post.

Crandall selected five paratroopers from the 506th PIR to secure the chateau. As the party approached, a shot came from the stable. A paratrooper collapsed to the ground. The other paratroopers retaliated and neutralized the threat. Crandall took cover in a ditch while a couple of the paratroopers hovered near him as bodyguards. A sniper's shot killed one of them. An American rifle team came into the yard, followed by reinforcements. The teams burst through the chateau door, but all they found was a French family, who welcomed them.

The paratroopers declared the house safe, so Crandall set up his hospital, but the paratroopers were dead wrong. More shots rang out in the courtyard, and enemy fire continued for the next four days. Crandall was too busy to worry about the danger: he set up an operating room in the milk house because it had a concrete floor, large windows, and a pump that provided spring water. He converted the living room into a shock ward, and the kitchen became a small operating room.

Even with enemy snipers lurking nearby, the courtyard became a reception station. For litters, the medics used window casings, feed troughs, kitchen tables, and ladders.[9] Surgeons worked at three tables, as the chateau courtyard filled with casualties brought in on improvised litters, horses, and captured trucks. By the day's end, the exhausted surgeons, who subsisted on chocolate bars and Benzedrine, had treated about three hundred patients.

Even though D-Day came to an end, the fighting intensified in the days and weeks that followed, translating into an even greater need for medics and chaplains and sympathetic French families—all Angels of Mercy.

27

The End of a Very Long Day

No one had ever seen Stuart Milner-Barry so excited.

For almost three years, Milner-Barry, a Cambridge University graduate, former stockbroker, and devoted chess player, had been in charge of Bletchley Park's Hut 6. He spent his days reading messages that his 450 codebreakers encrypted through the Germans' Enigma machine.

Not until late in the morning on June 6 did they know whether the fruits of their labor had affected the outcome of a battle—or even of a large-scale operation.

Such was the case a couple of weeks before D-Day: Intercepts showed that the German 91st Division had moved into Normandy and sat squarely in the middle of the three drop zones designated for Matthew Ridgway's 82nd Division. The deciphered data quickly made its way to Omar Bradley's First Army headquarters. Furiously, Bradley, the airborne commanders, and SHAEF staff worked to change the drop zones in hopes of averting the decimation of the All-Americans.

Milner-Barry excitedly relayed that message to his rapt, startled audience in Hut 6. Entering the Watch Room, he called for attention: "Ladies and gentlemen, may I interrupt you, please. I wish to congratulate you because you have just saved 15,000 American lives."[1]

Milner-Barry's number was off—by a lot: he'd more than doubled the number (the 82nd dropped more than six thousand men into Normandy). The difference was trivial, for every one of the six thousand paratroopers who survived on D-Day owed a debt of gratitude to the brilliant cryptanalysts at Bletchley, whose work has only recently been appreciated due to the Official Secrets Act that denied them publicity until now.

Back at the airfield in southern England, pilots and their crews were debriefed about their missions. In many instances, the same C-47s flew to Normandy twice. First, they flew during the main airborne drops; then, later that morning or in the evening, the planes went back, towing gliders full of Jeeps, heavy guns, and other supplies and equipment desperately needed by the paratroopers on the ground.

Some of the C-47s that flew double missions had been badly beat up by flak on the first run. A C-47 crewed by operations officer Major Thomas E. Nunn provided a glimpse of what he encountered during Operation Elmira in a short note to his wife, Anabel, after whom the plane was nicknamed "Tug Boat Annie." Disclaiming being a "philosopher" or "master of words," Nunn wrote, "Wish I could convey the thoughts we have on the run-in, twenty-four hours after unleashing a glider over Normandy on the evening of D-Day, with tracers whipping through the air like a big whip." While in the air over Normandy, he added, "in a way it is a beautiful sight, but darling, believe me, every one of us is scared as hell and you've never seen such a bunch of flying fools as our squadron. We are all praise for the airplane too. They'll fly with an awful lot of parts missing."[2]

The damaged C-47 reflected the sagas of Ridgway's and Taylor's experiences on June 6. Between the two divisions, rather than one long, hard fight, the day had seen between fifteen and twenty separate battles. Casualties were heavy (roughly 2,500 killed, wounded, and missing)— but, again, nowhere near what Leigh-Mallory had predicted.

On the afternoon of June 6, Leigh-Mallory apologized to Eisenhower for having stirred up the pot a week before over his fear of tremendous airborne casualties. "You can imagine my relief," he dictated in his diary entry on June 6, "when I heard that their (airborne) casualties had been light. A chance had been taken and it has come off. I am writing in this sense to the Supreme Commander-in-Chief."[3]

According to Eisenhower, Leigh-Mallory didn't send a message to him but had called "to express his regret that he had found it necessary to add to my personal burdens during the final tense days before D-Day."[4]

Scattered drops of men with loss of materiel hindered many of the day's goals. The unforgiving hedgerow terrain of Normandy complicated efforts to assemble men, who, in many instances, had dropped within a few hundred yards of each other. Units became entangled. It wasn't unusual to have paratroopers from both divisions fighting together for brief periods. Because radios were lost, communication, especially with the 82nd Division, was lost as well. The only way for Ridgway to maintain contact with his men was to hike to where they were fighting—not out of the ordinary for him (or for Taylor).

Despite these complications, most of the day's objectives were met. Sainte-Mère-Église had been liberated, although La Fière remained in German hands. The causeways from Utah Beach had been seized by the Screaming Eagles, allowing 4th Infantry Division to break out.

The scattered drops had been a blessing in disguise. German troop guards became confused when Americans landed all around, so the expected enemy aggressiveness, moderately weak at first, strengthened as the day progressed.

At the 6th Parachute Regiment Command Post in the village of Saint-Georges-de-Bohon, commander of 12 Company Oberleutnant Martin Pöppel rushed to his observation post after receiving reports that there had been parachute drops in the whole area.

This was confirmed when three wounded American paratroopers were brought in as prisoners and interrogated, but the Germans learned nothing from them. In response to every question, the Americans said, "I don't know." As more prisoners were brought in, the Germans enjoyed the American rations of cigarettes, chocolates, biscuits, and gum.

"These are big fellows from the United States," Pöppel recorded in his diary; they are "giants of men with beefy faces. Their equipment is only of moderate quality in general, but the medical equipment is impressive. Each soldier is carrying morphine and tetanus injections."

As the Germans fanned out into the countryside looking for more paratroopers, still unaware if the drops into Normandy were the main Allied assault or a diversion from a larger one in the Pas des Calais, they saw parachutes hanging all over the area and grabbed them. The Germans tore them into strips and turned them into scarves.[5]

Like the paratroopers' experiences that Colonel Barney Oldfield's airborne correspondents would write about, the reporters also had mixed results on D-Day. Oldfield stayed behind in London. By four in the morning on June 6, all the Airborne journalists had made the "short distance from static or tow-line to the ground."[6] Reuters correspondent Bob Reuben released his first story by carrier pigeon across the English Channel, but the frightened bird didn't know whether to "fly high or low." Phil Bucknell with *Stars and Stripes* landed hard after parachuting into Normandy, breaking his leg near Sainte-Mère-Église. After one of the paratroopers propped him up against a tree, Bucknell asked not to be left behind. The paratrooper responded abruptly, "If I were you, I'd just stay here real quiet-like. If you make any noise, you may attract someone you don't want to see." Then he left.

Like Bucknell, *Time* magazine's Bill Walton also had quite an experience on D-Day morning. Landing in a pear tree, he hung from a branch only a few feet from the ground. A small Hermes typewriter remained tightly strapped to his parachute harness, which had tightened so much it prevented him from grabbing his hunting knife, which he had placed in his breast pocket. Shortly afterward, he heard someone approach.

Paratrooper?

German soldier?

Unsure, Walton whispered the password: "Flash."

The voice in the dark responded in a Midwestern accent: "Thunder."

Walton replied, "Welcome."

The voice belonged to a sergeant with the last name of Auge, whom Walton had met back in England. Auge cut Walton down, who then set off with a mixed bag of paratroopers toward Sainte-Mère-Église. As he approached the town, he learned that it wasn't yet safe to enter, so he joined a group of paratroopers curled up under a tree.

Grabbing a parachute laying nearby, Walton lay down and fell fast asleep. Probably out for only a few moments, he was jolted awake by a soldier, who said they had orders to move out. Before leaving, Walton shook the other soldiers next to them.

They did not move.

They were dead.

Back on the road in the direction of Sainte-Mère-Église, Walton could see in the growing light of day that the picturesque Normandy that

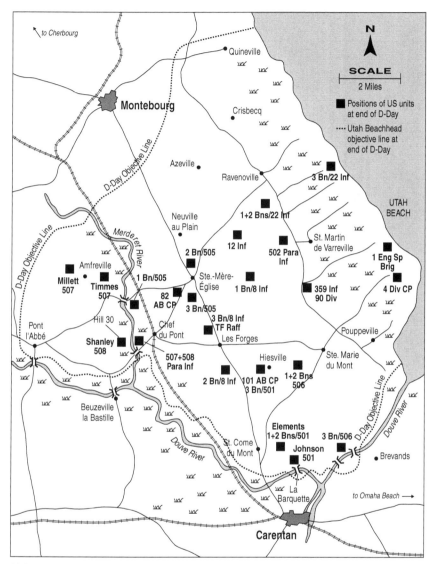

Airborne Units at the End of D-Day

he had heard so much about presented itself now as a shell-pocked war zone. Trees were splintered. Equipment lay smashed on the road and in ditches and fields. Black and white cows, as lifeless as the paratroopers he had left behind, lay in pastures.[7]

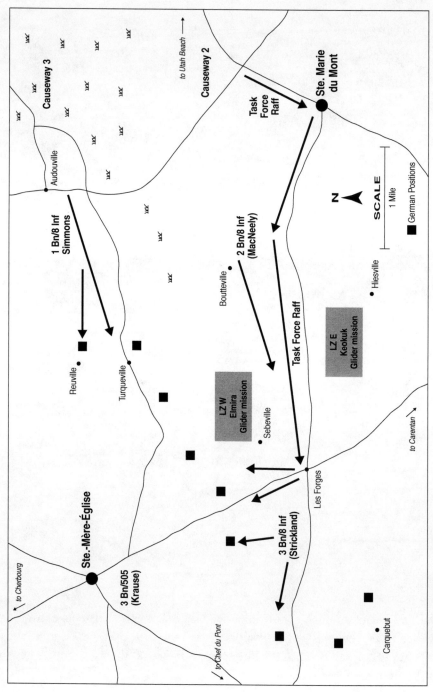

Evening Glider Missions on D-Day

Marshall Yarrow with Reuters bounced unhurt into a Normandy field near Sainte-Mère-Église after his glider clipped five of Rommel's "asparagus." Wright Bryan, the stringer for NBC/*Atlanta Journal-Constitution*, returned to Normandy that evening by glider; his historic broadcast had introduced the Airbornes' exploits that morning.[8]

Like the American Airborne divisions, the 5th and 3rd British parachute brigades elsewhere in Normandy experienced similarly poor drops and lost equipment; still, they also managed to achieve their objectives. They captured the Orne River and Caen Canal bridges and held them until reinforced by amphibious troops landing on Sword Beach. The "Paras," as the British Army nicknamed the paratroopers who captured the Merville Battery, blew up four key bridges over the Dives River. Like Ridgway's and Taylor's men, these paratroopers caught the Germans unaware, which led to panic.

In the late hours of June 5, Luftwaffe command alerted Oberleutenant Dietrich, a communications officer with 6 Paratrooper Regiment. "Allied troop carrier planes in England are active," Dietrich informed the regimental commander, Major Friedrich von der Heydte, who ordered his men to prepare for battle.

Shortly after midnight on June 6, paratroopers were spotted landing between the coast and Carentan. These were the 101st Division pathfinders.[9]

Private Paul Golz, a machine gunner stationed in Normandy with the German Grenadier Regiment 1057 of the 91st Air Infantry Division, tells that story from the Germans' point of view. Golz had grown up on a farm in Pomerania (now part of Poland) and had planned to be a farmer like his father. In August 1939, German troops came through Golz's village, and he played soccer with them.

When he turned sixteen in 1941, he attended agricultural school in Rummelsburg, Germany. Golz did not get very far in his studies because he was rounded up with nineteen other boys and taken to a doctor for a physical examination. Then he and the other young men had to take intelligence tests. Finally, Gloz was brought before a recruiting officer. "What branch of the SS do you want to join?" the officer asked the young man.

Golz had no interest in the Schutzstaffel, Hitler's paramilitary organization, and said so. "What?" responded the officer and added seductively, "You have a nice uniform! You get driven around!"

"No, I don't want to," Golz insisted.

The officer dismissed him. "Then pack your bags and get out of here."

Golz went back to his family farm, but two years later, in September 1943, he was forced into military training. His father, a World War I veteran, schooled him in ethics: "If the soldier from the other side has a weapon, then he is the enemy. But if you take his weapon away, he is a human being just like you and me."

During his initial training, Golz's machine-gun unit learned how to fire at gliders. "I thought they would be easy to shoot down," he later wrote; however, he added, "I did not like the idea of flying in them."

A year later, he was with his outfit in Normandy, and at night, the men were ordered to keep watch for enemy attack. Instead of billeting in the nearby villages, they dug holes along the ridges to camp. During the day, the Grenadiers were ordered to plant Rommel's "asparagus" (those green poles) along with the French laborers. Golz was jealous of them because they had bottles of wine to drink, while the Germans had only water.

On June 6, Golz was on guard duty from 2 a.m. to 6 a.m. At about three o'clock, the sky was colored like decorated *tannenbaums*. But the lights were not from Christmas trees: they were from flares dropped by Allied planes to mark preinvasion bombing sites. Then Golz saw "very many parachutes," so, he thought, the invasion must be on.

Later in the morning, Golz assembled with his unit, and they were sent to Sainte-Mère-Église. But it was too late: the 82nd Airborne had already liberated the town.

Dejected, they moved into a big field enclosed by hedgerows. In daylight, for the first time, Golz viewed the destruction from the early morning fighting. He saw crashed gliders, including two that had smashed into each other. The ground was covered in white, as though snow had fallen. Parachutes were everywhere in the grass. The Germans grabbed the material they thought was silk to send home to be made into wedding dresses. However, the United States was at war with Japan, the source of silk, so the American parachutes were actually made of nylon.

Hungry and thirsty, Golz sought chocolate and water. As he moved toward a hedge, he saw something moving, and as he edged closer, he could see it was a white sock on top of a rifle barrel—a sign of surrender. The American paratrooper trembled, his face covered in black. He put down his weapon, looked at Golz, and said, "Good water," or "*Gutes Wasser.*" The American was taken off to a POW collection point.

Golz, not sure who was in charge, marched off with his division, finding out later that his commander, General Wilhelm Falley, had been killed that day. On his way back from Rennes, where he had taken part in a war game, Falley was on the road leading to division headquarters at Picauville. That's where his vehicle was ambushed by Lieutenant Malcolm D. Brannen, who led Headquarters Company, 508th PIR.[10]

When Brannen told General Ridgway what he had done, the 82nd commander said, "Well, in our present situation, killing division commanders does not strike me as being particularly hilarious. But I congratulate you. I'm glad it was a German division commander you got."[11]

Golz and another soldier (surnamed Schneider) were ordered to look for other paratroopers in the fields where Golz had seen his first dead soldier, leaning against the stones at the foot of a hedgerow. Schneider picked the dead paratrooper's pockets, taking first his wallet containing a photo of the soldier standing next to a woman with blonde hair. Behind them was the New York skyline.

Golz remonstrated with Schneider: "It is not yours. Leave it."

Schneider said, "No, I like it. I will take it."

"No," Golz said angrily. "He needs it for identification."

Schneider then tried to take off a big gold ring from the American's finger, but the ring wouldn't budge from the stiff finger. Schneider pulled out a knife to cut it off. Golz had had enough. He pulled up his rifle and pointed it at Schneider.

"If you do that, then I will blow you away!" Schneider backed off. Golz figured later that Schneider would be glad Golz had stopped him.[12]

Elsewhere behind Utah Beach, other German troops were bewildered by the American paratroopers. There were so many of them scattered about that they were hard to track. They could not see the big picture that reporters like Bob Reuben provided of the 82nd and 101st Airborne on

D-Day: "The airborne forces had struck swiftly, destroying enemy installations, cleared vital areas so landings could be made without serious loss. And the paratroopers didn't stop there. They pushed on . . . fighting their style of fighting each inch of the way."[13]

This impressive showing had been accomplished even though only 10 percent of the paratrooper sticks had reached their drop zones. About half of the men landed four miles away; many others were dropped ten to twenty miles from where they should have been. Men and supplies, especially the prized radios, ended up in rivers and marshes. Only the 505th PIR from 82nd Division achieved accurate drops.

Of the combined thirteen thousand American paratroopers who had taken off from England in darkness on June 5, only 1,500 troopers from the 82nd and 1,100 men from the 101st were available to fight early on June 6. Another day or two passed before the straggling paratroopers lined up with their units.

Then—and only then—did the Germans feel the full brunt of Ridgway's and Taylor's forces.[14]

28

Crossing the La Fière Causeway

At first light on June 7, La Fière was still up for grabs.

Ridgway's paratroopers tenuously held on along the riverbank, by the bridge, the causeway, and the neighboring hamlet of Cauquigny. The Germans remained close by on their side of the river and continually reminded the Americans with mortar and artillery shelling that they hadn't left and had no intention of doing so.

Around ten that morning, the German firepower reached a new intensity, followed by two tanks and a couple of infantry battalions on the western end of the causeway. The enemy advanced behind the artillery barrage and reached the bridge. The lead tank was shattered by an antitank gun that Major Mark Alexander, 2nd Battalion, 505th PIR, had recovered the previous day. German infantry made repeated attempts to reach the American positions, but each time they were driven back.[1]

The fighting continued well into the afternoon until the Germans asked Major Alexander for a truce to collect their dead and wounded. Alexander agreed, and, for thirty minutes, some two hundred enemy soldiers were removed from the battlefield. The Germans also used the interlude to withdraw to Cauquigny. The Americans had likewise suffered in the fight: Red Dog Dolan had seventeen men killed and more than fifty wounded.[2]

General Gavin witnessed the day's action from a foxhole with war correspondent Bill Walton. Gavin encouraged him to leave: "You know, you don't have to stay here." Walton asked what he meant by that. Gavin responded, "We can't hold . . . but we are not going to give up. . . . We are going to keep at it."[3]

Now that the fighting seemed to have let up, at least temporarily, Gavin decided to take another crack at Chef-du-Pont. Lieutenant Colonel Thomas J. B. Shanley, in command of 2nd Battalion, 508th PIR, and three hundred men were holding a defensive position on Hill 30. The Germans had made several attempts to remove them from the small knoll west of the Merderet and north of the Chef-du-Pont causeway. So far, Shanley had driven off the enemy attacks, but he wasn't sure how long that would last. He informed Gavin that he was running out of food, water, and medical supplies.

Gavin sent Colonel Lindquist, commander of 508th PIR, to Chef-du-Pont. Lindquist relieved Captain Roy Creek, who had held the town despite taking heavy losses. Lindquist now had to secure the causeway and resupply Shanley on the west bank of the Merderet.

Lindquist contacted Shanley by radio and runner and advised him to clear the road, which ran southwest from the causeway to Pont-l'Abbé in Brittany. Lindquist would then send a rescue convoy across the causeway. Shanley agreed and deployed twenty-three men and two officers, who pushed out the Germans and continued fighting east across the causeway.

The party reported to Lindquist, but by the time they reached him, the causeway was under attack from German artillery. Lindquist refused to send the relief party, fearing it was too dangerous to attempt the mission. Shanley had to hold on for another two hours until he was relieved by a battalion of 90th Division.[4]

Back in La Fière, General Ridgway arrived at the heavily contested battleground on June 8 and ordered an attack to capture the causeway the next day. The plan was to reach Colonel Timmes, still isolated in the orchard east of Amfreville, as well as four hundred paratroopers northwest of that town with 507th PIR commander Colonel George Millet. Major Teddy Sanford from 1st Battalion, 325th Glider Infantry Regiment, would lead the operation.[5]

Sanford would move north along the railway, cross the river above La Fière, and then head south to capture the west end of the causeway. There, he would establish a bridgehead and connect with Timmes and Millett. By that time, Millett would have joined Timmes east of Amfreville.[6]

After sunset on June 8, Sanford and Millett simultaneously converged on Timmes's position, but Millett's men never made it. Their column came under fire in the dark and fell apart. Millett and several other officers and men became separated from the main column and were captured. Germans firing from a group of buildings sent the rest of the group fleeing northwest toward the river.

Sanford's battalion was initially much more successful. It was guided by a paratrooper from Timmes's patrol across the marshes and onto dry ground. As Sanford's men approached Timmes's position, they took fire from the same Germans who had harassed Millett's men. One company from Sanford's battalion veered off to clear the buildings while the rest of the battalion tried to seize the west end of the causeway but failed. German defenders stopped the paratroopers cold, forcing them back, with numerous casualties to Timmes's lines.

Under the cover of darkness, Sanford and Timmes's combined force headed toward Cauquigny, but their attack failed. The Germans were well entrenched, so couldn't be budged. Sanford alerted Ridgway of their predicament and that they were withdrawing back to Timmes's position and preparing for an expected counterattack.

One of Sanford's men, twenty-three-year-old Private Charles N. DeGlopper from Company C, stood up in the face of the enemy. He fired his Browning automatic rifle (BAR) to cover the withdrawal until a German bullet killed him. For his bravery that day, DeGlopper, from Grand Island, New York, would posthumously receive the Medal of Honor, the only man in the 82nd to receive his country's highest decoration.[7]

In reflecting on Sanford's failure to take the causeway, Gavin had this to say: "It was a great deal to ask of a battalion that had not been in combat. . . . The Germans counterattacked violently and by sheer numbers overwhelmed the inexperienced glidermen."[8]

Captain Roy Creek had taken part in separate fighting near Chef-du-Pont. Following an exchange of heavy artillery fire, the attack commenced about ten in the morning on June 8. Captain Creek later recalled that the incoming fire was so intense that the thought "passed through his mind that no one would survive it." Creek moved about the area, checking on the men. Gavin was also in the thick of it. Creek remembered he "seemed to be everywhere, sometimes exhorting reluctant troops to heroic action."

When the shelling increased, Creek thought it wise to seek protection. He jumped into the nearest foxhole and found it "already occupied by a frightened young soldier." Creek didn't recognize him, nor did the soldier know who Creek was. Regardless, they reassured each other that "unless one had your name on it, you would surely survive."

Creek got up to leave and bent down to thank the young paratrooper for letting him share the foxhole: he saw that a large shell fragment had penetrated the top of his helmet. "He was dead, killed while we were talking," Creek recalled, "and I never learned his name. Incidents like these are the horrible things one remembers about war."[9]

On June 9, when Ridgway learned that the latest effort to take La Fière had failed, he told Gavin "to get the Merderet crossing . . . [and] get it without delay." Ridgway now had extra pressure to seize the causeway because, at the same time, the 90th Infantry Division was attacking westward across the base of the Cotentin Peninsula through the 82nd Division sector. It would need to cross the La Fière causeway heading toward Sainte Sauveur-le-Vicomte in order to commence the advance on Cherbourg.

Gavin would spearhead the attack with the division reserve, Lieutenant Colonel Charles Carrell's 2nd Battalion, 401st Glider Battalion. Carrell would be supported by Sherman tanks from Task Force Raff that were positioned overlooking the high ground while the 90th Division would provide artillery support.

The attack began precisely at 10:30 a.m. with an intense bombardment. "For about fifteen minutes," Gavin recalled, "we poured everything we had right on top of the German positions." Forty-five minutes later, Gavin looked at Carrell and told him it was time to go. "I don't think I can do it," Carrell replied. "I'm sick." He was replaced by Major Arthur Gardner. Ridgway later had Carrell transferred from the 82nd, and he ended up in 90th Division.

Gardner may not have been the best choice to lead the attack. Most of the men didn't know him, and when he shouted "Go! Go! Go!" only a few paratroopers heeded his command.

Before relieving Carrell, Gavin had selected Captain John Sauls's G Company to lead the attack. Gavin gave him the order, and Sauls took off, jumping through a hole in the stone wall in the causeway and over the bridge. His second platoon followed closely behind him, but the remainder of G Company got held up by German machine guns fired from the far bank. Some of enemy weapons zeroed in on the hole in the wall where Sauls and the other troopers passed through.

Next up was Captain Charles Murphy's E Company. It blazed the same trail as Sauls' Company G into the causeway. The German fire had now become ruthless, with guns from both flanks cutting down the charging paratroopers. Because there were so many dead and wounded on the roadway, it was slow going for Captain James M. Harney's F Company. His men were also blocked by German POWs, who were coming from the opposite direction after tossing aside their weapons and heading to the American lines unescorted.[10]

As the German fire raked the paratroopers, Captain Robert D. Rae and Colonel Maloney led about ninety men into the causeway, screaming at them to keep moving. As men dropped all around them, Rae directed the survivors to the west bank, where they fanned out and took cover.

During the midst of the battle, General Ridgway could be seen on the causeway carrying his .30-06 rifle. An American tank had been disabled after hitting a mine, which prevented other tanks from passing through. With mortar shells exploding all around him, Ridgway grabbed a towline and cleared the wreckage and pushed his men forward.

At Cauquigny, the Americans were gaining ground against fierce German opposition. Late that afternoon, the Germans counterattacked against the 325th Glider Regiment, causing them to fall back. Gavin watched what was happening with absolute disbelief and called for his men to launch their own counterattack.

The paratroopers rushed down the fields and hedgerows to the next town, Le Motey, a stone's throw from Amfreville and believed to be the German assembling point. Artilleryman John Devine's long-range 155mm howitzers supported the assault. To the right, Timmes and Sanford attacked in the same direction. As one of Ridgway's biographers put it, "the counterattack was not a model of perfection." Indeed, the battle saw much confusion, but by nightfall, Le Motey had been reoccupied and the final threat to La Fière eliminated.

Ridgway's paratroopers were relieved the next morning by the 90th Division. The last of Ridgway's main objectives had been reached, but there was still plenty of hard fighting ahead.

29

Seizing the Carentan Causeway

On the morning of June 7, 1944 (D+1), Colonel Sink spearheaded the day's attack. His 1st Battalion, 506th PIR, would strike at the railroad bridges across the Douve River to keep German armor from passing over them and threatening the American flank. This operation prepared the 101st for an assault on Carentan.

Between his 1st Battalion under Lieutenant Colonel William L. Turner and the 2nd Battalion under Lieutenant Colonel Robert L. Strayer, Sink had roughly 525 men for the operation. Sink also had about forty men from 82nd Airborne, some 326th Engineers, and a battery from the 81st Airborne AAA (American Anti-Aircraft) Battalion carrying eight six-pound antitank guns.[1]

This was a far greater concentration of Screaming Eagles than any of Taylor's other regiments. After being scattered far from their DZs, many of Sink's paratroopers had missed the first day's fighting. They began trickling into regimental headquarters on D-Day afternoon, during the night, and well into the predawn hours of June 7.

Master Sergeant Lloyd E. Willis from Sink's regiment was among the cluster of latecomers. Willis dropped into an orchard and didn't know that, beyond the soaring hedgerows all around him, the 506th PIR assembly was only four hundred yards away. Willis stripped off his parachute harness and set out in the dark to find other paratroopers. He wandered aimlessly for several hours, becoming trapped within the maze of tall vegetation, seldom seeing "more than one hundred yards in any direction."

Eventually, he stumbled upon a group of twenty-five men, including some from his regiment's Headquarters Company. The others belonged to various 82nd Division units. This mixed bag of lost paratroopers was drawn into a couple of small skirmishes. "You go along and join a group," Wills wrote. "The group goes along and is fired upon. Then you engage. Everybody has to wait until the road is clear again. The larger the group, the harder it is to get by without fighting." Willis eventually reached Culoville at 10:30 a.m. on June 7.[2]

Captain Laurence Critchell sympathized with the plight of Willis and other paratroopers lost in the dense landscape of Normandy. In his history of the 506th, Critchell wrote that "for a man to crawl through the hedgerows was almost impossible." The "twisted roots," Critchell recalled, "were close together and immovable." A soldier could try and climb over the hedgerows, but, if he did, "it was unlikely that he would be alive to reach the ground on the other side."[3]

At 4:30 a.m., Sink's paratroopers started their advance toward the railroad bridge. As Critchell noted, this attack would be the first attempt by the 101st "to act with forces in excess of the scattered Indian bands" that had done the fighting on D-Day.[4] Sink led his 1st Battalion down the road from Culoville to Vierville. Right from the start German snipers harassed the men, firing at them for the front and flanks. Sink made a brief stop at Vierville to clear the houses of enemy troops. General Taylor arrived in the town, and while he conferred with Sink, they could see several hundred troops about two thousand yards to the southeast.

Bunched together, Sink thought, they would make an easy target, but he hesitated firing on them until he was certain they were enemy. He sent out a patrol to get a better read on the soldiers, but before the patrol came back, the column of troops was out of sight.

Before departing Vierville, Sink split his battalion so that the 1st headed toward Beaumont and the 2nd veered left in the direction of Angoville-au-Plain. Neither battalion got very far. German machine-gun and small-arms fire put a halt to the advances. A platoon of Sherman medium tanks from Company A, 746th Tank Battalion, which had come ashore in Utah Beach right before noon the previous day, came to their aid. Still, 1st Battalion continued to take enemy fire on its right flank by

German soldiers who hid behind trees and hedges on a ridge that paralleled the road. Eventually, 1st Battalion made its way into Beaumont, but two enemy counterattacks stalled any further advance.

Support from a company of paratroopers from 2nd Battalion and a platoon of M5 Stuart light tanks from Company D, 70th Tank Battalion freed 1st Battalion to push ahead to a crossroads about five hundred yards east of Saint-Côme-du-Mont. After firing at the Germans, one of the tanks ran out of ammunition, and its commander, Lieutenant Walter T. Anderson, ordered it back to the rear to reload. Instead of returning by the same route, which was through the hedges and into a field, the tanker took the road and rolled up in front of a house being used as a German aid station. An enemy antitank crew was on the property: one blast placed an armor-piercing shell through the tank's turret.

Private Donald Burgett, a paratrooper with the 506th PIR, watched in horror as "the small tank erupted in a violent explosion and started to burn." The tank crew died instantly. "We could smell their flesh cooking in the flames," Burgett later wrote, "along with the heavy, oily smoke." In the explosion, Lieutenant Anderson's body was thrown half out of the tank's turrett. For several days, the tank with Anderson's corpse in full view remained on the road. Soldiers who passed by this intersection referred to it as "Dead Man's Corner."[5]

It being too dangerous to remain in the open, 1st Battalion moved to higher ground east of the town, but the nearby enemy strength made this position equally treacherous. Sink ordered 1st Battalion to withdraw back to Beaumont, and he would take another stab at Saint-Côme-du-Mont the next morning.

At dawn on June 8, the new attack on Saint-Côme-du-Mont strengthened to four battalions. On the right, Sink's 1st and 2nd Battalions headed directly from Beaumont to the town. The 3rd Battalion, 501st PIR, advanced from the southeast at les Droueries to the main highway south of Saint-Côme-du-Mont. To the left, 1st Battalion, 401st Glider Infantry, headed from the east of les Droueries. As the entire force of paratroopers descended upon Saint-Côme-du-Mont, the glidermen would slant off to the south, go down the highway, and blow up the causeway bridge to prevent German reinforcements.

Private Robert Hillman was among the wounded on June 8. The machine gunner, who three days before had proudly proclaimed to war correspondent Wright Bryan that he had no fear about landing safely in Normandy because his mother worked at the Pioneer Parachute Company, had indeed survived the jump. Hillman quickly recovered from his injury and fought with the 502nd PIR until the Germans surrendered on May 8, 1945. After the war, he went back to Manchester, Connecticut, where the townsfolk could see Hillman riding his bike while wearing his paratrooper boots.[6]

The 3rd Battalion, 501st PIR, easily cleared les Droueries and moved quickly toward an intersection east of Saint-Côme-du-Mont. Colonel Ewell, 3rd Battalion commander, thought he saw German troops withdrawing from Saint-Côme-du-Mont and took his men south along the Carentan Highway to capture the causeway and the bridges. Just when the men moved on to the highway, they were hit by small-arms, machine-gun, and antitank fire coming from buildings near the first bridge and 88mm shelling from Carentan.

Just as Ewell pulled the battalion back to the highway, a German counterattack hit him. Ewell's men drove back the enemy, but they were still in force on a small hill to the west. Ewell dug his men in on an east/west line facing north. The Germans attacked the position five times, almost piercing the American line on each occasion, but Ewell's men hung tough and never wavered. The enemy withdrew, leaving a clear route into Saint-Côme-du-Mont. Now General Taylor's 101st could concentrate on destroying the causeway bridges that led to Carentan.

Taylor ordered the main attack to commence on June 10, 1944, with two crossings over the Douve River. His left wing would start at 1 a.m. and cross in the vicinity of Brevands. A detachment from this force would link up near the Vire River Bridge southwest of Isigny with V Corps coming from the direction of Omaha Beach. The 101st's right wing would cross the causeway northwest of Carentan, bypass the city, and seize Hill 30 to the southwest.

By taking Hill 30, the American paratroopers would have a clear view of the main German escape route from Carentan. As the operation unfolded, the left and right wings would coordinate and form a ring around the city and then press into the city itself.[7]

Now, with Saint-Côme-du-Mont no longer a threat, the 101st's right wing was ready to attack with Lieutenant Colonel Cole's 3rd Battalion, 501st PIR. His force would approach Carentan over a four-and-a-half-mile asphalt causeway, about forty feet wide with dirt shoulders, that elevated from six to nine feet above the marshes and crossed over the Douve and Madeleine rivers, as well as two Douve canals. Cole would have no protection should his men take fire from the front and both flanks.[8]

Shortly after midnight, Cole's battalion started out but was ordered to halt. Engineers deployed to repair Bridge 2 took heavy fire. A patrol sent to investigate determined that a stronger-than-expected German force with mortars and machine guns was positioned on the highway and on higher ground directly south and west of the highway. Cole would now attack in the afternoon with artillery support from two field artillery battalions.

At noon on June 9, the engineers had still not finished repairing a twelve-foot gap at Bridge 2. Cole and three of his men improvised a footbridge to allow his battalion to start crossing single file in the middle of the afternoon. Cole's force was repeatedly hit by the projectiles of an 88mm gun fired from Carentan, but there were no casualties, and the battalion continued along at a steady pace by keeping low and crawling along an embankment.

Three hours down the highway, when the last of Cole's battalion had crossed three of the bridges and most of his men were over Bridge 2, the Germans opened fire from two directions, the hedgerows and a large farmhouse to their right front. Cole's men on point tried ducking in the ditches. As they attempted to advance, an enemy machine gun perched behind a hedgerow only one hundred yards away blasted into the ditches and struck three men, forcing the group to withdraw.

Now the entire battalion was under small-arms fire and couldn't maneuver to either flank. They were a totally exposed long, thin column. The only way to advance was to send one man at a time through the heavy steel fence, known as a "Belgian Gate," at Bridge 2. It stretched almost completely across the bridge, and the men would have to slip under an opening that was only about eighteen inches wide. This would be attempted, of course, under heavy enemy fire.

American artillery from the 377th Field Artillery Battalion (with two captured German guns); the 907th Glider Field Artillery Battalion, armed with twelve-pack howitzer 75mms; and the 65th Armored Field Artillery, with its eighteen self-propelled 105mms, helped neutralize the German guns. A portion of Company G, which led Cole's battalion, deployed to the left of the bridge and provided cover fire while the remainder of the unit tried squeezing through the narrow gate opening. Only six men got through; the seventh was wounded. The company temporarily ceased its attempt to cross and instead set up a fire position with mortars. The small artillery pieces made little impact. German fire kept coming, and casualties mounted within the American ranks, as the men had nowhere to take cover on the bare ground.[9]

Now four in the morning on June 11, Cole ordered the 3rd Battalion to attack, using the darkness as cover. His plan worked. Three companies made it across Bridge 4, and the battalion deployed on both sides of the highway. Because there were so many casualties along the causeway that day, the Americans named it "Purple Heart Lane."[10]

Scouts were sent out to determine the main source of enemy strength. It was the large farmhouse beyond Bridge 2, well defended by mortars, machine guns, and rifles. American artillery concentrated on the building, but it had little effect. Cole decided his only option was to rush the house, and he ordered a bayonet charge. Cole called to his second in command across the road, executive officer Major John P. Stopka, to have the order passed along.

Even though it was still dark, Cole ordered artillery units to put down smoke in a wide arc around the farmhouse to conceal the attack. "What made the job so difficult, I believe," Cole explained afterward, "was that hedges were filled with snipers. . . . Artillery was not heavy enough to knock them out unless you got a direct hit. . . . The shells burst above them." The Germans also made practical use of an orchard behind the house by using woodpiles to climb up into the trees and hide themselves in the branches.[11]

At 6:15 a.m. on June 11, 1944, as the artillery laid down fire, Cole blew his whistle, drew his pistol from its holster, and charged forward. But he was practically by himself. Instead of the 250 men who should have been right behind him, only twenty left cover with him. Another ten were behind Major Stopka. The other two hundred men, spread all around, had not heard the order for a bayonet charge.

Some troops from Company G ignored Cole and Stopka for good reason: they were busy tangling with enemy soldiers in a meadow east of the highway. Some of the men in Company G didn't hear Cole's whistle, but when they realized what was happening, they took off after the others to catch up.

None of them had charged an enemy position before, and their inexperience showed. They bunched up while running across a ditch into a field raked with fire to the east of the farmhouse. Several times, Cole had to stop, "waving both arms at them," trying to "get them to fan out." He fired his Colt .45 "wildly" in the general direction of the farmhouse, while at the same time yelling, "Goddam, I don't know what I am shooting at, but I gotta keep on."[12]

The first men to reach the farmhouse found it abandoned. The German soldiers had withdrawn to the west on higher ground and were entrenched in rifle pits and concrete machine-gun emplacements strategically placed along a hedgerow and pointed at right angles toward the road.[13]

Cole's men refused to be deterred. With shear momentum, they charged the Germans and wiped out their position with bayonets and grenades, Cole had hoped to keep the initiative going and take advantage of the enemy's disorganization, but this was asking too much of his men. All the paratroopers in his battalion had found their way across the causeway and assembled in a field near the farmhouse.[14]

For his bravery that day in leading the bayonet charge, fully exposed to enemy fire, Cole would later be awarded the Medal of Honor in October 1944, the only soldier with the 101st Airborne to receive such acclaim. Unfortunately, Cole was killed on September 18, 1944, by an enemy sniper in Operation Market Garden, so his mother accepted the medal on his behalf on the Fort Sam Houston parade ground where he had played as a child.[15]

The companies and platoons were mixed, and many of the soldiers had been torn up by artillery and small-arms fire. Cole sent a runner to

Colonel Cassidy's 1st Battalion, 502nd PIR, with a message requesting he come up, pass through his battalion, and continue attacking south from Hill 30 through the hamlet of la Billonerie.

Cassidy's battalion was north of Bridge 4 when Cole's message arrived. Crossing the bridge under heavy fire, Cassidy deployed the men across the field toward the farmhouse, but his men were in just as bad shape as Cole's. So instead of relieving 3rd Battalion, Cassidy stayed put and placed his men to the right of Cole's battalion. More men arrived to defend the right flank, where a few German troops had remained. Another small group appeared and set up a machine-gun position behind the farmhouse that covered all directions.

Even with the ground heavily defended by a mix of paratroopers, Cole remained concerned. He was unaware of the situation on his flanks: his communications had failed, and he didn't trust the artillery support. The men had their backs to the Douve River and had no rear area and no reserves close by. The artillery observers couldn't see where their shells were landing because of the dense hedgerows and had to adjust their fire unreliably by sound.

Cole's worries turned out to be justified. In the middle of the morning, the Germans counterattacked. A large enemy force rushed through the orchard and placed American paratroopers south and east of the farmhouse in peril, but the machine guns that were placed south of the house repelled the assault. There was still sporadic firing throughout the morning, but around noon regimental headquarters sent a message that the enemy had requested a truce. In reality, that message had been misunderstood.

Brigadier General McAuliffe, who had been directing the operations for the 101st, had requested the truce for his own men so casualties could be removed. The 502nd regimental surgeon, Major Douglas T. Davidson, escorted by two Germans, had walked through enemy lines to ask the military commander in Carentan to allow a brief lull in the fighting to evacuate the wounded. But Davidson wasn't allowed to speak to the German commander, and as he returned to Bridge 4, the enemy launched an all-out assault with what seemed like every gun in its arsenal—small arms, machine guns, mortars, and artillery.[16]

Cole asked regimental headquarters for permission to return fire but was told to wait until definitive word was received from Davidson. Cole's men took matters in their own hands, however, and retaliated with their arsenal. They were certain, having observed movement by the Germans during the truce, as well as the accuracy of the enemy guns, that the interlude had been used to strengthen German positions for an attack.

Cole's men were at a breaking point. German fire kept coming and became more intense the longer the attack continued. Observing the battle from a second-floor window in the farmhouse, Cole told regimental headquarters that his only option was to withdraw, and he requested cover fire and smoke when the time came to vacate the positions. His artillery observer, Captain Julian Rosemond, tried to send the message, but his radio had jammed.

Throughout the day, the battle seesawed. Just when the exhausted Americans believed the Germans were finished, they would counterattack. By afternoon, what remained of Cole's battalion was barely holding on in and around the farmhouse. Cole stood near a window and watched the fighting. Without artillery support, there was little chance of driving off the enemy.

But that changed when Rosemond finally reached the artillery command post, and a short time later, the German fire subsided. The 506th PIR had increased its artillery fire, lobbing shells over the farmhouse into a field were the enemy had positioned. American patrols determined that the enemy had fled, likely to Carentan. Around eight that evening, 2nd Battalion arrived and relieved the 1st and 3rd Battalions.[17]

Enemy defenders blocking the road to Carentan from the north were no longer a threat, but the 502nd was too exhausted to continue the attack. Carentan would have to wait another day.

30

Carentan

Taking the city of Carentan was General Maxwell Taylor's last major objective in the Normandy campaign, and his most important.

Bob Reuben remembered how much in awe the Screaming Eagles were of the battle for Carentan. In the marshaling area back in England, Taylor's staff officers stressed that the town "was the channel through which Germany could pour its hordes upon our landing forces while they struggled through the water and sought a shaky foothold on the beaches."[1]

Before the war, Carentan had thrived on dairy farming. On the outskirts of town, cows grazed on the lush greenery, their milk processed at the Carnation Evaporated Milk dairy on the site of an old creamery. Now American forces needed to take the town in order to consolidate the beachheads at Omaha and Utah. Although only a small city of 4,100 civilians, Carentan was larger than any other community in the lower Cotentin Peninsula. Straddling the main highway from Cherbourg to Caen and St. Lô, the double-tracked railroad from Paris to Cherbourg cut through the center of town, making it strategically important for German communications.

During a June 8 meeting, Taylor informed VII Corps Major General J. Lawton Collins that, earlier in the day, Colonel Robert Sink's 506th PIR, plus reinforcements from Lieutenant Colonel Julian Ewell's 3rd Battalion, 501st PIR, and a battalion of glider infantry, had captured Saint-Côme-du-Mont on the Carentan-Cherbourg road. Now in Allied hands, the village was no longer a threat from the Germans, who were slowing the American breakout from Utah Beach.

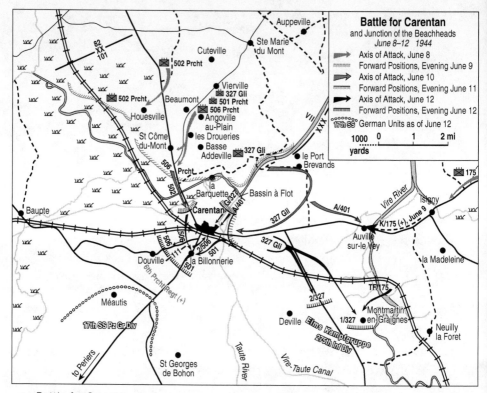

Battle for Carentan

Taking Carentan would help facilitate the link between the American V Corps at Omaha Beach and Collins's VII Corps forces at Utah. The only sound approach to Carentan was down the slope from Saint-Côme-du-Mont and along an exposed causeway supporting the main road. Carentan was mostly defended by the German 6th Parachute Regiment, the same unit that Bletchley Park's codebreakers had discovered in late May, forcing the 82nd Division to alter its D-Day drop plan.

Taylor's men launched the attack on Carentan in the early morning hours of June 10 from two directions. The 502nd PIR advanced from the south along the Cherbourg Road, while the 327th Glider Regiment crossed the Taute River to strike from the northeast.

At 1:45 a.m., a brief artillery and mortar bombardment preceded the advance of the 1st Battalion, 327th, across the Taute. Soon after, the glider troops tangled with Germans trying to block their advance. The 3rd Battalion of the 502nd PIR had commenced its southeast movement along the causeway road toward Carentan until it met heavy resistance from the 6th Parachute Regiment, firing from behind hedgerows and farm buildings.

At 6 p.m., German bombers struck one American company of the 502nd, killing and wounding scores of Taylor's men. By nightfall, two more glider battalions were across the Taute River. The next morning, the glider soldiers renewed their attack southwestward but were stopped cold on the northern outskirts of Carentan.

Early the next morning, June 11, a battalion of the 502nd renewed its attack under cover of a smokescreen. Reinforced by another of the regiment's battalions, hand-to-hand fighting ensued for almost six hours. Because the casualties began piling up, Taylor had his officers in the field negotiate a truce at noon to collect the dead and wounded. Taylor exploited the opportunity to send a message to the German commander, Major Friedrich von der Heydte, to offer him a chance to surrender. Strict orders from Hitler to hold Carentan at all costs meant that Heydte couldn't even consider Taylor's offer.

Right after the truce expired, the Germans repeatedly counterattacked until 10:30 p.m., forcing all three battalions of the 502nd Parachute Infantry Regiment to withdraw under cover of artillery and mortar fire. By late afternoon on the next day, June 12, the Germans had run out of ammunition, so von der Heydte ordered his troops to abandon Carentan under the cover of darkness and under fire.

Around midnight on June 11, however, as the Germans began pulling out of Carentan, Brigadier General Anthony C. McAuliffe's men pelted the enemy with large artillery, naval guns, and air power. Six hours later, McAuliffe's firepower had cleared the town of Germans. Snipers continued firing, but the jubilant French citizens came out of hiding to greet the American liberators. The French skillfully uncorked the bottles of wine that hadn't fallen into enemy hands.[2]

Two days later, on June 13, Major John J. Maginnis, a fifty-year-old World War I veteran and coal dealer from Worcester, Massachusetts, led Civil Affairs Detachment C2B1 into Carentan. Civil Affairs detachments were charged with keeping order in the occupied towns and cities. Their interactions with civilians could be friendly one day, hostile the next.

One of fifty detachments assigned to the various corps and divisions under Bradley's First Army, Maginnis's detachment was the first to operate in France. The War Department assigned it to the 101st Airborne. Colonel David Marcus joined Maginnis as an observer. His job was not to assist or interfere with Maginnis but to serve as the Pentagon's keen eyes and ears in order to report back to Washington the effectiveness of managing civil affairs.[3]

Forty-three-year-old Marcus, better known as "Mickey" on Manhattan's Lower East Side, had made headlines as a West Point cadet for his skills as a boxer, gymnast, and ballroom dancer. Marcus stayed in the army only a few years, switched to the reserves, went to law school, and then worked for the Treasury and Justice Departments. At the outbreak of World War II, he went back to the Army full time as a judge advocate general before transferring to Civil Affairs and heading to Normandy in 1944. Four years later, he died from friendly fire while fighting with the Israeli Army against the Arabs.

Maginnis and Marcus boarded a naval vessel at Southampton, England, transferred to a landing craft tank (LCT) and landed on Utah Beach the morning of June 8. Forty-eight hours had passed since D-Day; yet Utah remained hostile. German artillery fire and strafing from Luftwaffe planes hammered the beach. The LCT dropped Maginnis and Marcus a fair distance from shoreline. Their Jeep became submerged, forcing them to wade across the rough surf while carrying their gas masks and briefcases.[4] Surrounded by thousands of lifesavers, they stood on Utah Beach soaking wet. Without warning, a German plane appeared out of the low clouds. While Marcus looked skyward, Maginnis dove for cover under a nearby truck. When he crawled out, a sergeant looked down upon him and remarked, "That won't help you much under there, Major. The truck is loaded with ammunition."

Recovered from their first taste of combat, they drove to VII Corps headquarters in Audouville-la-Hubert, where General Collins's staff briefed them on the situation since D-Day. Next, they motored to the 101st Airborne command post in Hiesville.

When they arrived, the obvious signs of the paratroopers' landings surrounded Maxwell Taylor's headquarters. Parachutes hung from trees and gliders lay at "crazy angles in the fields and against the hedgerows," recalled McGinnis. Taylor's chief of staff, Colonel Gerald Higgins, greeted Maginnis and Marcus and advised them to watch out for mines and booby traps and to stay clear of any position that might draw enemy fire.

Maginnis and Marcus entered Caranten on June 13 at 11:00 a.m., where the situation was hostile. The German 17th SS Panzergrenadier Division mounted a heavy assault to overtake the 101st by way of the Carentan-Baupte-Périers road. The Americans were overrun by German infantry armed with self-propelled guns, but Colonel Robert Sink's 506th PIR managed to hold on until relief came from tanks, half-trucks, and heavy guns manned by an element of the 2nd Armored Division.[5]

Even though Carentan was a war zone, Maginnis and Marcus drove near the cattle market, where they heard rifle, machine-gun, and mortar fire. American soldiers taking cover in doorways yelled and waved for the party to quickly get out, but they refused. Maginnis asked an officer what was going on. "The krauts have counterattacked," he warned, "and things don't look good."[6]

The two men settled into the damaged Hôtel de Ville. The town looked every bit a war zone: German bodies, destroyed equipment, and rubble clogged the streets. The civilians who remained during the fighting were left with no water or electricity, rotting garbage, and decaying animals that filled the air with a nauseous stench. Despite Carentan barely being habitable, the Germans wanted to reoccupy the town.

Maginnis and Marcus remained for several hours until a shell hit the middle of the road they were on. One of Taylor's staff officers, Colonel Bryant Moore, ordered them to withdraw to Sainte-Marie-du-Mont, about a mile to the rear. Moore explained, "I want to recheck the situation. You're no good to me dead and I certainly don't want to have to run Carentan myself."[7]

On the way back into Carentan, Maginnis and Marcus stopped at the crossroads by Saint-Côme-du-Mont, known as Dead Man's Corner. Because of the constant shelling, they agreed to walk the several miles back to Carentan. A Jeep carrying Maxwell Taylor approached and slowed down. The two men saluted the general. Marcus, who had been at West Point at the same time as Taylor, turned to Maginnis and said, "If he lives long enough, there goes a future Chief of Staff."[8]

On June 14, the 101st drove off the final German counterattack: Carentan and the link between Omaha and Utah were now secure.

No longer worried about German shelling, the Civil Affairs detachment set up its headquarters on the second floor of the Hotel de Ville. The hotel had a long history, including as an Augustinian nuns' convent before being taken over by the local government. The detachment's temporary office had an American flag on an end wall and was furnished with, according to McGinnis, "captured German stuff and not too good." Through three windows, each missing glass, the crew could look out into what was once a small garden but was "now a jumble of trenches and shell holes."[9] Artillery shelling had destroyed much of the building, although the southwest section containing the public offices was useable. Curfew hours were set from 10 p.m. to 6 a.m.

That afternoon, Maginnis and Taylor met for about twenty minutes. The 101st commander "cross-examined" him with "impressive, probing questions" on how Civil Affairs planned to work his troops. Maginnis responded that his immediate concerns were disposing of the dead cattle and other animals, preventing contamination of the water supply, and keeping the narrow and crowded roads open for military traffic.

On June 15, as the 506th PIR, 3rd Battalion, left Carentan, Private Harold Stedman, one of the "Filthy Thirteen," took special notice of the Carnation milk factory that lay in ruins. First led by Lieutenant Charles Mellen, Stedman's unit had been trained as a demolition team tasked with blowing up bridges over the Douve. After Mellen was killed on D-Day, Sergeant Jake McNiece took command of the unit. McNiece, who was half Choctaw Indian, encouraged the other paratroopers in the unit to wear war paint and cut their hair Mohawk-style.

Stedman stepped out of the column and plucked some labels with the Carnation logo and placed them in his pack to give to his parents. Before the war, Stedman had worked at the Carnation plant in Massachusetts.[10]

Taylor concluded the meeting by telling Maginnis, "I am satisfied that you know what you are doing and have the situation under control."

Taylor and Maginnis convened a meeting with city officials and the new mayor, M. Joret, an "old, crippled man" with a white beard who dressed in black and walked hunched over with help from a cane.

Joret had replaced the previous mayor, Dr. Caillard, who was killed by a bomb dropped by an American plane (Joret's Christian name and that of his predecessor are lost to history). Speaking perfect French in his clipped bass, Taylor apologized to the group for the damage and mortality that war brings to local places and asked the officials to give all possible assistance and cooperation to the division.[11]

Maginnis and Marcus quartered in the eastern section of the city in a building owned by a brick manufacturer "of some substance in the community." They shared the same room, sleeping on ancient cots. They drew water from a public hand pump and used a latrine in a palm garden to the rear of the building.[12]

On June 19, no longer worried about a German counterattack, the paratroopers were treated to their first movie since arriving in France. *Andy Hardy's Blonde Trouble*, starring Mickey Rooney, was shown at the Jeanne d'Arc Theatre, which had been run by German soldiers during their occupation of Carentan. Just released, the film provided comic relief as clueless Andy was alternately flirted with or slapped by a blonde (Bonita Granville) on a train.

That evening, a brawl broke out between some of the Screaming Eagles and First Army military police. Shooting, fighting, and destroying property were fueled by large amounts of wine and Calvados, the local brandy made from apples. Resentment had been building among Taylor's men toward the constabulary. Their thinking, according to McGinnis, was "It's our town, and no outsiders are going to tell us how to act here." Some of Taylor's staff stepped in to prevent serious injuries or even deaths. Taylor took a hard line to prevent further outbreaks: he established curfew at 10:00 p.m. and limited the sale of alcohol.[13]

At the end of June, General Lawton Collins withdrew Maxwell Taylor and the 101st from Carentan and removed the forces north to Cherbourg for occupation duty.

31

Ridgway's Final Attacks

After four days of nonstop fighting, Major General Ridgway was exhausted, and so were his men.

The 82nd Airborne had accomplished its main objective, the securing of the Merderet bridgehead, but it had taken longer than planned. The toll in terms of men killed, wounded, and taken prisoner was heavy.

If any of the War Department brass had taken note of existing Airborne doctrine, then it would be obvious that Ridgway's paratroopers had already done their fair share in the liberation of Europe and that they should be relieved and sent back to England for refitting and training.

As far as Ridgway was concerned, the remaining tasks were more appropriate for traditional infantry divisions. But VII Corps commander General J. Lawton Collins had other ideas, and he coaxed General Bradley into allowing him to utilize the 82nd in the drive west across the Cotentin Peninsula. Cherbourg had become a tough objective to reach, and if the Allies didn't reach it soon, the Germans could easily reinforce its port.[1]

One of Ridgway's biographers thinks that, in reality, Ridgway didn't put up much of a fight and may have "welcomed the new challenge." Collins and Bradly revised the plan to cut the Cotentin, and the All-Americans would help spearhead the drive to split the peninsula. After regrouping, the 82nd would pass through the 90th Division and head southwest along the lower Douve River from Pont-l'Abbé to Sainte Sauveur-le-Vicomte. The 9th Division would attack abreast of Ridgway's men.

The first engagement in this new campaign, from June 11 to June 13, sent the 508th PIR southward over the Douve. On the third day of the fighting, Lieutenant Colonel Shields Warren, commander of the regiment's 1st Battalion, motored down to inspect the assault. He recalled Ridgway's visit:

"After we crossed the Douve, my objective was to occupy the area around Coigny," Warren wrote. "We came upon the largest clearing I had seen in Normandy. Two hundred yards into the clearing, between us and our objective, were five Renault tanks, eight other tanks armed with low-powered 40mm guns and one machine gun."

Warren watched the tanks get "air bursts in the trees [near us] with the 40mms and dusting the hedgerows with the machine guns." As he continued to watch the attack unfold through his field glasses, "a familiar voice at my elbow said, 'Well, Shields, how are things going?'" Warren was "quite aghast" to see his division commander take such risks. He could have been "hit by hot lead and steel flying around," the battalion commander thought.

Warren and Ridgway had small talk about the battle, and he explained to the division commander his men didn't have antitank guns but shot at the German armor instead with bazookas. Ridgway advised him to "be careful how you used that heavy stuff." He turned around to leave, but not before adding one more comment: "Isn't that sort of like swatting a fly with a sledgehammer?"[2]

Beginning on June 14, three of Ridgway's regiments were committed to an attack on St. Sauveur-le-Vicomet. The operation launched about noon with the 325th Glider Regiment and 507th PIR side-by-side on the road between St. Sauveur-le-Vicomet and Pont-l'Abbé. The 507th took the brunt of a vicious German attack. The fighting died down around dark, with bodies of dead paratroopers strewn on the road.

Sergeant Spencer Wurst of 505th PIR and some of the men from his unit headed to where the dead 507th troopers lay. Wurst's unit had not received rations for some time, and they searched the bodies for food. Crawling out of the hedgerows, careful to not alert Germans to the north of them, Wurst and soldiers from his squad uncovered some K rations the Germans had missed earlier that day.

The next afternoon, 505th PIR under Colonel Edman attacked right through the remaining 507th. Lieutenant Colonel Alexander's 1st Battalion took the right flank, while Lieutenant Colonel Vandevoort's 2nd Battalion held the left.

According to Private Wurst, "the battle itself was the same old story." The Germans had tanks, and the Americans "were fighting it out hedgerow by hedgerow." The paratroopers ran into direct fire by 37mm flak cannons, as well as 75mm antitank guns and the usual machine guns and mortars.

Alexander lent Vandervoort two Sherman tanks, and he used them to great effect. The armor supported a platoon from Company D that eclipsed the German stronghold. The 505th pushed on to St. Sauveur-le-Vicomet, but when it got dark, the regiment halted about two miles outside the town.

The next morning, June 16, the attack on St. Sauveur-le-Vicomet started at 7 a.m., with the 505th on the right and the 325th Glider Regiment advancing from the left. Infantry divisions provided the paratroopers with artillery. The objective was to hold a defensive line at the Douve River on the heights across from the St. Sauveur-le-Vicomet, but not to capture the bridge or the town.

That morning, Colonel Vandervoort with a forward artillery observer surveyed the area from a bluff by the river. He had an excellent vantage point from which to see the highway, which was "crammed" with German troops fleeing the town. Vandervoort passed the information on down the line, and it ended up with Ridgway. The 82nd commander came to Vandervoort's position with General Bradley. They recognized the opportunity to rush the bridge and ordered the 505th PIR to attack down the slope and across the river, seize the bridge, and clean out the town.

A large artillery barrage aimed at the Germans started the attack, but it also blew up part of the town. After the barrage lifted, the paratroopers advanced and were met by small-arms and machine-gun fire. As they got to within 150 yards of the town, they were also hit with heavy artillery. The Germans had ceased withdrawing and took a position on the other side of the river to the left and right front on slightly elevated ground.

Casualties began to mount as the paratroopers rushed across the bridge under blasts of artillery. Ridgway and Bradley watched the attack with amazement. Bradley was heard to say, "My God, Matt, can't anything stop those men?" By the end of the day, after a long struggle, St. Sauveur-le-Vicomet had been taken by the Americans.[3]

On June 19, the 82nd Airborne had been detached from VII Corps and was now attached to General Troy Middleton's VIII Corps with the mission of clearing the Bois de Limors. The ground would serve as jump off point for an attack on the Germans holding La-Haye-du-Puits.

The assault took the men of 505th PIR through swampy ground and back into the hedgerow areas, all the time under careful watch from the Germans holding Hill 131. The paratroopers eventually dug in at the base of the hill and waited for orders to attack the high ground. This would be delayed because a storm lasting four days dumped buckets of rain on Normandy. For the men holed up in the woods, the conditions were miserable. The Germans made things worse with constant artillery and mortar fire that knocked trees on the helpless paratroopers. The regiment lost 293 men over a two-week period.[4]

After two weeks of muddy, wet conditions, the regiment was relieved, but only for a few days. On July 2, Colonel Vandervoort ordered an assault on Hill 131. The following day, the 505th attacked by platoon. The men made their way through brush and in between tall trees to a line of departure. Along the way, Sergeant Wurst caught a glimpse of Colonel Vandervoort, who had preceded the men. He was wearing a raincoat and leaning on a crutch, his bad leg still not healed.[5]

By 8:20 a.m., the men had reached the line of departure. About halfway up Hill 131, the paratroopers captured some prisoners. Wurst, who was with the groups rounding up the Germans, got annoyed when one of them, an officer who spoke English, asked, "Aren't you a bit young to be a sergeant in the parachute troops?" Wurst, who was only twenty years old, told the German to shut up and took his watch.[6]

By the afternoon, the paratroopers had crested the hill just as the sky cleared, providing them a picture-perfect view of the German-held territory. The day after taking Hill 131 was the Fourth of July. Every artillery piece in the American arsenal fired simultaneously to celebrate. Four days later, the 8th Infantry Regiment relieved 505th PIR, and on July 11, 1944, the entire 82nd Airborne had been placed in First Army reserve.[7]

Word spread that the regiment and the entire 82nd Airborne would soon return to England.

32

Conclusion

After more than thirty days of uninterrupted combat, the Paratrooper Generals and the Airborne troops they led from the 82nd and 101st Airborne Divisions were relieved from combat in Normandy and sent back to England.

Both divisions had proven as worthy or better than any other American fighting force in the European Theater of Operations (ETO). They had captured all of the key objectives assigned to them as part of Operation Neptune, but their contribution to the Allied victory in Normandy had come at an enormous cost.

Of the nearly twelve thousand men who fought under Ridgway (including the main body of paratroopers and men brought in later by glider and landing craft), nearly 50 percent showed up on the rolls as casualties—meaning killed, wounded, or missing. Almost 1,300 died in Normandy, and another 2,300 were wounded or severely injured. Taylor's Screaming Eagles suffered similar losses of just over 3,100 men killed and wounded.[1]

Lost for almost twenty-four hours, the fact that they could even find their units is a testament to the solid training they received in England. Since early 1944, many hours had been spent jumping into mock drop zones, learning how to use a compass, and reading maps with unpronounceable French locations.

In the marshaling areas, men stood over sand tables crafted to look exactly like the drop zones. Using aerial reconnaissance photos as a guide, the men studied every tree and hedgerow, memorizing the location of where each unit would assemble in the dark and then attack against likely fierce resistance. All of that preparation paid off.

But lingering questions remain over why the vast majority of the 101st and 82nd Airborne paratroopers were scattered so far from their intended drop zones. The parachutists who struggled for hours, sometimes days, to link up with their units were quick to blame the pilots of General Williams's Troop Carrier Command. Even Ridgway and Taylor questioned the Troop Carrier Command's ability to transport troops into a combat zone.

The Normandy Operation "certainly drove home the fact that the great danger to airborne troops is not only the enemy," Taylor told a group of West Point cadets. "It is dispersion."[2]

As a recent Air Force study suggests, many factors caused the Airborne to be scattered that day (in a few instances, up to twenty miles from the drop zones). Dropping the paratroopers and gliders at night was the first problem. Pilots and crew did not have modern technology and had to rely on moonlight when they weren't flying in a cloudbank. There were pathfinder ground lights, but they weren't always accurately placed; in some drop zones, they were nonexistent.

Flak from German antiaircraft fire caused pilots to change course by going right or left, or climbing or descending. Lack of navigational aids also caused dispersal of the men; only the lead plane in each formation carried any sort of navigation equipment, and only a handful of C-47s was equipped with GEE, which relied on radio beams transmitted from ground stations. Finally, high winds from the front that had delayed D-Day pushed planes faster than they were supposed to fly, resulting in paratroopers dropping beyond the intended drop zones.

Despite the unfair criticism levied at the troop carrier pilots, they successfully dropped thirteen thousand paratroopers behind enemy lines, and as the author of the Air Force study submits, "more than half of the men landed within two miles of their designated zones, and four out of five of them within five miles."[3]

Both divisions would be combat tested again two months later in Holland. General Ridgway had been promoted to command the newly formed XVIII Airborne Corp, and, not surprisingly, Jim Gavin took over the 82nd. Maxwell Taylor remained at the helm of the 101st until the end of the war. Both Ridgway and Taylor were promoted to higher commands later in their careers.

Ridgway would first lead the 8th Army in Korea until General MacArthur was sacked, and he then took over as United Nations commander. From 1953 to 1955, he served as Army Chief of Staff. When he retired, Taylor, his former assistant division commander, replaced him. Taylor also became chairman of the Joint Chiefs of Staff and military advisor to President John Kennedy. When reflecting on his military career, Taylor considered his association with the 101st to be the highlight. "That great division," he told historian S. L. A. Marshall, "put a lazy, ordinary fellow into orbit."[4]

Despite all their later accomplishments, their service as the Paratrooper Generals during the Normandy campaign would be their most rewarding.

Appendix

Order of Battle, June 6, 1944

82ND AIRBORNE DIVISION
Commanding General: Major General Matthew B. Ridgway
Assistant Commander: Brigadier General James M. Gavin
505th Parachute Infantry Regiment: Colonel William E. Ekman
507th Parachute Infantry Regiment: Colonel George V. Millett
508th Parachute Infantry Regiment: Colonel Roy E. Lindquist
325th Glider Regiment: Colonel Harry L. Lewis
82nd Division Artillery: Colonel Francis A. March

101ST AIRBORNE DIVISION
Commanding General: Major General Maxwell D. Taylor
Assistant Commander: Brigadier General Don F. Pratt
501st Parachute Infantry Regiment: Colonel Howard R. Johnson
502nd Parachute Infantry Regiment: Colonel George Mosele
506th Parachute Infantry Regiment: Colonel Robert Sink
327th Glider Infantry Regiment: Colonel George S. Wear
101st Division Artillery: Brigadier General Anthony C. McAuliffe

9TH AIR FORCE
Commander: Lieutenant General Lewis H. Brereton

IX TROOP CARRIER COMMAND
Commander: Major General Paul Williams
50th Troop Carrier Wing: Colonel Julian M. Chappell
52nd Troop Carrier Wing: Brigadier General Harold L. Clark
53rd Troop Carrier Wing: Colonel Maurice M. Beach

Notes

Prologue: June 6, 1944
1 Mitchell Yockelson, "The Radio Reporter Who Witnessed D-Day and Told the World What He Saw," *Washington Post*, June 6, 2019, https://www.washingtonpost.com/history/2019/06/06/nbc-radio-reporter-who-witnessed-d-day-told-world-what-he-saw/; John McDonough, "The Longest Night: Broadcasting's First Invasion," *American Scholar* 63, no. 2 (spring 1994): 203.
2 Hugh Richardson Jr., "Forty Years Ago," unknown publication, 1984, William Wright Bryan Papers, Clemson University Special Collections Unit.
3 John Huey, "Watching History from the Blister," *Atlanta Journal-Constitution*, June 6, 1974.
4 Wright Bryan, "Script of June 6, 1944, NBC Broadcast," Wright Bryan Papers, Clemson University, 10.

Chapter 1: General Lee's Airborne
1 In 1917, during World War I, Winston Churchill, then minister of munitions, suggested the possibility of flying airborne troops to destroy the enemy's communications. That same year, a Russian colonel made a similar pitch to his government. Both Churchill and the colonel were rebuffed.
2 William Mitchell, *Memoirs of World War I: From Start to Finish of Our Greatest War* (New York: Random House, 1960), 268.
3 Major General William C. Lee, USA Retired, "The Pioneering of American Airborne," Records of the Adjutant General's Office (Record Group 407), 101st Infantry Division Historical Files, 3101-0.6, National Archives and Records Administration.
4 E. M. Flanagan Jr., *Airborne: A Combat History of American Airborne Forces* (New York: Ballantine Books, 2002), xi.
5 Sig Christenson, "Brooks Stunt Gave Birth to Airborne Infantry," *San Antonio Express-News*, August 7, 2018.
6 Flanagan, *Airborne*, 13.
7 Ed Cray, *General of the Army: General George C. Marshall, Soldier and Statesman* (New York: Cooper Square Press, 2012), 62.
8 Cray, *General of the Army*, 68.
9 Cray, *General of the Army*, 69–78.

10 David L. Roll, *George Marshall: Defender of the Republic* (New York: Caliber, 2019), 10–11.

11 See https://www.marshallfoundation.org/marshall/essays-interviews/george-c -marshall-study-character/.

12 James Gavin, *Airborne Warfare* (Washington, DC: Infantry Journal Press, 1947), vii–viii.

13 Gerard M. Devlin, *Paratrooper! The Saga of U.S. Army and Airborne Parachute and Glider Troops during World War II* (New York: St. Martin's Press, 1979), 34–35.

14 Devlin, *Paratrooper!*, xi.

15 Charles E. Kirkpatrick, *An Unknown Future and a Doubtful Present: Writing the Victory Plan of 1941* (Washington, DC: US Army Center of Military History, 1992), 1–2, http://www.ibiblio.org/hyperwar/USA/USA-Victory/index.html.

16 Flanagan, *Airborne*, 19. Much gratitude goes to historian Tim Mulligan for his analysis of the Crete operation and for providing me with the casualty statistics.

Chapter 2: Matthew Bunker Ridgway

1 George C. Mitchell, *Matthew B. Ridgway: Soldier, Statesman, Scholar, Citizen* (Mechanicsburg, PA: Stackpole Books, 2002), 26–27.

2 Carlo D'Este, *Patton: A Genius at War* (New York: HarperCollins, 1995), 401.

3 Mitchell, *Matthew B. Ridgway*, 20.

4 Mitchell, *Matthew B. Ridgway*, 22.

5 Clay Blair, *Ridgway's Paratroopers: The American Airborne in World War II* (Garden City, NY: Doubleday, 1985), 3–5.

6 Blair, *Ridgway's Paratroopers*, 4.

7 Matthew B. Ridgway, *Soldier: The Memoirs of Matthew B. Ridgway* (New York: Harper and Brothers, 1956), 23.

8 Ridgway, *Soldier*, 24–25.

9 Blair, *Ridgway's Paratroopers*, 4.

10 Mitchell, *Matthew B. Ridgway*, 15.

11 Mitchell, *Matthew B. Ridgway*, 12, 16.

12 Ridgway, *Soldier*, 30–31.

13 Ridgway, *Soldier*, 32.

14 Ridgway, *Soldier*, 34; Matthew B. Ridgway "Efficiency Report (1922)," National Personnel Records Center, National Archives and Records Administration.

15 Ridgway, *Soldier*, 39.

16 Ridgway, *Soldier*, 47.

Chapter 3: Maxwell Davenport Taylor

1 Maxwell D. Taylor, *Swords and Plowshares* (New York: W. W. Norton, 1972), 22.

2 Colonel Richard A. Manion, "Interview with General Maxwell Taylor," transcribed, October 19, 1972, United States Military History Institute.

3 Manion, "Interview with General Maxwell Taylor," 6.

4 John M. Taylor, *General Maxwell Taylor: The Sword and the Pen* (New York: Doubleday, 1989), 12–13.

5 Manion, "Interview with General Maxwell Taylor," 4.

6 Manion, "Interview with General Maxwell Taylor," 14.

7 Manion, "Interview with General Maxwell Taylor," 3.

8 Manion, "Interview with General Maxwell Taylor," 4.

9 Manion, "Interview with General Maxwell Taylor," 13.

10 Manion, "Interview with General Maxwell Taylor," 13.

11 Manion, "Interview with General Maxwell Taylor," 15.

12 Manion, "Interview with General Maxwell Taylor," 16.

13 Taylor, *Swords and Plowshares*, 27.

14 Taylor, *Swords and Plowshares*, 28.

15 Taylor, *Swords and Plowshares*, 28.

16 Taylor, *Swords and Plowshares*, 28.

17 Taylor, *Swords and Plowshares*, 28.

18 Manion, "Interview with General Maxwell Taylor," 17.

19 Manion, "Interview with General Maxwell Taylor," 26.

20 Taylor, *Swords and Plowshares*, 34.

21 Taylor, *Swords and Plowshares*, 32.

22 Taylor, *Swords and Plowshares*, 33.

23 Taylor, *Swords and Plowshares*, 35–36; Maxwell Taylor "Efficiency Report (1937)," National Personnel Records Center, National Archives and Records Administration.

24 Taylor, *Swords and Plowshares*, 37.

25 Taylor, *Swords and Plowshares*, 37.

26 Taylor, *Swords and Plowshares*, 42; Manion, "Interview with General Maxwell Taylor," 30.

Chapter 4: War

1 John M. Taylor, *General Maxwell Taylor: The Sword and the Pen* (New York: Doubleday, 1989), 36; Maxwell Taylor, *Swords and Plowshares* (New York: W. W. Norton, 1972), 40–41.

2 Leonard Mosley, *Marshall: Hero for Our Times* (New York: Hearst Books, 1982), 175.

3 Clay Blair, *Ridgway's Paratroopers: The American Airborne in World War II* (Garden City, NY: Doubleday, 1985), 8. Eventually, the structures were abandoned, and the various military offices moved to the Pentagon.

4 Taylor, *Swords and Plowshares*, 41.

5 Taylor, *Swords and Plowshares*, 40.

6 Matthew B. Ridgway, *Soldier: The Memoirs of Matthew B. Ridgway* (New York: Harper and Brothers, 1956), 49.

7 Maurice Matloff, ed., *American Military History* (Washington, DC: Office of the Chief of Military History, 1969), 435; Guy LoFaro, *The Sword of St. Michael: The 82nd Airborne Division in World War II* (Cambridge, MA: Da Capo Press, 2011), 28.

8 Jonathon W. Jordan, *Brothers, Rivals, Victors: Eisenhower, Patton, Bradley, and the Partnership That Drove the Allied Conquest in Europe* (New York: Caliber, 2011), 30.

9 Steven L. Ossad, *Omar Nelson Bradley: America's GI General, 1893–1981* (Columbia: University of Missouri Press, 2017), 22.

10 Ossad, *Omar Nelson Bradley*, 46.
11 Blair, *Ridgway's Paratroopers*, 15.
12 Ridgway, *Soldier*, 49–50.
13 Blair, *Ridgway's Paratroopers*, 21.
14 Stephen R. Taafe, *Marshall and His Generals: U.S. Army Commanders in World War II* (Lawrence: University of Kansas Press, 2011), 272.
15 Taylor, *General Maxwell Taylor*, 37–38.

Chapter 5: The Birth of American Airborne Divisions

  1 Guy LoFaro, *The Sword of St. Michael: The 82nd Airborne Division in World War II* (Cambridge, MA: Da Capo Press, 2011), 34.

  2 John M. Taylor, *General Maxwell Taylor: The Sword and the Pen* (New York: Doubleday, 1989), 41; Maxwell Taylor, *Swords and Plowshares* (New York: W. W. Norton, 1972), 44.

  3 LoFaro, *The Sword of St. Michael*, 34; Jonathan M. Soffer, *General Matthew B. Ridgway: From Progressivism to Reaganism, 1895–1993* (Westport, CT: Praeger, 1998), 37.

  4 Clay Blair, *Ridgway's Paratroopers: The American Airborne in World War II* (Garden City, NY: Doubleday, 1985), 25; Matthew B. Ridgway, *Soldier: The Memoirs of Matthew B. Ridgway* (New York: Harpers and Brothers, 1956), 54.

  5 Blair, *Ridgway's Paratroopers*.

  6 Blair, *Ridgway's Paratroopers*, 31.

  7 See https://www.switlik.com/information/ourstory and https://www.thisdayinaviation.com/tag/irwin-parachute-company/; Napier Crookenden, *Dropzone Normandy* (New York: Charles Scribner's Sons, 1976), 18; James A. Huston, *Out of the Blue: U.S. Army Airborne Operations in World War II* (West Lafayette, IN: Purdue University Press, 1972), 102–3.

  8 Crookenden, *Dropzone Normandy*, 19.

  9 Richard Meade, *General "Boy": The Life of Lieutenant General Sir Frederick Browning* (South Yorkshire, UK: Pen & Sword Books, 2017), 14.
10 Meade, *General "Boy."*
11 Meade, *General "Boy,"* 78–79.
12 Meade, *General "Boy."*
13 Blair, *Ridgway's Paratroopers*, 32.
14 Blair, *Ridgway's Paratroopers*.
15 Ridgway, *Soldier*, 56–57.
16 Ridgway, *Soldier*, 58.
17 Blair, *Ridgway's Paratroopers*, 63.
18 Blair, *Ridgway's Paratroopers*, 61.
19 Groves and Ridgway Papers, speech delivered to the 82nd Airborne Division by Ridgway upon its movement from Claiborne, Louisiana, to Fort Bragg, North Carolina. Folder: Speeches to His Troops: 1942–1944, Box 4; Blair, *Ridgway's Paratroopers*, 38.
20 T. Michael Booth and Duncan Spencer, *Paratrooper: The Life of General James M. Gavin* (Philadelphia: Casemate, 2013), 15.

Chapter 6: "Become a Paratrooper!"

1 See https://www.thecrimson.com/article/1942/8/24/all-creeds-study-together-at-army.

2 Francis L. Sampson, *Paratrooper Padre* (Washington, DC: Catholic University of America Press, 1948), 3.

3 Sampson, *Paratrooper Padre.*

4 *Life Magazine*, "U.S. Trains More Parachute Troops," May 12, 1941, 110–17; Edward M. Coffman, *The Regulars: The American Army, 1898–1941* (Cambridge, MA: Belknap Press of Harvard University Press, 2004), 403.

5 See the Internet Movie Database, https://www.imdb.com/title/tt0034000/.

6 Gerard M. Devlin, *Paratrooper! The Saga of U.S. Army and Airborne Parachute and Glider Troops during World War II* (New York: St. Martin's Press, 1979), 85.

7 Sampson, *Paratrooper Padre*, 5.

8 Spencer F. Wurst and Gayle Wurst, *Descending from the Clouds: A Memoir of Combat in the 505 Parachute Infantry Regiment, 82nd Airborne Division* (Haverton, PA: Casemate, 2004), 35.

9 Bob Bearden, *To D-Day and Back: Adventure with the 507th Parachute Infantry Regiment and Life as a World War II POW* (Minneapolis, MN: Zenith Press, 2007), 23.

10 Francis L. Sampson Oral History, Army Heritage Education Command, 10; Sampson, *Paratrooper Padre*, 6.

11 Kate Eschner, "Meet the Daredevil Parachutist Who Tested the First Nylon Parachute 75 Years Ago," *Smithsonian.com* (June 6, 2017), https://www.smithsonianmag.com/smart-news/meet-daredevil-parachutist-who-tested-duponts-first-nylon-parachute-180963527/.

12 Wurst and Wurst, *Descending from the Clouds*, 37.

13 Michael E. Haskew, *The Airborne in World War II: An Illustrated History of America's Paratroopers in Action* (New York: Thomas Dunne Books, 2017), 13; Eugene G. Piasecki, "The Knollwood Maneuver: The Ultimate Test," *Veritas* 4, no. 1 (2008).

14 Haskew, *The Airborne in World War II*, 38; Sampson, *Paratrooper Padre*, 8.

15 Wurst and Wurst, *Descending from the Clouds*, 38.

16 Sampson, *Paratrooper Padre*, 10.

17 Sampson, *Paratrooper Padre*, 11–13.

18 Wurst and Wurst, *Descending from the Clouds*, 43.

19 Wurst and Wurst, *Descending from the Clouds*, 44; Sampson, *Paratrooper Padre*, 14.

20 Wurst and Wurst, *Descending from the Clouds*, 44.

21 Sampson, *Paratrooper Padre*, 14.

Chapter 7: James Gavin

1 Matthew B. Ridgway, *Soldier: The Memoirs of Matthew B. Ridgway* (New York: Harper and Brothers, 1956), xvi–xviii, 62.

2 Ridgway, *Soldier*, 20.

3 Author interview with James Gavin's daughter, Chloe Gavin, 2019.

4 Author interview with James Gavin's daughter, Barbara Gavin Fauntleroy, 2019.

5 Author interview with Chloe Gavin.

6 T. Michael Booth and Duncan Spencer, *Paratrooper: The Life of James M. Gavin* (Philadelphia: Casemate, 2013), 64–65; General James M. Gavin, *On to Berlin: Battles of an Army Commander, 1943–1946* (New York: Bantam Books, 1979), 1–2; James Gavin, *Airborne Warfare* (Washington, DC: Infantry Journal Press, 1947), viii–ix.

7 Booth and Spencer, *Paratrooper*, 52–56.

8 Booth and Spencer, *Paratrooper*, 74.

9 Gavin, *On to Berlin*, 6.

10 Phil Nordyke, *All American All the Way from Sicily to Normandy: A Combat History of the 82nd Airborne in World War II* (Minneapolis, MN: Zenith Press, 2005), 17.

11 Nordyke, *All American All the Way from Sicily to Normandy*.

Chapter 8: Sicily and Italy

1 Captain Harry F. Jost, "Airborne Operations in Sicily, July 1943," *Advanced Infantry Officers Course*, 1948–1949, Fort Benning, Infantry School.

2 Steve J. Zaloga, *U.S. Airborne Divisions in the ETO: 1944–45* (Oxford: Osprey Publishers, 2007), 9–11.

3 Eugene G. Piasecki, "The Knollwood Maneuver: The Ultimate Test," *Veritas* 4, no. 1 (2008); Michael E. Haskew, *The Airborne in World War II: An Illustrated History of America's Paratroopers in Action* (New York: Thomas Dunne Books, 2016), 29–43.

4 Carlo D'Este, "Jim Gavin's War, Part 2," *Armchair General* (April 23, 2015).

5 D'Este, "Jim Gavin's War, Part 2"; Clay Blair, *Ridgway's Paratroopers: The American Airborne in World War II* (Garden City, NY: Doubleday, 1985), 53.

6 Matthew B. Ridgway, *Soldier: The Memoirs of Matthew B. Ridgway* (New York: Harper and Brothers, 1956), 60.

7 For Operation Husky, the 505th Parachute Infantry Regiment was renamed the 505th Regimental Combat Team (RCT) because it temporarily included a battalion from the 504th Infantry Regiment, now also known as the 504th RCT.

8 Blair, *Ridgway's Paratroopers*, 70.

9 Blair, *Ridgway's Paratroopers*, 71.

10 Thomas M. Fairfield, Chief Curator, 82nd Airborne Museum, to General James Gavin, January 6, 1978, Collections of the 82nd Division Airborne Division Memorial Museum.

11 *Bing Wood Memoirs*, March 28, 1992, 314th Troop Carrier Group, Air Mobility Museum Collections.

12 Captain Harry F. Jost, "Airborne Operations in Sicily, July 1943," *Advanced Infantry Officers Course*, 1948–1949, US Army Infantry School; Colonel Charles Hutchinon Young, *Into the Valley: The Untold Story of USAF Troop Carrier in World War II: From North Africa through Europe* (Flint, MI: PrintComm, 1995), 14–15.

13 John M. Taylor, *General Maxwell Taylor: The Sword and the Pen* (New York: Doubleday, 1989), 46–47.

14 Jerry Autry, *General William C. Lee: Father of the Airborne* (San Francisco: Airborne Press, 1995), 140.

15 General James M. Gavin, *On to Berlin: Battles of an Army Commander, 1943–1946* (New York: Bantam Books, 1979), 22.

16 Major General James M. Gavin, Assistant Chief of Staff, G-3, to General Farrell, September 22, 1954, Collections of the 82nd Division Airborne Division Memorial Museum.

17 Maxwell Taylor, *Swords and Plowshares* (New York: W. W. Norton, 1972), 52; Taylor, *General Maxwell Taylor*, 49.

18 Ridgway, *Soldier*, 74–75; Taylor, *General Maxwell Taylor*, 49.

19 Taylor, *General Maxwell Taylor*, 56–59.

20 Taylor, *General Maxwell Taylor*, 65–66.

21 Michael E. Haskew, *The Airborne in World War II* (New York: Thomas Dunne Books, 2016), 77–79.

Chapter 9: Eisenhower

1 Stephen Ambrose, *D-Day, June 6, 1944: The Climactic Battle of World War II* (New York: Simon and Schuster, 1994), 59.

2 Jean Smith, *Eisenhower: In War and Peace* (New York: Random House, 2012), 294.

3 Winston Churchill, *Closing the Ring: The Second World War*, vol. 5 (London: Cassell, 1951), 85.

4 See http://liberationtrilogy.com/the-road-to-d-day/who-will-command-this-operation/.

5 Stephen Ambrose, *Eisenhower: Soldier and President* (New York: Simon and Schuster, 1990), 22.

6 Dwight D. Eisenhower, *At Ease: Stories I Tell to Friends* (Garden City, NY: Doubleday, 1967), 166.

7 Carlo D'Este, *Eisenhower: A Soldier's Life* (New York: Henry Holt, 2002), 208.

8 D'Este, *Eisenhower*, 220–21; Smith, *Eisenhower: In War and Peace*, 111.

9 Smith, *Eisenhower: In War and Peace*, 101.

10 Lecture by Professor Brad Coleman, Virginia Military Institute, Lexington, Virginia, June 17, 2017.

11 John S. D. Eisenhower, *General Ike: A Personal Reminiscence* (New York: Free Press, 2003), 100; Smith, *Eisenhower: In War and Peace*, xii; Clifford Williams, "Supreme Headquarters for D-Day," *After the Battle*, no. 84: 1.

Chapter 10: Planning for Neptune

1 See https://winstonchurchill.org/publications/churchill-bulletin/bulletin-070-apr-2014/montys-clash-with-churchill/.

2 David Chandler, ed., *The D-Day Encyclopedia* (New York: Simon & Schuster, 1994), 369.

3 Carlo D'Este, *Eisenhower: A Soldier's Life* (New York: Henry Holt, 2002), 304–5.

4 General Montgomery to Lieutenant General Sir Oliver Leese, January 12, 1944, in Stephen Brooks, ed., *Montgomery and the Battle of Normandy* (Stroud-Gloucestershire, UK: History Press and Army Records Society, 2008), 39.

5 Bill Newton Dunn, *Big Wing: The Biography of Air Chief Sir Trafford Leigh Mallory* (Shrewsbury, UK: Airlife, 1992), 15–17; David Irving, *The War between the Generals* (Key West, FL: Parforce UK, 2010), 70.

6 James M. Gavin, *On to Berlin: Battles of an Army Commander, 1943–1946* (New York: Viking Press, 1978).

7 Gavin, *On to Berlin.*

8 Richard Meade, *General "Boy": The Life of Lieutenant General Sir Frederick Browning* (South Yorkshire, UK: Pen & Sword Books, 2017), 101.

9 Omar N. Bradley, *A Soldier's Story* (New York: Modern Library, 1988), 228 H. Paul Jeffers, *Taking Command: General J. Lawton Collins from Guadalcanal to Utah Beach to Victory in Europe* (New York: NAL Caliber, 2009), 161.

10 Gerard M. Devlin, *Paratroope! The Saga of U.S. Army and Marine Parachute and Glider Troops during World War II* (New York: St. Martin's Press, 1979), 368.

11 Sam Gibbons, "June 6, 1944—I Was There," Sam W. Gibbons Papers, University of South Florida Special Collections, 3.

12 Joseph Balkoski, *Utah Beach, June 6, 1944: The Amphibious Landing and Airborne Operation on D-Day* (Mechanicsburg, PA: Stackpole Books, 2005), 296.

13 Devlin, *Paratrooper!*, 369–91; Russell Miller, *Nothing Less Than Victory: An Oral History of D-Day* (New York: William Morrow, 1993), 119, 197.

14 Much gratitude to the Utah Beach Museum for supplying me with the historical summary of the Cotentin Peninsula causeways.

15 Steven J. Zaloga, *Battles of World War II: D-Day 1944: Utah Beach & the US Airborne Landings* (Oxford, UK: Osprey Publishing, 2010), 7, 14.

16 Bradley, *A Soldier's Story*, 234–35.

Chapter 11: The American Airborne in England

1 Leonard Rapport and Arthur Norwood Jr., *Rendezvous with Destiny: History of the 101st Airborne Division* (Old Saybrook, CT: Konecky & Konecky, 1948), 43–45.

2 Adam G. R. Berry, *And Suddenly They Were Gone: An Oral and Pictorial History of the 82nd Airborne Division in England, February–September 1944* (Boston: Overlord Publishing, 2015), 7.

3 Jerry Autry, *General William C. Lee: Father of the Airborne, Just Plain Bill* (San Francisco: Airborne Press, 1995), 148.

4 Martin Wolfe, *Greenlight: A Troop Carries Squadron's War from Normandy to the Rhine* (Philadelphia: University of Pennsylvania Press, 1989), 54–56.

5 Wolfe, *Greenlight*, 60.

6 Juliette Gardiner, *Overpaid, Oversexed and Over Here* (New York: Canopy Books, 1992), 33–36.

7 Air Mobility Command Museum, "Daily Chronicles of a USAAF Unit in England for the Invasion of Europe," 3, https://amcmuseum.org/history/daily-chronicles-of-a-usaaf-unit-in-england-for-the-invasion-of-europe/.

8 Len Lebenson, *Surrounded by Heroes: Six Campaigns with Division Headquarters, 82nd Airborne, 1942–1945* (Philadelphia: Casemate, 2007).

9 Roger A. Freeman, *UK Airfields of the Ninth: Then and Now* (London: After the Battle, 1994), 124; John R. Johnson Jr., *Un-Armed, Un-Armored and Un-Escorted: A World War II C-47 Airborne Troop Carrier Pilot Remembers* (Bennington, VT: Meriam Press, 2014), 122.

10 Spencer F. Wurst and Gayle Wurst, *Descending from the Clouds: A Memoir of Combat in the 505th Parachute Infantry Regiment, 82nd Airborne Division* (Haverton, PA: Casemate, 2004), 111.

11 Wurst and Wurst, *Descending from the Clouds.*

Chapter 12: C-47s

1 Dwight D. Eisenhower, *Crusade in Europe* (New York: Doubleday, 1948), 163.

2 Boeing Aircraft "Historical Snapshot" of the C-47, http://www.boeing.com/history/products/c-47-skytrain.page.

3 See https://corescholar.libraries.wright.edu/cgi/viewcontent.cgi?referer=https://www.google.com/&httpsredir=1&article=1002&context=following.

4 Arthur Pearcy, *The Dakota: A History of the Douglas Dakota in RAF and RCAF Service* (London: Allan, 1972), 11.

5 Douglas J. Ingalls, *The Plane That Changed the World* (Fallbrook, CA: Aero Publishers, 1966), 21.

6 Pearcy, *The Dakota*, 7.

7 Pearcy, *The Dakota*, 11–12.

8 Carroll V. Glines, *The Legendary DC-3* (New York: Von Nostrand Reinhold, 1979), 42.

9 Thanks to Bob Leicht for this information.

10 Glines, *The Legendary DC-3*, 43.

11 Roger E. Bilstein, *Airlift and Airborne Operations in World War II* (Arlington, VA: Air Force History and Museums Program, 2005), 16.

12 W. F. Craven and J. L. Cate, eds., *The United Army Air Forces in the World War*, vol. 6 (Washington, DC: Department of the Air Force), 360.

13 Ingalls, *The Plane That Changed the World*, 144.

14 Pearcy, *The Dakota*, 21–22.

15 *Business Week*, April 2, 1943, in Douglas J. Ingells, *The Plane That Changed the World: A Biography of the DC-3* (Fallbrook, CA: Aero Publishers, 1966), 148–51, 165–66.

16 Thanks to Bob Leicht for providing information on the C-53.

Chapter 13: Gliders

1 Matthew B. Ridgway, *Soldier: The Memoirs of Matthew B. Ridgway* (New York: Harper and Brothers, 1956), 56.

2 David Polk, *World War II Army Airborne Troop Carriers* (Paducah, KY: Turner Publishing Company, 1992), 13; https://www.airspacemag.com/daily-planet/last-words-otto-lilienthal-180960084/.

3 Gerard M. Devlin, *Paratrooper! The Saga of U.S. Army and Airborne Parachute and Glider Troops during World War II* (New York: St. Martin's Press, 1979), 132.

4 See https://www.asme.org/topics-resources/content/the-flying-coffins-of-world-war-ii.

5 See http://www.avalanchepress.com/Gliders.php.

6 Text courtesy of the 101st Airborne Division Museum, Fort Campbell, Kentucky.

7 See https://www.asme.org/topics-resources/content/the-flying-coffins-of
-world-war-ii.

8 See https://www.asme.org/topics-resources/content/the-flying-coffins-of-world
-war-ii; Walter Cronkite, *A Reporter's Life* (New York: Ballentine Books, 1997), 108–9;
101st Airborne Museum, Exhibit Text, Fort Campbell, Kentucky.

9 Text courtesy of the Bill Lee Museum, Dunn, North Carolina.

10 Jonathan Falconer, *D-Day Operations Manual: "Neptune," "Overlord" and the Battle of
Normandy—75th Anniversary Edition: Insights into How Science, Technology and Engineering Made the Normandy Invasion Possible* (Sparkford, UK: Haynes Publishing, 2013), 130.

11 Gerard M. Devlin, *Silent Wings: The Story of the Glider Pilots of World War II* (London:
W. H. Allen, 1985), 64.

12 See https://www.asme.org/topics-resources/content/the-flying-coffins-of
-world-war-ii.

13 Michael Ingrisano, *Valor without Arms: A History of the 316th Troop Carrier Group,
1942–1945* (Bennington, VT: Merriam Press, 2001), 45.

Chapter 14: Eisenhower's Parachuting Correspondents

1 Barney Oldfield obituary, *British Broadcasting Newspaper*, April 28, 2003.

2 *Evening State Journal* (*Lincoln Journal Star*), March 24, 1938.

3 *Macon Chronical Herald*, July 15, 1942.

4 *Atlanta Journal-Constitution*, September 27, 1978.

5 James M. Gavin to Mr. Clifford F. Berry Jr. (editor, *Armed Forces Journal*), October
27, 1975, Barney Oldfield Papers, Nebraska Historical Museum.

6 Robert Reuben, "Unpublished Manuscript of Experience during World War II,"
Reuters News Agency Archives, 4–6.

Chapter 15: Brereton's 9th Air Force

1 William B. Breuer, *Geronimo: American Paratroopers in World War II* (New York: St.
Martin's Press, 1989), 326.

2 Gerald M. Devlin, *Paratrooper! The Saga of U.S. Army and Marine Parachute and
Glider Combat Troops during World War II* (New York: St. Martin's Press, 1979), 468.

3 Carlo D'Este, *Eisenhower: A Soldier* (New York: Henry Holt, 2002), 295; Geoffrey
Perret, *Winged Victory: The Army Air Forces in World War II* (New York: Random House,
1993), 176–77.

4 Napier Crittenden, *Dropzone Normandy* (New York: Charles Scribner's Sons, 1976),
65.

5 Michael N. Ingrisano Jr., *Valor without Arms: A History of the 316th Troop Carrier
Group, 1942–1945* (Bennington, VT: Merriam Press, 2001), 40.

6 George Collins, *Into Fields of Fire: The Story of the 438th Troop Carrier Group during
World War II* (Bloomington, IN: Xlibris, 2004), 19, Kindle.

7 Crittenden, *Dropzone Normandy*, 29.

8 "Barney Oldfield, Journal and Star Columnist," *Evening Star Journal*, March 24,
1944.

9 Frank A. King, "Paratroopers Thrill Mr. Churchill: Realistic Training," *London Evening Standard*, March 24, 1944.
10 Guy LoFaro, *The Sword of St. Michael: The 82nd Airborne Division in World War II* (Cambridge, MA: Da Capo Press, 2011), 187.
11 Martin Wolfe, *Green Light: A Troop Carrier Squadron's War from Normandy to the Rhine* (Philadelphia: University of Pennsylvania Press, 1989), 49.
12 J. Lawton Collins, *Lightning Joe: An Autobiography* (Novato, CA: Presidio Press, 1979), 189.
13 "Report of Exercise Eagle," 101st Airborne Division, May 11, 1944, G-3 for Air, Records of the Adjutant General's Office (Record Group 407), National Archives and Records Administration; Peter Caddick-Adams, *Sand & Steel: The D-Day Invasion and the Liberation of France* (Oxford: Oxford University Press, 2019), 211–12; Devlin, *Paratrooper!*, 367.

Chapter 16: The Unbearable Burden of a Conscience
1 Captain Harry C. Butcher, USNR, *My Three Years with Eisenhower: The Personal Diary of Naval Aide to General Eisenhower, 1942–1945* (New York: Simon & Schuster, 1946), 51.
2 Guy LoFaro, *The Sword of St. Michael: The 82nd Airborne Division in World War II* (Cambridge, MA: Da Capo Press, 2011), 192; Dwight D. Eisenhower, Memorandum for Diary, 22 May 1944, in *Papers of Eisenhower, The War Years*, vol. III, ed. Alfred D. Chandler (Baltimore: Johns Hopkins University Press, 1970), 881.
3 John S. D. Eisenhower, *General Ike: A Personal Reminiscence* (New York: Free Press, 2003), 177.
4 Winston G. Ramsey, "Supreme HQs for D-Day," *After the Battle*, no. 84, October 23, 1944.
5 Joseph Balkoski, *Utah Beach: The Amphibious Landing and Airborne Operation on D-Day* (Mechanicsburg, PA: Stackpole Books, 2005), 43.
6 LoFaro, *The Sword of St. Michael*, 182–83.
7 F. H. Hinsley, *British Intelligence in the Second World War: Its Influence on Strategy and Operations*, vol. 3 (New York: Cambridge University Press, 1988), 797–98.
8 Text courtesy of Bletchley Park.
9 Thomas Parrish, *The Ultra Americans: The U.S. Role in Breaking the Nazi Codes* (Briarcliff Manor, NY: Stein and Day, 1986), 109; David Kenyon, *Bletchley Park and D-Day: The Untold Story of How the Battle for Normandy War Was Won* (London: Yale University Press, 2019), 23–24, 45–46, 52.
10 Kenyon, *Bletchley Park*, 23–24, 45–46, 52.
11 Kenyon, *Bletchley Park*, 197.
12 Kenyon, *Bletchley Park*.
13 Parrish, *The Ultra Americans*, 117–21.
14 Parrish, *The Ultra Americans*, 124.
15 Omar N. Bradley, *A Soldier's Story* (New York: Henry Holt, 1951), 181.

16 Letter, HQ, VII Corps, 30 May 44, Subject: Modification of VII Corps Plan to CG FUSA, APO 230, VII Corps Historical File, Records of the Adjutant General's Office (Record Group 407), National Archives and Records Administration.
17 "Gavin Diary," May 26–May 30, 1944, James M. Gavin Papers, United States Army Military History Institute (USMHI). Thanks to historian Joe Balkoski for lending me his copy of the diary.
18 Major L. F. Ellis, *Victory in the West: The Battle of Normandy*, vol. 1 (Nashville, TN: Battery Press, 1993), 139.
19 Clay Blair, *Ridgway's Paratroopers: The American Airborne in World War II* (Garden City, NY: Doubleday, 1985), 207–9.
20 Dwight D. Eisenhower, *Crusade in Europe* (New York: Doubleday, 1948), 245–47.
21 Bradley, *A Soldier's Story*, 235–36.

Chapter 17: "A Rendezvous with Destiny"
1 James Lee McDonough and Richard S. Gardner, *Sky Riders: History of the 327th/401st Glider Infantry* (Nashville, TN: Battery Press, 1980), 24, 43.
2 Bill Lee to Dava Lee, March 26, 1944, Bill Lee Museum, Dunn, North Carolina.
3 "Operation Neptune"—History of the 101st A/B Division, File 3101-0.3, Records of the Adjutant General's Office (Record Group 407), National Archives and Records Administration.
4 "Operation Neptune"—History of the 101st A/B Division.
5 Don Forrester Pratt, "Biography," July 1, 1944, Don Pratt Papers, 101st Airborne Museum, Fort Campbell, Kentucky.
6 Clay Blair, *Ridgway's Paratroopers: The American Airborne in World War II* (Garden City, NY: Doubleday, 1985), 18.
7 Blair, *Ridgway's Paratroopers*, 197.
8 Dwight D. Eisenhower, *Crusade in Europe* (Garden City, NY: Doubleday, 1948), 183–84.
9 James M. Gavin Diary, February 14, 1944, James M. Gavin Papers, Army Heritage and Education Center.
10 Colonel Richard A. Manion, "Interview with General Maxwell Taylor," transcribed, October 19, 1972, United States Military History Institute.
11 Jack Raymond, "Taylor Returns to the Front," *New York Times*, May 7, 1961; author interview with Kathy Shiabani, 2019; Robert Reuben, "Unpublished Manuscript of Experience during World War II," Reuters News Agency Archives, 41.
12 Reuben, "Unpublished Manuscript of Experience during World War II," 130–31.

Chapter 18: Pathfinders
1 Associated Press, "Proud Mama," *Atlanta Journal-Constitution*, June 9, 1944.
2 Robert V. Roberts, "18-Man Invasion D-Day Spearhead," *New York Daily News*, August 2, 1944.
3 James Gavin, *On to Berlin: Battles of an Army Commander, 1943–1946* (New York: Viking Press, 1978), 54.

4 Phil Nordyke, *All American All the Way: From Sicily to Normandy* (Minneapolis, MN: Zenith Press, 2005), 104.

5 Benoit Rondeau, *Airborne Operations on D-Day* (Rennes, France: Quest-France, 2014), 22–23.

6 Colonel Charles H. Young, *Into the Valley: The Untold Story of USAAF Troop Carrier in World War II, from North Africa through Europe* (Flint, MI: PrintComm, 1995), 96–97.

7 Joe Balkoski Papers, 29th Division Museum, "Utah Beach Collection."

8 Associated Press, "Proud Mama."

9 See https://www.historynet.com/first-in-france-the-world-war-ii-pathfinder-who-led-the-way-on-d-day.htm.

10 George E Koskimaki, *D-Day with the Screaming Eagles* (New York: Ballantine Books, 2006), 41.

11 Guy LoFaro, *The Sword of St. Michael: The 82nd Airborne Division in World War II* (Cambridge, MA: Da Capo Press, 2011), 200.

12 LoFaro, *The Sword of St. Michael*, 200–201.

Chapter 19: Readying the Skytrains

1 Interview with Mr. John Cornish conducted by the author on March 27, 2019; Roger A. Freeman, *UK Airfields of the North, Then and Now* (London: After the Battle, 1978), 186.

2 Peter Bergh, *The Art of Ogden M. Pleissner* (Boston: David R. Godine, 1984), 21, 24.

3 Michael N. Ingrisano Jr., *Valor without Arms: A History of the 316th Troop Carrier Group, 1942–1945* (Bennington, VT: Merriam Press, 2001), 45.

4 Colonel Charles D. Young, *Into the Valley: The Untold Story of the USAAF Troop Carrier in World War II, from North Africa through Europe* (Flint, MI: PrintComm, 1995), 114.

Chapter 20: The Paratrooper Generals Make Final Preparations

1 Clay Blair, *Ridgway's Paratroopers: The American Airborne in World War II* (Garden City, NY: Doubleday, 1985), 240.

2 Francis L. Sampson, *Paratrooper Padre* (Washington, DC: Catholic University of America Press, 1948), 161–67.

3 Sampson, *Paratrooper Padre*, 44.

4 Maxwell D. Taylor, *Swords and Plowshares* (New York: W. W. Norton, 1972), 74–75.

5 Blair, *Ridgway's Paratroopers*, 216.

6 Blair, *Ridgway's Paratroopers*, 213.

7 Matthew B. Ridgway, *Soldier: The Memoirs of Matthew B. Ridgway* (New York: Harper and Brothers, 1956), 2.

Chapter 21: Delay

1 Dwight D. Eisenhower, *Crusade in Europe* (Garden City, NY: Doubleday, 1948), 245–47.

2 See http://archive.commercialmotor.com/article/3rd-november-1944/30/general-eisenhowers-trailer-headquarters.

3 Lecture presented by Southwick House historian, Richard Culligan, September 5, 2019.

4 Wright Bryan, "Letter to His Family," courtesy of Keely Jurgovan, Wright Bryan's granddaughter.

5 Charles McNab, ed., *The D-Day Training Pocket Manual, 1944* (Havertown, PA: Casemate Books, 2019), 65–97.

6 James Gavin, "Notes on Eisenhower," *Papers of James M. Gavin*, American Heritage and Education Command.

7 Carlo D'Este, *Eisenhower: A Soldier's Life* (New York: Henry Holt, 2002), 2, 481.

8 Clay Blair, *Ridgway's Paratroopers: The American Airborne in World War II* (Garden City, NY: Doubleday, 1985), 225.

9 Major Knut H. Runstein, "The Operations of the 1st Battalion, 506th Parachute Infantry (101st Airborne Division) in the Vicinity of Carentan, 6–8 June 1944—Personal Experience of a Company Commander" (Infantry School Advanced Infantry Officers School, Fort Benning, Georgia, 1948–1949), 6.

10 "Eisenhower Dud Won Photo Job," *Los Angeles Times*, June 14, 1946.

11 See https://www.northcountrypublicradio.org/news/story/25048/20140604/star-lake-d-day-vet-remembers-scared-stiff.

Chapter 22: The Paratrooper Generals Take Off

1 Maxwell D. Taylor, *Swords and Plowshares* (New York: W. W. Norton, 1972), 77–79; John M. Taylor, *General Maxwell Taylor: The Sword and the Pen* (New York: Doubleday, 1989), 78–79; Maxwell Taylor, "Talk to the Garrison on the Normandy Invasion," United States Military Academy, West Point, October 9, 1947, Maxwell Taylor Papers, National Defense University Special Collections.

2 Matthew B. Ridgway Papers, "Operation Neptune After Action Reports," Army Heritage and Education Center.

3 Clay Blair, *Ridgway's Paratroopers: The American Airborne in World War II* (Garden City, NY: Doubleday, 1985), 229; Matthew B. Ridgway, *Soldier: The Memoirs of Matthew B. Ridgway* (New York: Harper and Brothers, 1956), 7–9; Ridgway Papers located in the Joseph Balkoski Papers, 29th Division Museum, "Utah Beach Collection."

Chapter 23: Scattered in Streams and Cow Pastures

1 See https://www.dday-overlord.com/en/d-day/air-operations/usa/albany.

2 See https://www.dday-overlord.com/en/d-day/air-operations/usa/boston.

3 Dr. John C. Warren, *Airborne Operations in World War II, European Theater* (Washington, DC: USAF Historical Division, Research Studies Institute, Air University, 1956), 16.

4 Martin Wolfe, *Green Light: A Troop Carrier Squadron's War from Normandy to the Rhine* (Philadelphia: University of Pennsylvania Press, 1989).

5 Francis L. Sampson, *Paratrooper Padre* (Washington, DC: Catholic University of America Press, 1948), 46.

6 Guy Remington, "Second Man Out," in *The New Yorker Book of War Pieces* (New York: Schocken Books, 1947), 339–40.

7 Mary Louise Roberts, *D-Day through French Eyes: Normandy, 1944* (Chicago: University of Chicago Press, 2014), 36.

8 Bob Bearden, *To D-Day and Back: A Memoir* (Minneapolis, MN: Zenith Press, 2007), 117–20.

9 See http://www.baseballinwartime.com/in_memoriam/brewer_lefty.htm.

10 Congressman Sam Gibbons, "June 6, 1944—I Was There," Sam W. Gibbons Papers, the University of South Florida Special Collections.

11 Gibbons, "June 6, 1944—I Was There," 10.

12 Escape and Evasion Report No. 908, Record Group 498, Records of Headquarters, European Theater of Operations, US Army, National Archives and Records Administration.

13 Escape and Evasion Report No. 836, Record Group 498, Records of Headquarters, European Theater of Operations, US Army, National Archives and Records Administration.

14 Spencer F. Wurst and Gayle Wurst, *Descending from the Clouds: A Memoir of Combat in the 505 Parachute Infantry Regiment, 82nd Airborne Division* (Haverton, PA: Casemate, 2004), 35, 124–26.

Chapter 24: The All-Americans on D-Day

1 Clay Blair, *Ridgway's Paratroopers: The American Airborne in World War II* (Garden City, NY: Doubleday, 1985), 244–46.

2 Phil Nordyke, *All American All the Way from Sicily to Normandy: A Combat History of the 82nd Airborne in World War II* (Minneapolis, MN: Zenith Press, 2005), 29.

3 Alexandre Renaud, *Sainte-Mère-Église: D-Day, June 6, 1944* (Paris: Julliard, 1986), 20.

4 US Army, *Utah Beach to Cherbourg*, 30–34.

5 Stephen E. Ambrose, *Band of Brothers: E Company 506th Regiment, 101st Airborne from Normandy to Hitler's Eagle's Nest* (New York: Touchstone, 2001), 206.

6 Robert M. Murphy, *No Better Place to Die: Sainte-Mère-Église, June 1944, and the Battle for La Fière Bridge* (Philadelphia: Casemate, 2009).

7 Guy LoFaro, *The Sword of St. Michael: The 82nd Airborne Division in World War II* (Cambridge, MA: Da Capo Press, 2011), 209.

8 Charles J. Masters, *Glidermen of Neptune: The American D-Day Glider Attack* (Carbondale: Southern Illinois University Press, 1995), 51–52; Blair, *Ridgway's Paratroopers*, 235.

9 Charles J. Masters, *Glidermen of Neptune*, 53–54, 70–74.

10 Spencer F. Wurst and Gayle Wurst, *Descending from the Clouds: A Memoir of Combat in the 505 Parachute Infantry Regiment, 82nd Airborne Division* (Haverton, PA: Casemate, 2004), 128.

11 Ridgway, *Soldier*, 80.

12 Murphy, *No Better Place to Die*, 29.

13 Blair, *Ridgway's Paratroopers*, 251.

14 LoFaro, *The Sword of St. Michael*, 222.

15 Murphy, *No Better Place to Die*, 50–51.

16 Blair, *Ridgway's Paratroopers*, 267.

17 Blair, *Ridgway's Paratroopers*, 150.

18 LoFaro, *The Sword of St. Michael*, 241.

19 General James M. Gavin, *On to Berlin: Battles of an Army Commander, 1943–1946* (New York: Bantam Books, 1979), 121.

Chapter 25: The Screaming Eagles on D-Day

1 Maxwell D. Taylor, *Swords and Plowshares* (New York: W. W. Norton, 1972), 79.

2 "Operation Neptune," *History of the 101st A/B Division, Allied Invasion of Western Europe, June 6-30, 1944*, Record Group 407, National Archives and Records Administration, Historical Files of the 101st Airborne Division, 3101-0.3.

3 Taylor, *Swords and Plowshares*, 80.

4 S. L. A. Marshall, *Night Drop: The American Airborne Invasion of Normandy* (Boston: Little, Brown, 1962), 271.

5 "Interview with Brigadier General Gerald Higgins on Normandy Operation," Army Historical Education Committee, 2–3.

6 Taylor, *Swords and Plowshares*, 80; Robert Reuben, "Unpublished Manuscript of Experience during World War II," Reuters New Agency Archives, 76.

7 Reuben, "Unpublished Manuscript of Experience during World War II," 78.

8 Reuben, "Unpublished Manuscript of Experience during World War II," 79–80.

9 Taylor, *Swords and Plowshares*, 79–81; Omar N. Bradley, *A Soldier's Story* (New York: Modern Library, 1988), 276.

10 General J. Lawton Collins, *Lightning Joe: An Autobiography* (Novato, CA: Presidio, 1979), 204–5.

11 Flint Whitlock, *If Chaos Reigns: The Near-Disaster and Ultimate Triumph of the Allied Airborne Forces on D-Day, June 6, 1944* (Philadelphia: Casemate, 2014), 166.

12 "The Fight at the Lock," History Section, US Army European Theater of Operations, 8-3.1 BB 2.

13 "The Fight at the Lock," 26–28.

14 Project Vigil. See http://www.projectvigil.com/robert-lee-bull-wolverton.

15 S. L. A. Marshall, *Night Drop: The American Airborne Invasion of Normandy* (Boston: Little, Brown, 1962), 286–87; "Robert Sink to Brigadier General S.L.A. Marshall, November 5, 1952," S. L. A. Marshall Papers, University of Texas, El Paso, Special Collections.

16 John M. Taylor, *General Maxwell Taylor: The Sword and the Pen* (New York: Doubleday, 1989), 82; Napier Crookenden, *Dropzone Normandy* (New York: Scribner's Sons, 1976), 108.

17 Reuben, "Unpublished Manuscript of Experience during World War II," 133–34.

18 Leon F. Spencer, "The Death of General Don F. Pratt," http://worldwar2gliderpilots.blogspot.com/2009/03/death-of-general-don-f-pratt.html; Reuben, "Unpublished Manuscript of Experience during World War II," 133–34.

19 Reuben, "Unpublished Manuscript of Experience in World War II," 134.

20 The Lee and Eisenhower letters are included among the collections of the 101st Airborne Museum at Fort Campbell, Kentucky.

21 Leonard Rappaport and Arthur Norwood Jr., *Rendezvous with Destiny: History of the 101st Airborne Division* (Old Saybrook, CT: Konecky & Konecky, 2001), 134.
22 Private Jim "Pee Wee" Martin, "Interview with American Veteran's Center," November 8, 2014, https://www.youtube.com/watch?v=B-jMt8Rftn0.
23 Crookenden, *Dropzone Normandy*, 110.

Chapter 26: The Airborne Angels of Mercy

1 Phil Nordyke, *All American All the Way from Sicily to Normandy: A Combat History of the 82nd Airborne Division in World War II* (Minneapolis, MN: Zenith Press, 2005), 32.
2 See https://history.amedd.army.mil/booksdocs/wwii/Overlord/Overlord/Overlord ETO.html#Assault, 204.
3 Francis L. Sampson, *Paratrooper Padre* (Washington, DC: Catholic University of America Press, 1948), 37.
4 Escape and Evasion Report 948, Record Group 498, Records of Headquarters, European Theater of Operations, US Army, National Archives and Records Administration.
5 See https://vocationblog.com/2014/06/d-day-chaplain-remembered and https://www.catholic.com/magazine/online-edition/father-ignatius-maternowski-d-day-chaplain.
6 Sampson, *Paratrooper Padre*, 46–53; *The Hall of Valor Project*, "DSC Citation for Francis L. Sampson," https://valor.militarytimes.com/hero/22634.
7 See https://history.amedd.army.mil/booksdocs/wwii/Overlord/Overlord/Overlord ETO.html#NEPTUNE.
8 George E. Koskimaki, *D-Day with the Screaming Eagles* (Haverton, PA: Casemate, 2008), 356.
9 George Koskinaki Papers, "Front Line Surgeons," Army Heritage and Education Command, 141.

Chapter 27: The End of a Very Long Day

1 Thomas Parrish, *The Ultra Americans: The U.S. Role in Breaking the Nazi Codes* (New York: Stein and Day, 1986), 203.
2 Major Thomas E. Nunn to Anabel Nunn, June 7, 1944. Much appreciation to Jenny Nunn Brawley for sharing the letter between her father and mother.
3 Bill Newton Dunn, *Big Wing: The Biography of Air Marshal Sir Trafford Leigh-Mallory* (Shrewsbury, UK: Airlife Publishing, 1992), 121.
4 Dwight D. Eisenhower, *Crusade in Europe* (NewYork: Doubleday, 1948), 247.
5 Martin Pöppel, *Heaven and Hell: The War Diary of a German Paratrooper* (Gloucestershire, UK: Spellmount, 2010), 175–77.
6 Barney Oldfield, *Never a Shot in Anger* (Santa Barbara, CA: Capra Press, 1956), 77–79.
7 Mary Hackett, *Bill Walton: A Charmed Life* (Tucson, AZ: Branden Books, 2013), 62.
8 Oldfield, *Never a Shot in Anger*, 77–79.

9 Volker Griessner, *The Lions of Carentan: Fallschirmjäger Regiment 6*, 1943–1945 (Philadelphia: Casemate, 2011), 84–85.

10 Paul Golz, *The Pomeranian Grenadier and the Invasion of Normandy* (self-pub., 2014), 2–9.

11 Clay Blair, *Ridgway's Paratroopers: The American Airborne in World War II* (Garden City, NY: Doubleday, 1985), 277.

12 Golz, *The Pomeranian Grenadier*, 10–13. Three days later, on June 9, Golz's unit covered the retreat from the rest of the 1057th Regiment after it had been pushed from Cauquigny by La Fière Bridge. Along with three other soldiers, including Schneider, they were taken prisoner by an American tank officer as they hid in a cow pasture.

13 Robert Reuben, "Unpublished Manuscript of Experience during World War II," Reuters News Agency Archives, 85.

14 Benoit Bondeau, *Airborne Operations on D-Day* (Rennes-Lille: Quest-France, 2014), 130–31.

Chapter 28: Crossing the La Fière Causeway

1 Guy LoFaro, *The Sword of St. Michael: The 82nd Airborne Division in World War II* (Cambridge, MA: Da Capo Press, 2011), 224–26.

2 Robert M. Murphy, *No Better Place to Die: The Fight for La Fière Bridge* (Philadelphia: Casemate, 2009), 91.

3 Bill Walton interview by Cornelius Ryan, March 10, 1958, Ryan Collection, Ohio University Special Collections; LoFaro, *The Sword of St. Michael*, 231.

4 Clay Blair, *Ridgway's Paratroopers: The American Airborne in World War II* (Garden City, NY: Doubleday, 1985), 299.

5 Blair, *Ridgway's Paratroopers*, 276.

6 "History of the 507th Parachute Infantry Participation in Normandy," Historical File of the 82nd Airborne, Record Group 407, National Archives and Records Administration.

7 Phil Nordyke, *All American All the Way from Sicily to Normandy: A Combat History of the 82nd Airborne in World War II* (Minneapolis, MN: Zenith Press, 2005), 336.

8 James Gavin, *On to Berlin: Battles of an Army Commander, 1943–1946* (New York: Viking Press, 1978), 127.

9 82nd Airborne Division Papers, 82nd Airborne Museum.

10 LoFaro, *The Sword of St. Michael*, 236–37.

Chapter 29: Seizing the Carentan Causeway

1 Leonard Rapport and Arthur Norwood Jr., *Rendezvous with Destiny: History of the 101st Airborne Division* (Old Saybrook, CT: Konecky & Konecky, 1968), 163–64.

2 History Section, European Theater of Operations, *Regimental Unit Study Number 3: 506 Parachute Infantry Regiment in Normandy Drop*, 13.

3 Laurence Critchell, *Four Stars of Hell: With U.S. Paratroopers in Combat from the Night Drop at Normandy to the Battle of the Bulge* (New York: Ballantine Books, 1947), 69.

4 "History of the 101st Division Neptune," Record Group 407, Records of the Adjutant General's Office, 101st Division Historical Files, 3.

5 John C. McManus, *The Americans at Normandy: The Summer of 1944—The American War from the Normandy Beaches to the Falaise Pocket* (New York: Forge, 2004), 103, 105; Donald R. Burgett, *Currahee: A Screaming Eagle at Normandy* (Novato, CA: Presidio, 1999), 133–34; "History of the 70th Tank Battalion," Record Group 407, Records of the Adjutant General's Office, Armored Historical Files.

6 Robert C. Hillman, "Enlisted Record and Report of Separation"; Robert C. Hillman "Separation Qualification Record," courtesy of Hillman's daughter, Karen Costantini.

7 US Army, Fort Benning Infantry School, "Carentan Causeway Fight," https://www.benning.army.mil/Library/Donovanpapers/wwii/index.html.

8 Arve Robert Pisani, *The Carentan Causeway: Normandy 1944* (self-pub., 2012), 23.

9 Rapport and Norwood, *Rendezvous with Destiny*, 173–80.

10 Rapport and Norwood, *Rendezvous with Destiny*, 218.

11 "Lieutenant-Colonel Robert G. Cole—Carentan," interview, https://www.youtube.com/watch?v=jhUkxKa7DxE.

12 Rapport and Norwood, *Rendezvous with Destiny*, 189.

13 Rapport and Norwood, *Rendezvous with Destiny*, 189.

14 Rapport and Norwood, *Rendezvous with Destiny*, 188–89.

15 See http://www.cmohs.org/recipient-detail/2685/cole-robert-g.php.

16 "History of the 501st Parachute Infantry Regiment June 1944," Record Group 407, Records of the Adjutant General's Office, 101st Division Historical Files.

17 John McManus, "The Battle to Control Carentan," *World War II Magazine*, July/August 2006, https://www.historynet.com/battle-to-control-carentan-during-world-war-ii.htm.

Chapter 30: Carentan

1 Robert Reuben, "Unpublished Manuscript of Experience during World War II," Reuters News Agency Archives, 141.

2 Reuben, "Unpublished Manuscript of Experience during World War II," 17.

3 Steven L. Ossad, "Out of the Shadow and into the Light: Col. David 'Mickey' Marcus and U.S. Civil Affairs in World War II," *Army History* (winter 2016): 13.

4 John J. Maginnis, "My Service with Colonel David Marcus," *American Jewish History* 69, no. 3 (March 1980): 309–10.

5 Maginnis, "My Service with Colonel David Marcus," 29–20.

6 Maginnis, "My Service with Colonel David Marcus," 12

7 Maginnis, "My Service with Colonel David Marcus," 9.

8 Major General John J. Maginnis, *Military Government Journal: Normandy to Berlin*, ed. Robert A. Hart (Boston: University of Massachusetts Press, 1971), 8.

9 Maginnis, *Military Government Journal*, 12.

10 Ian Gardner and Roger Day, *Tonight We Die as Men: The Untold Story of the Third Battalion, 506th Parachute Infantry Regiment from Toccoa to D-Day* (Havertown, PA: Casemate, 2011), 300–301.

11 Maginnis, *Military Government Journal*, 13–14.

12 Maginnis, *Military Government Journal*, 15.
13 Maginnis, *Military Government Journal*, 20–21.

Chapter 31: Ridgway's Final Attacks

  1 Clay Blair, *Ridgway's Paratroopers: The American Airborne in World War II* (Garden City, NY: Doubleday, 1985), 282; H. Paul Jeffers, *Taking Command: General J. Lawton Collins from Guadalcanal to Utah Beach and Victory in Europe* (New York: NAL Caliber, 2009), 92; General J. Lawton Collins, *Lightning Joe: An Autobiography* (Novato, CA: Presidio, 1979), 210.
  2 Blair, *Ridgway's Paratroopers*, 253–54.
  3 Guy LoFaro, *The Sword of St. Michael: The 82nd Airborne Division in World War II* (Cambridge, MA: Da Capo Press, 2011), 250–53.
  4 LoFaro, *The Sword of St. Michael*, 256–57.
  5 Spencer F. Wurst and Gayle Worst, *Descending from the Clouds: A Memoir of Combat in the 505 Parachute Infantry Regiment, 82nd Airborne Division* (Haverton, PA: Casemate, 2004), 158.
  6 Wurst and Wurst, *Descending from the Clouds*, 158.
  7 Phil Nordyke, *All American All the Way from Sicily to Normandy: A Combat History of the 82nd Airborne in World War II* (Minneapolis, MN: Zenith Press, 2005), 396–97.

Chapter 32: Conclusion

  1 Clay Blair, *Ridgway's Paratroopers: The American Airborne in World War II* (Garden City, NY: Doubleday, 1985), 294–95; Maxwell Taylor, *Swords and Plowshares* (New York: W. W. Norton, 1972), 83.
  2 Maxwell Taylor, "Talk by Major General M. D. Taylor to First Class," December 12, 1945.
  3 Daniel L. Haulman, "Before the D-Day Dawn: Reassessing Troop Carriers at Normandy," *Air Power History* (summer 2004): 22–29.
  4 "Maxwell Taylor to S. L. A. Marshall, April 9, 1972," S.L.A. Marshall Papers, University of Texas, El Paso, Special Collections.

Selected Bibliography

ARTICLES AND BOOKS

Air Force Public Affairs Alumni Association. *Colonel Barney Oldfield Oral History Interview.* East Peoria, IL: Air Force Public Affairs Alumni Association, 1994.

Ambrose, Stephen E. *Band of Brothers: E Company 506th Regiment, 101st Airborne from Normandy to Hitler's Eagle's Nest.* New York: Touchstone, 2001.

————. *D-Day: The Climactic Battle of World War II.* New York: Simon & Schuster, 1994.

Autry, Jerry. *General William C. Lee: Father of the Airborne, Just Plain Bill.* San Francisco: Airborne Press, 1995.

Balkoski, Joseph. *Utah Beach, June 6, 1944: The Amphibious Landing and Airborne Operation on D-Day.* Mechanicsburg, PA: Stackpole Books, 2005.

Bando, Mark A. *The 101st Airborne at Normandy.* Osceola, WI: Motorworks Books, 1994.

Bearden, Bob. *To D-Day and Back: Adventure with the 507th Parachute Infantry Regiment and Life as a World War II POW.* Minneapolis, MN: Zenith Press, 2007.

Bennett, Ralph. *Ultra in the West: The Normandy Campaign of 1944–45.* New York: Charles Scribner's Sons, 1985.

Bernarge, Georges, and Dominique Francois. *Utah Beach: Ste.-Mère-Église and Ste.-Marie-du Mont.* Bayeux, France: Editions Heimdal, 2004.

Blair, Clay. *Ridgway's Paratroopers: The American Airborne in World War II.* Garden City, NY: Doubleday, 1985.

Booth, T. Michael, and Duncan Spencer. *Paratrooper: The Life of General James M. Gavin.* Philadelphia: Casemate, 2013.

Bradley, Omar N. *A Soldier's Story.* New York: Modern Library, 1988.

Brereton, Lewis H. *The Brereton Diaries: The War in the Air in the Pacific, Middle East and Europe, 3 October 1941–8 May 1945.* Boston: Da Capo Press, 1976.

Breuer, William B. *Geronimo: American Paratroopers in World War II.* New York: St. Martin's Press, 1989.

Buchanan, Austin J., and W. L. George Collins. *Into Fields of Fire: The Story of the 438th Troop Carrier Command during World War II.* Bloomington, IN: Xlibris, 2014.

Buffetaut, Yves. T*he 101st Airborne in Normandy: June 1944.* Philadelphia: Casemate, 2018.

Burgett, Donald M. *Curahee: A Screaming Eagle at Normandy*. Novato, CA: Presidio, 1999.

Butcher, Harry C. My *Three Years with Eisenhower: The Personal Diary of Captain Harry C. Butcher, Naval Aide to General Eisenhower, 1942–1945*. New York: Simon & Schuster, 1946.

Caddick-Adams, Peter. *Sand and Steel: The D-Day Invasion and the Liberation of France*. New York: Oxford University Press, 2019.

Center of Military History. *Utah Beach to Cherbourg, 6–27, 1944*. Washington, DC: Department of the Army, Historical Division, 1947.

Chandler, David, ed. *The D-Day Encyclopedia*. New York: Simon & Schuster, 1994.

Collins, General J. Lawton. *Lightning Joe: An Autobiography*. Novato, CA: Presidio, 1979.

Cray, Ed. *General of the Army: George C. Marshall, Soldier and Statesman*. New York: Cooper Square Press, 2012.

Critchell, Laurence. *Four Stars of Hell: With U.S. Paratroopers in Combat from the Night Drop at Normandy to the Battle of the Bulge*. New York: Ballantine Books, 1947.

Crookenden, Napier. *Dropzone Normandy*. New York: Charles Scribner's Sons, 1976.

D'Este, Carlo. *Decision in Normandy*. New York: Harper Perennial, 1994.

———. *Eisenhower: A Soldier's Life*. New York: Henry Holt, 2002.

———. "Jim Gavin's War, Parts 1 and 2." *Armchair General*. April 23, 2015.

Devlin, Gerard M. *Paratrooper! The Saga of U.S. Army and Airborne Parachute and Glider Combat Troops during World War II*. New York: St. Martin's Press, 1979.

———. *Silent Wings: The Story of the Glider Pilots of World War II*. London: W. H. Allen, 1985.

Dunn, Bill Newton. *Big Wing: The Biography of Air Chief Sir Trafford Leigh Mallory*. Shrewsbury, UK: Airlife, 1992.

Eisenhower, Dwight D. *At Ease: Stories I Tell to Friends*. Garden City, NY: Doubleday, 1967.

———. *Crusade in Europe*. New York: Doubleday, 1948.

Eisenhower, John S. D. *General Ike: A Personal Reminiscence*. New York: Free Press, 2003.

Eschner, Kate. "Meet the Daredevil Parachutist Who Tested the First Nylon Parachute 75 Years Ago." *Smthsonian.com* (June 6, 2017).

Flanagan, E. M., Jr. *Airborne: A Combat History of American Airborne Forces*. New York: Ballantine Books, 2002.

Fauntleroy, Barbara Gavin. *The General and His Daughter: The Wartime Letters of General Gavin to His Daughter*. New York: Fordham University Press, 2007.

Gardner, Ian, and Roger Day. *Tonight We Die as Men: The Untold Story of the Third Battalion, 506th Parachute Infantry Regiment from Toccoa to D-Day*. Havertown, PA: Casemate, 2011.

Gavin, James M. *Airborne Warfare*. Washington, DC: Infantry Journal Press, 1947.

———. *On to Berlin: Battles of an Army Commander, 1943–1946*. New York: Viking Press, 1978.

Glines, Carroll V. *The Amazing Gooney Bird: The Saga of the Legendary DC-3/C-47*. Atglen, PA: Schiffer, 1996.

Griessner, Volker. *The Lions of Carentan: Fallschirmajager Regiment 6, 1943–1945*. Philadelphia: Casemate, 2011.

Hackett, Mary. *Bill Walton: A Charmed Life*. Tucson, AZ: Branden Books, 2013.

Haskew, Michael E. *The Airborne in World War II: An Illustrated History of America's Paratroopers in Action*. New York: Thomas Dunne Books, 2017.

Harrison, Gordon A. *Cross-Channel Attack*. Washington, DC: Center of Military History, US Army, 1951.

Haulman, Daniel L. "Before the D-Day Dawn: Reassessing the Troop Carriers at Normandy." *Air Power History* (summer 2004).

Huston, James A. *Out of the Blue: U.S. Army Airborne Operations in World War II*. West Lafayette, IN: Purdue University Press, 1972.

Hymel, Kevin M. "D-Day Dilemma: General Ridgway Needed an Armored Force to Help Him Hold Sainte-Mère-Église. But Could He Rely on Its Commander?" *World War II History*, September 2008.

———. "Screaming Eagles at Brécourt Manor: The 'Band of Brothers' Faced Off Against German Artillerymen in a Fight for a Crucial Battery on D-Day." *World War II History*, Special Edition, 2018.

Ingrisano, Michael, Jr. *Valor without Arms: A History of the 316th Troop Carrier Group, 1942–1945*. Bennington, VT: Merriam Press, 2001.

Irving, David. *The War between the Generals*. Key West, FL: Parforce UK, 2010.

Johnson, John R. *Unarmed, Un-Armored, and Un-Escorted: A World War II C-47 Airborne Troop Carrier Remembers*. Bennington, VT: Merriam Press, 2014.

Keffers, H. Paul. *Taking Command: General J. Lawton Collins from Guadalcanal to Utah Beach and Victory in Europe*. New York: Caliber, 2009.

Kenyon, David. *Bletchley Park: The Untold Story of How the Battle for Normandy Was Won*. New Haven, CT: Yale University Press, 2019.

Kershaw, Ian. *First Wave: The D-Day Warriors Who Led the Way to Victory in World War II*. New York: Caliber, 2019.

Koskimaki, George E. *D-Day with the Screaming Eagles*. Haverton, PA: Casemate, 2008.

Lebenson, Len. *Surrounded by Heroes: Six Campaigns with Division Headquarters, 82nd Airborne, 1942–1945*. Philadelphia: Casemate, 2007.

LoFaro, Guy. *The Sword of St. Michael: The 82nd Airborne Division in World War II*. Cambridge, MA: Da Capo Press, 2011.

Marshall, S. L. A. *Night Drop: The American Airborne Invasion of Normandy*. Boston: Little, Brown, 1962.

Masters, Charles J. *Glidermen of Neptune: The American D-Day Glider Attack*. Carbondale: Southern Illinois University Press, 1995.

McDonough, James Lee, and Richard S. Gardner. *Sky Riders: History of the 327th/401st Glider Infantry*. Nashville, TN: Battery Press, 1980.

McKenzie, John. *On Time, On Target: The World War II Memoir of a Paratrooper in the 82nd Airborne*. New York: Ballantine Books, 2004.

McKeogh, Michael, and Richard Lockride. *Sgt. Keogh and General Ike*. New York: G. P. Putnam's Sons, 1946.

McManus, John C. *The American Army at Normandy: The Summer of 1944—The American War from the Normandy Beaches to Falaise.* New York: A Tom Doherty Associates Book, 2004.

Miller, Merle. *Ike the Soldier: As They Knew Him.* New York: G. P. Putnam's Sons, 1987.

Miller, Russell. *Nothing Less Than Victory: An Oral History of D-Day.* New York: William Morrow, 1993.

Mitchell, George C. *Matthew B. Ridgway: Soldier, Statesman, Scholar, Citizen.* Mechanicsburg, PA: Stackpole Books, 2002.

Mosley, Leonard. *Marshall: Hero for Our Times.* New York: Hearst Books, 1982.

Nordyke, Phil. *All American All the Way from Sicily to Normandy: A Combat History of the 82nd Airborne in World War II.* Minneapolis, MN: Zenith Press, 2005.

———. *Four Stars of Valor: The Combat History of the 505th Parachute Infantry Regiment in World War II.* Minneapolis, MN: Zenith Press, 2010.

Oldfield, Barney. *Never a Shot in Anger.* Santa Barbara, CA: Capra Press, 1956.

Ossad, Steven L. *Omar Nelson Bradley: America's GI General, 1893–1981.* Columbia: University of Missouri Press, 2017.

Parrish, Thomas. *The Ultra Americans: The U.S. Role in Breaking the Nazi Codes.* New York: Stein and Day, 1986.

Polk, David. *World War II Army Airborne Troop Carriers.* Paducah, KY: Turner Publishing Company, 1992.

Pöppel, Martin. *Heaven and Hell: The War Diary of a German Paratrooper.* Gloucestershire, UK: Spellmount, 2010.

Rapport, Leonard, and Arthur Norwood Jr. *Rendezvous with Destiny: History of the 101st Airborne Division.* Old Saybrook, CT: Konecky & Konecky, 1948.

Renaud, Alexandre. *Sainte-Mère-Église: D-Day, June 6, 1944.* Maurice Renarud, France: Sainte-Mère-Église, 2014.

Ridgway, Matthew B. *Soldier: The Memoirs of Matthew B. Ridgway.* New York: Harper and Brothers, 1956.

Roberts, Mary Louise. *D-Day through French Eyes: Normandy 1944.* Chicago: University of Chicago Press, 2014.

Roll, David L. *George Marshall: Defender of the Republic.* New York: Dutton-Caliber, 2019.

Rondeau, Benoit. *Airborne Operations on D-Day.* Rennes, France: Quest France, 2014.

Sampson, Francis L. *Paratrooper Padre.* Washington, DC: Catholic University of America Press, 1948.

Shilleto, Carl, and Mike Tolhurst. *A Traveler's Guide to D-Day and the Battle for Normandy.* New York: Interlink Books, 2000.

Smith, Jean. *Eisenhower: In War and Peace.* New York: Random House, 2012.

Smith, General Walter Bedell. *Eisenhower's Six Great Decisions: Europe, 1944–1945.* This Kindle edition published by Pickle Partners Publishing, 2013.

Soffer, Jonathan M. *General Matthew B. Ridgway: From Progressivism to Reaganism, 1895–1993.* Westport, CT: Praeger, 1998.

Taaffe, Stephen A. *Marshall and His Generals: U.S. Army Commanders in World War II.* Lawrence: University Press of Kansas, 2011.

Taylor, John M. *General Maxwell Taylor: The Sword and the Pen.* New York: Doubleday, 1989.

Taylor, Maxwell D. *Swords and Plowshares.* New York: W. W. Norton, 1972.

Warren, John C. *Airborne Operations in World War II, European Theater.* Washington, DC: USAF Historical Division, Research Studies Institute, Air University, 1956.

Welchman, Gordon. *The Hut Six Story: Breaking the Enigma Codes.* New York: McGraw Hill, 1982.

Whitlock, Flint. "Airborne at La Fière: Slugfest in Normandy." *World War II History,* Special Edition, 2018.

———. *If Chaos Reigns: The Near-Disaster and Ultimate Triumph of the Allied Airborne Forces on June 6, 1944.* Philadelphia: Casemate, 2011.

Wolfe, Martin. *Green Light: A Troop Carrier Squadron's War from Normandy to the Rhine.* Philadelphia: University of Pennsylvania Press, 1989.

Wurst, Spencer F., and Gayle Wurst. *Descending from the Clouds: A Memoir of Combat in the 505 Parachute Infantry Regiment, 82nd Airborne Division.* Haverton, PA: Casemate, 2004.

Young, Colonel Charles Hutchinson. *Into the Valley: The Untold Story of USAAF Troop Carrier in World War II, from North Africa through Europe.* Flint, MI: PrintComm, 1995.

Zaloga, Steve J. *U.S. Airborne Divisions in the ETO: 1944–45.* Oxford: Osprey Publishers, 2007.

MANUSCRIPT COLLECTIONS AND ARCHIVAL RECORDS

Air Mobility Museum
Bing Wood Memoirs

Army Heritage and Education Command
James Gavin Papers
Harry W. O. Kinnard Papers
George Koskimaki Papers
Roy E. Lindquist Papers
Patrick J. Lindsay Papers
Matthew B. Ridgway Papers
Francis L. Sampson Papers
Maxwell D. Taylor Papers

Atlanta History Center
Judge George Hillyer Papers
Veterans Oral History Project

Clemson University Library Special Collections Unit
Wright Bryan Papers

Fort Benning, Donvan Library
Infantry School Student Papers

**Fort Leavenworth, Command and General Staff College
Combined Arms Research Library**
Digital Library

29th Division Museum
Joseph Balkoski Papers (Utah Beach Collection)

National Defense University
Maxwell D. Taylor Papers

Don Pratt Memorial Museum
101st Airborne Division Historical Papers

82nd Airborne Division Memorial Museum
82nd Airborne Collections

Nebraska Historical Museum
Barney Oldfield Papers

Ohio University Special Collections
Cornelius Ryan Collection

National Archives and Records Administration
Record Group 92, Records of the Office of the Quartermaster General
Record Group 111, Records of the Office of the Chief Signal Officer
Record Group 112, Records of the Office of the Surgeon General
Record Group 208, Records of the Office of War Information
Record Group 331, Records of the Supreme Command Allied Expeditionary Force
    (SHAEF)
Record Group 407, Records of the Adjutant General's Office
Record Group 498, Records of Headquarters, European Theater of Operations, US Army

Dwight D. Eisenhower Presidential Library
James Lawton Collins Papers

Franklin D. Roosevelt Presidential Library
President's Personal Files

Reuters News Agency Archives
Robert Reuben, "Unpublished Manuscript of Experience in World War II"

University of South Florida Library–Special Collections
Congressman Sam Gibbons Papers

INTERVIEWS
Ms. Chloe Beatty
Karen Constantini
Mr. John Cornish
Ms. Barbara Gavin Fauntleroy
Ms. Caroline G. McNeil
Kathy Shiabani
Mary Lane Sullivan
John M. Taylor

WEBSITES
https://www.americanveteranscenter.org/
https://amcmuseum.org/history/daily-chronicles-of-a-usaaf-unit-in-england-for-the
    -invasion-of-europe/
https://www.newspapers.com/
https://www.dday-overlord.com/en/
http://www.6juin1944.com/
https://amcmuseum.org/
https://www.historynet.com/jim-gavin-the-general-who-jumped-first.htm
https://www.med-dept.com/veterans-testimonies/veterans-testimony-duane-j-pinkston/
https://www.med-dept.com/unit-histories/307th-airborne-medical-company/
https://www.med-dept.com/unit-histories/326th-airborne-medical-company/
http://airpower.airforce.gov.au/APDC/media/PDF-Files/Pathfinder/PF013-
http://www.rcaf-arc.forces.gc.ca/en/article-template-magazine.page?doc=d-day-the
    -rcaf-and-bomber-command/jw26nhjt
http://www.projectvigil.com/

NEWSPAPERS
Atlanta Journal-Constitution
Baltimore Sun
Evening State Journal (Lincoln Journal Star)
Macon Chronicle Herald
Washington Post

Index

Stagg, J. M., 141, 142
Stalin, Joseph, 63
Steadman, Patricia, 112
Stedman, Harold, 234
Steinway and Sons, 93
stick, term, xiii
Stillwell, Joseph, 22–23, 29, 51, 53
Stimson, Henry L., 7, 26, 53
Stopka, John P., 224, 225
Strayer, Robert L., 190, 219
Strobel, Wally, 148
Sturgis, William, 143, 148
Summerall, Charles P., 3
Summers, Harrison, 189
Summersby, Kathleen ("Kay"), 107, 144, 145
Supreme Headquarters Allied Expeditionary Force (SHAEF), x, xiii, 64, 110
Swing, Joe, 35
Swingler, Harold D., 176
Switlik, Stanley, 33
Switlik Parachute Company, 33

Taylor, Lydia Happer, 20, 21–22, 25
Taylor, Maxwell Davenport: background of, 17–23; and boarding, 149; and Carentan, 229, 233–34; and Carentan Causeway, 220; and casualties, 195; character of, 20, 56, 122; and command, 120–21; and D-Day, 185–96; and delay, 141, 142, 144; as front-line leader, ix, 60; and jumps, 151–54; and Pearl Harbor, 25, 29; and planning for D-Day, x, 121; and Pratt, 193, 195; and preparations, 135, 137; and promotion, 242; and Ridgway, 16, 23, 30, 31, 60, 121; and risks of D-Day, 115; and Rome, 60–61, 121; and Sicily, 57, 59, 60
Taylor, Robert E., xvii
Tedder, Arthur, 116
Telecommunications Research Establishment, 124
Tester, Ralph, 114

Tighe, Dixie, 100
Timmes, Charles J., 181, 214–15, 217
Todd, Michael, 97
towers, training, 43
training, 35–36, 39–45, 241; in England, 99, 105; with gliders, 94, 105; importance of, Gavin on, 62; for pathfinders, 124, 125
Troop Carrier Command, xiv, 57, 97, 105, 107, 129, 132–33, 242; D-Day, 131f, 160, 162f
Tucker, Reuben, 58, 59, 60, 62
Tunisia, 36
Turing, Alan, 112
Turnbull, Turner B., 176–77
Turner, William L., 219

Urquhart, Brian, 34
US Military Academy. See West Point
Utah Beach. See D-Day

V Corps, xi
VII Corps, xi, 74–75, 106
VIII Corps, 240
Vandervoort, Benjamin H., 157, 175–76, 238, 239, 240
Victory Plan, 8
Vire River Bridge, 222

Waco Aircraft Company, 91, 93–94
Wallace, C. D., 100
Walton, Bill, 99, 138, 206–7, 213
war correspondents, xv, 95–101, 106–7, 205–9; and delay, 142–43; at drop, xiii–xx
war paint, 148, 234; aircraft and, 132
Warren, Shields, 237–38
Watson, Edwin Martin ("Pa"), 25
weapons, 176, 178–78; of flight crews, 130
weather: D-Day, 161–63; and delay, 141–42; and dispersion, 242
Wedemyer, Albert, 8
West Point (US Military Academy), 11–13, 14, 19–21, 28, 50–51, 65